"*The Big Weird* is an excellent read, charming, amusing, insightful, complex, localised yet startlingly universal in its themes."
—*Guide of Bangkok*

"A good read, fast-paced and laced with so many of the locales so familiar to the expat denizens of Bangkok."
—*Art of Living* (Thailand)

"Like a noisy, late-night Thai restaurant, Moore serves up tongue-burming spices that swallow up the literature of Generation X and Cyberpsace as if they were merely sticky rice."
—*The Daily Yomiuri*

"Whether you are a local, resident or a tourist, there are golden nuggets to be found in *The Big Weird*."
—Bangkok Post Sunday Magazine

"Highly entertaining."
—*Bangkok Post*

"*The Big Weird* exemplifies a writer who is in control of his material. [It] demonstrates that at last we have an author who understands the abyss between the dreams and aspirations of westerners hoping for a new life in an Asian land and the often-harsh reality that they find."
—Professor Paul Wilson, Criminologist and Dean, Humanities and Social Science, Bond University, Australia

The Big Weird

CHRISTOPHER G. MOORE

Heaven Lake Press

Distributed in Thailand by:
Asia Document Bureau Ltd.
P.O. Box 1029
Nana Post Office
Bangkok 10112 Thailand
Fax: (662) 260-4578
Website: www.heavenlakepress.com
email: editorial@heavenlakepress.com

First published 1996 by BookSiam
Mass paperback edition published in Thailand by Heaven
Lake Press

Jacket design: K. Jiamsomboon
Cover photograph: Ralf Tooten © 2010

ISBN 978-616-7503-09-7

For David Walls
and
John Blank

Norman Smith once again was called upon to bring his expertise as the wise old Asia hand to the manuscript, and he spent a great deal of time pointing out the small details which needed refinement.

David Walls generously contributed his time and stories, and provided me with the benefit of his wisdom on an earlier draft. He conceived the concept of the Mermaid-ium, which was executed by Nicholas J. Bell, designer, and Stephen Dunn, engineer

Now war is a game of deception.

Know your enemy and know yourself and you can fight a hundred battles without peril. If you know neither the enemy nor yourself, you are bound to be defeated in every battle.

Sun Tzu
The Art of War

[The persona] is only a mask for the collective psyche, a mask that feigns individuality, and tries to make others and oneself believe that one is individual, whereas one is simply playing a part in which the collective psyche speaks.

Carl Jung
Two Essays on Analytical Psychology

FOREWORD

I was in Asia when I first read a Christopher G. Moore book. The novel was called *A Killing Smile* and once I started reading it, I could not stop. With subsequent Moore books, including *The Big Weird,* it has been exactly the same. The plots and characters force you to turn the pages until you finish.

Moore's writings are addictive for a variety of reasons. The first is that his novels continue that tradition of American private detective stories so cleverly exemplified by Raymond Chandler. Like Chandler, Moore allows you almost to smell the streets and to visualise the frail but very human characters that occupy his literary landscape. But where Moore differs from Chandler is that he exports the private eye genre to Asia, a region with quite different smells and scenes from the more familiar surrounds of North America. Indeed, there is a razor-sharp edge to the settings that act as a background to his books—and also a real sense that the reader is part of this background, a fly-on-the-wall almost, soaking up the action that comes from the bars, homes or offices of the principal characters.

Vinny Calvino, for example, Moore's crusty but perceptive private detective in The Big Weird, is someone the reader appears to have known for years. Calvino may not be your best friend, but you can at least understand where he comes from and some of the reasons why he has given up his Big Apple heritage for the fleshpots of Bangkok. And the fleshpots of Bangkok feature prominently in all of Moore's books, including *The Big Weird*. The bars and brothels buzz with the erotic tension of foreigners and hookers playing mind games with each other in pre-sexual rituals that are a far cry from the romantic couplings found in a Mills and Boon novel.

What Moore does so cleverly is to give us a real sense of "the sickness" that a rootless class of foreigners suffer from when they wash up onto the soils of Thailand. This rootless class of foreigners, some veterans from the Vietnam War and some more recent refugees from western cities, have an obsession with the rich tapestry of sex so readily available in their new home. This sickness is addictive, psychologically troubling and sometimes deadly.

Though Moore's books have a decidedly sexual tone about them he is not concerned with just gratuitous sex alone. Rather, the erotic elements in *The Big Weird* have to be seen in the context of a wider sub-text that explores the cultural and psychic undertones that characterise Thai society.

For Moore is one of the few Westerners writing stories about an Asian country who understands the way in which the world is perceived by both foreigners and Thai alike— and the huge gap between the misperceptions that both parties harbour. For foreigners, Thai women are often vehicles for the unlimited expression of their wildest and most deviant sexual and romantic fantasies. The dark and slim bodies of the bar *ying*s embody that unique mixture of loving subservience and fleshy exuberance that stands in sharp contrast to what foreigners perceive as the controlling and sexually inhibited mind-set and bodies of Western women.

But Moore's books are not just disguised cultural dissertations on Asian society and life. There are pounding, adrenalin-charging episodes that throb through the pages as Thai and Western men and women struggle to survive in a society where life is often brutal and short. *The Big Weird* exemplifies a writer who is in control of his material. This book, like his others, demonstrates that at last we have an author who understands the abyss between the dreams and aspirations of Westerners hoping for a new life in an Asian land and the often-harsh reality that they find.

As I said at the beginning, Christopher G. Moore is a compelling writer. Much like Thailand itself, his stories become part of our own psyches, forcing us to return to that uncomfortable space in our souls where the erotic and the violent live side by side. In that sense, his books explore universal questions about the meaning of love, life and sometimes death. These are therefore stories that transcend all cultures.

20 January 2000

Professor Paul Wilson
Criminologist and Dean Humanities and Social Sciences
Bond University, Gold Coast, Queensland
Australia

ONE

WHY WOULD YOU choose to live in Bangkok? It was a question a lot of *farang*s asked. Those who lived in the city asked themselves around the time of a visa run. This ritual renewal for another ninety days required the farangs to leave the country and then return. Four times a year Calvino asked himself during the twenty-seven kilometer taxi ride out to the airport whether he should return. Each ninety days he rolled over the big decision to move out of Thailand for one more visa run. Authorities had slapped on restrictions. The message was: we don't want you; don't come back, and if you do, bring money and stay silent. After all, it was only another three months in the city. A series of three-month visas had turned into more than ten years.

In the expat community were the Vichy *farang* who wrote letters to the local newspapers urging that any *farang* who had a beef with life in the Big Weird should get out and stay out. They had it all figured out, the way simple minds figure out how the world works, "Love it or leave it."

Private eye Vincent Calvino neither loved this part of Southeast Asia nor could he bring himself to leave it, except to renew his visa. He had made forty visa runs. That was not even considered a good start among the old hands. He had friends who had done eighty runs, and others who had passed the one hundred-run mark—men and women of the permanently impermanent *farang* underclass of Thai visa runners—and they were no more reconciled than Calvino. Thailand was like the wife you couldn't live with and you couldn't live without; and every three months for the rest of your life, you left her only to return and try the relationship all over again.

It was as if someone had hooked up a hose to millions of faulty catalytic converters and coal burning hibachis and sprayed the sky with the exhaust. Looking upward, where the sky should have been blue, Calvino remembered something else. Something he wanted to forget. His lungs were sucking in millions of microbes, which had been hatched from permanent colonies in the air. As Calvino stared at the atmospheric catastrophe, which enveloped the city, he had a flashback. An image of death. The kind of violent death that came with the job and, as hard as he had tried to extinguish it from his memory, it was always there, above him, following him until nightfall.

A dome of smoke from more than half a dozen shopping mall fires mingled with a cocktail of car fumes, corporate leakage, cesspool evaporation, slaughterhouse spillage, fungi and bacteria—the F&B of the Big Weird—gathering into a seamless hive with a three hundred kilometer circumference and Sukhumvit Road was the epicenter for this sexually active microbe empire.

The color, yes, that was a good question—what color could capture the Bangkok sky, he asked himself? Then the flashback broke through, harder this time, straight into his face: the color of a five-day-old corpse. He had *waited* on the banks of the Chao Phraya River, watching as two police divers dragged out the body. Earl Luce was perched on the muddy bank, snapping pictures of the chubby, swollen body. *Farang*s with too much history of death tried to keep out of the daytime sky. Sometimes they avoided the nights as well, fighting their fears, staying locked inside small rooms. The sky brought back too many memories that Calvino had wanted to lose.

Bangkok was a sprawl of thousands of half-empty, square, box-like whitish gray structures, high-rises belched out of bloated, chemically dulled egos as suspect as the money that lifted them upward to the sky of greed. A mind-numbing urban horizon of building cranes and building machines giving birth to more and more boxes fashioned from concrete, steel, and glass; home to ten million people, most of whom appeared to occupy the roads for twenty hours a day. Going where? No one knew, and no one cared.

Calvino had an interview for a new case five days into the New Year, the Chinese New Year of the Rat. If Bangkok had a mascot, it had to be the rat, and its year had come up on the twelve-year cycle like a bubble coughed up from the sewers. There were rats in the garbage, rats running in the gutters, more rats camping in restaurant kitchens.

There were other kinds of rats, too. Sometimes they turned out to be a client. It was that kind of business, and that kind of city. The morning Calvino got a telephone call for a new case, the Big Weird had that mortally ill look as if it had been hooked up overnight to a life-support system and it just might not make it through the day. The ranks of the old hands had been thinned by the usual attrition—death or moving on to other places upcountry. A few brave old hands had returned to a place they called home, a place which no longer recognized or wanted them.

The half-Jewish, half-Italian private eye sat at the table in his kitchen, peeling an overripe banana, tipping one end into a plastic bowl of gefilte fish. His German Shepherd, Joy, sat clocking his every move, her head cocked to the side, tensing each time his hand came up with a piece of banana. She froze, not moving her eyes. He listened to Dame Kiri Te Kanawa singing Canteloube's "La Wally" as the piledriver across the lane pounded like a bad headache. He wondered how much longer citizens could go on breathing the two hundred and eighteen different chemicals, the thirty-eight different germs and the infinite buffet of dust particles before they became the color of the sky.

Opened on the table was *The Art of War*. The book had been a birthday gift from Col. Prachai Chongwatana, or Pratt, as his close friends called him. On his last birthday, Pratt had given him the collected edition of Shakespeare's plays; that volume lay unopened. Living in the Thai capital, *The Art of War* had far more relevance that morning in the kitchen.

The book was two books in one: Sun Tzu's version and

the second version by Sun Bin. He was reading the Sun Tzu words as he ate breakfast: "He who first occupies the field of battle and awaits his enemy is rested and prepared; he who comes late to the scene and hastens into battle is weary and passive. Therefore, those skilled in war move the enemy rather than being moved by him." Calvino thought the passage might be applied to the local bar scene with the *farang* cast in the role of the enemy.

"Joy, are you staring at my gefilte fish or what?" asked Calvino.

The German Shepherd barked.

"That's what I thought. But German Shepherds aren't supposed to eat gefilte fish."

Joy yawned, eyes closed, then barked again.

"So, you admit that you are not a wholly gentile dog. I suspected as much all along," he said, tossing her a piece of banana with gefilte fish smashed on to the top.

Joy didn't even bother to chew; it went straight down her gullet, her thick, wet tongue circling around her mouth as she waited for the next offering.

"You eat too fast. Even for a dog." Calvino knelt down, stroked the dog. "Joy, you gotta learn to enjoy your food. And, remember, we are all part of this wonderful food chain. You and me, buddy. I was reading how we are all freaks of nature. Dogs are a freak of nature. Though German Shepherds had a little help becoming freaky from human beings. But it don't matter, Joy, because people are pretty much freaks, too. There was no real reason for any of us to appear on the planet. All those atoms, protein, carbons, and some stardust bonded randomly together like this gefilte fish on this banana, and boom, we got a dog."

He threw another piece of banana and gefilte fish,

which Joy snapped out of the air and inhaled in one breath.

"Your species came together like those little plastic bricks kids play with. My species came together from another set of tiny bricks. And here we are in Bangkok sharing a banana with gefilte fish not having the slightest idea how we ever got here. It could have turned out altogether different. A little more stardust and we would've been something else. But it turned out the way it turned out. Of all the millions of possibilities we are just one that happened to emerge. Here. In the kitchen. Eating together, wondering who is gonna get the final piece of banana. You or me?"

Mrs. Jamthong, for a large woman, slipped in and out of the apartment with the silence of a sniper moving into range on a target.

"Joy don't speak English, Khun Vinny," said Mrs. Jamthong, his maid.

She had been Calvino's maid for nearly a decade. Her hair had gone gray, the skin sallow, the jaw line slack, and a thickness had overtaken her waist. She had begun to think of Calvino as her younger brother who needed a great deal of advice about the ways of the world. She loomed large in the door of his apartment, hands on her hips, a disapproving look in her eye. At her feet were two plastic bags filled with oranges, bananas, pineapple, and apples.

"Dogs don't eat gefilte fish either. But Joy loves it," he said, the last piece of banana arching into the air as Joy's head went up to make a perfect catch.

Mrs. Jamthong sneezed, then sneezed again. "It's the air," she said, screwing up her face. "Very dirty." She removed a large handkerchief from her dress pocket and blew her nose. She gasped for her next breath. Her asthma had been flaring up for days and she had been to the clinic where the doctor advised her to take antihistamines. "The rains used to clear the dust. Not any more," she said.

On New Year's Eve, acid rain had fallen over the city, ushering in the Year of the Rat with a torrent of muddy, black water sluicing down Calvino's soi. Mrs. Jamthong was right: the air pollution was no better after the rain; nothing was ever better than the year before in the city. Life in the city was a slide into suffering, a slide into the allergy of living where none of the measurement devices any longer registered the upper ranges of misery.

Sun Tzu had written, "It is a rule in war that you must not count on the enemy coming, but always be ready for him; that you must not count on the enemy attacking, but make yourself so strong that you are invincible." The problem with Sun Tzu was that he never had planned to fight a war in a battlefield like in the sprawl of a place like Bangkok, a place where the enemy included invisible emissions, thought Calvino.

Calvino stared at himself in the mirror, wondering if the blackness under his eyes meant that the gefilte fish had gone off, and then he looked out of the window at the sky as if it were another mirror, checking for signs to explain the decay, the ghostly pallor that slowly crept into his face and into the faces of others he had known for years. He wondered why so many *farang*s had refused to see that daily life had become a drag race between hope and despair, between drinking and inhaling foreign bodies, between violence and tenderness. This required some thinking. But how could anyone think with all the pounding noise echoing from hundreds of construction sites across the city; the large machine at the construction site no more than twenty meters away struck the earth like a huge, angry fist. His floor and walls vibrated as if rolling from an earthquake and the wave of sound echoed in his temples. He noticed that overnight the cracks in his ceiling were growing wider. With a slice of bread, he cleaned the bottom of the bowl containing the gefilte fish and washed it down with a glass of orange juice as his maid hung his wash on the outside balcony. Before nightfall, the clothes would be dry and full of more dirt than when they were thrown in the laundry.

It was a morning for reflection as he strapped on his leather holster and checked his . 8 police revolver. He shoved the gun into the leather shoulder holster. Glanced at himself in the mirror. Time for work, he thought. Time to face the enemy, time to face eternity. Time for an interview, a new client, another job, another pay check, and the calendar turned over on yet another Chinese New Year, a new embryo of time had been born inside the Big Weird. Out of the door and down the steps, he knew one powerful reason that kept many *farang*s living and trying to breathe air bathed in most toxins known to man.

The Sickness; it wouldn't let them leave, no matter how hard it was to breathe, or how many pills they had to take to keep breathing. The condition had doomed some of them to life within the dungeon walls surrounding the playgrounds of Soi Cowboy, Nana Plaza, Patpong. They didn't so much live in either Bangkok or Thailand but had been sentenced to playground areas—and in a fair number of cases, this translated into a life sentence without parole. Sentenced by whom would be the sensible question. There was no simple answer other than most had no more feeling of imprisonment than sparrows in small wooden cages outside of temples, released to gain merit, returning to their cages time and time again because it was what they knew, where they felt safe.

His client was Quentin Stuart, someone he had done a job for in the past—the Year of the Dog. That year Quentin had suffered from a bad case of The Sickness—meaning his primitive lymphatic system kicked into overdrive, easily defeating reason and rationality like the Visigoths sacking Rome—and if history were any guide, the chances were stacked high that Quentin, like Rome, would fall. This time around, Calvino figured that the case had to be more serious. An American woman close to Quentin had died. She had apparently shot herself in the head. After taking Quentin's call, Calvino had made a few discreet inquiries of his own. The main finding was from the Thai police: they had no reason to suspect it was anything other than suicide.

Pratt came on the line himself. "Samantha McNeal shot herself at the house of her ex-boyfriend, an American named Benjamin Nakamura. He was away at the time she pulled the trigger. We talked to him."

"Domestic problems, don't tell me," said Calvino.

"It is a good place to start, don't you agree?" Pratt asked. "Nakamura had broken her heart. She shot herself. Samantha McNeal was an angry person. She sent enough hate mail. That establishes that she had problems. She was unbalanced. Emotionally she was falling apart."

"Pratt, you know I met her two years ago. Her nickname was Sam."

"Sam?" asked Pratt.

"Short for Samantha. I only talked with her once.

But I remember her well. And she didn't strike me as the suicidal type."

"What is the suicidal type?"

"Sad, unstable."

"I said she was unstable. Sad? What is sad? I think that maybe she changed from last year. Everyone changes, Vincent," said Pratt.

"Her father was already in Bangkok to make the funeral arrangements. He's gone back to Los Angeles with her belongings and ashes. So, I guess, you are working for him?"

"No, I am not working for Sam's father. Tell Manee and the kids I said hello. Are we still having dinner on Sunday?"

"Come over about five," said Pratt. "Not the father? I just thought it would be the father."

"Not the father. I have been hired by Quentin Stuart. He was a close friend of Sam's," said Calvino. He could tell that Pratt was trying everything short of a direct question to find out who his client was.

"I assumed you were working for Mr. McNeal." Pratt didn't need an explanation of who Quentin Stuart was; two years earlier, Quentin had asked for help in the production of a movie. He had given Pratt a small walk-on role. "Is Quentin making another film?"

"From my recollection, he's always making a film."

"Tell him I said hello," said Pratt.

"And that I'm sorry about his friend. But suicide is always a big shock."

"I'll tell him," said Calvino.

That's what the police assumed—suicide. Calvino had

made a few assumptions of his own, including that Sam was connected to Quentin's Sickness. The problem with assumptions was the tendency to assume either too much or too little. The safe play was to find the middle path. Calvino had found the problem with the middle path: it often led to nowhere.

Quentin Stuart had The Sickness but, at the same time, he was also mortally ill. In the eyes of truth and justice, not all sicknesses were equal. Some came with moral debts attached; others, as the result of self-abuse; and still others were the hounds of age, genetics having caught the pant leg of the average Joe, pulling him down, devouring him like a mongoose slowly devouring a cobra for a mid-afternoon snack.

TWO

TWO YEARS EARLIER, Calvino had taken the lift to Quentin's penthouse off Sukhumvit Road and rung the bell. A maid opened the door and waited until he removed his shoes. A huge wall was three stories high, and on it were gallery-sized Vietnamese oils and watercolors, portraying sleek women in bamboo hats and clothed in white *ao dai,* clinging to the contours of the body. A five-foot wooden Burmese Buddha was at the end of the foyer with a spotlight above it, and Persian carpets covered the wooden floor. An art deco lamp of a naked ebony woman was against another wall. Khmer lions carved from teak were placed like guards on either side of the staircase leading down to the sitting room.

The penthouse reeked of big money, success, power. He followed the maid as they glided past the teak lions which were larger than his dog, as she led him down a second flight of stairs to a huge study with filing cabinets, bookcases, a bank of telephones and fax machines.

Quentin Stuart stood behind a large teak desk, his reading glasses on the end of his nose; he leaned forward putting his weight on his fingertips. He was flanked on either side by a number of framed photographs. Concentration had frozen his features into total stillness as he turned the page of the script on his desk. Continuing to read, Quentin made no effort to look up, even though the maid had cleared her throat for the second time and finally said, "Boss, Khun Vinny come to see you."

Calvino used the time to look around the room. Mostly he studied the photographs, which were on a table behind Quentin Stuart's desk. On the left side of the table in one photo, Quentin—with long, black hair—carried a picket sign, and was smiling into the camera with one arm hooked over the hood of a silver gray Mercedes Benz convertible. In the back of the car was a white poodle, with a tiny fuzzy black collar around its throat, and beyond the poodle, in the street, were other people carrying picket signs. The poodle had the pained expression of a snake that had eaten a pig but had trouble passing anything larger than a raisin. The background was filled with trees, a wide, clean street, shiny 1960s cars, and tanned, smiling faces with perfect teeth meant that it could have only been in one place: Southern California. Calvino had thought at the time that Quentin must have been mid-forties, about his own age.

The succeedingthirty-fiveyearshadturned Quentin's hair pure white. His body remained youthful, trim, like someone who had spent a lifetime taking care of himself. His clear, cool blue movie star eyes had the kind of determined gaze of someone who had survived strikes, wars, jungles, and sailing misadventures.

Three decades plus later in Bangkok, he had exchanged his 60s outfit for a white tailored Chinese silk shirt with a Mao collar, a white raw silk jacket and white cotton trousers, and a five-baht gold chain with a large Buddha amulet swung like a pendulum beneath his unbuttoned shirt as he leaned over his desk.

"Chinese wear white for mourning," said Calvino.

"And white is the color for innocence in America. I am in mourning for the death of my innocence." Quentin's eyes looked away from the page. He smiled as he removed his reading glasses.

From that moment onward, it was to be like that with Quentin Stuart: each phrase nicely turned like a woman with bulging calf muscles standing tall in a pair of four-inch high heels; all muscle, muscle with a pulse, a flex-like beat, muscle that caught all eyes and entranced the brain with a hundred different possibilities of excitement.

Quentin Stuart's Oscar statue, along with other statues—Golden Globe awards, Critics awards, and others that Calvino didn't recognize—had been lined up like bowling pins in a v-shape. Calvino's eyes had scanned the room, taking it in, pulling it apart, looking for the structure, the underlying values projected by the owner. People in Bangkok didn't usually have a room with themselves in photographs with internationally famous actors and directors, or all the glamor trophies that Hollywood could bestow.

"You like the composition I take it?"

Calvino wasn't certain if Quentin was talking about the Frank Sinatra song playing in the background or the award statues. Later he found out that Quentin had known Frank and just about every other performer over the age of seventy who had ever worked in Hollywood. He knew more dead movie stars and singers than he knew live ones; that was understandable, it came from outliving almost everyone he knew.

"Hey, I am just a guy from Brooklyn. But isn't the idea something like making a bowling alley of awards?"

The old man looked pleased.

"A writer is defined by his metaphors, and awards should be aligned in a metaphorical way. Ten-pin bowling captures the basic concept of how awards are won. You throw the ball. Most of the time you throw the goddamn thing, it goes straight into the gutter. Not a single pin falls. Most people at that point just say fuck it and throw in the towel. Fools like me just keep bowling. Then, if you are lucky, and luck is a big part of it, you spend a life mastering the game, and people look at these things and draw the crazy conclusion that you have thrown strikes all your life," he smiled, nodding at the photograph on his desk. "So someone has given you some goddamn award? And you think, what does it mean? Any writer with half a brain knows it means squat other than you make a lot of money for a few years before you are back throwing gutter balls on cable TV, and you have a new generation of twenty-three-year-old assholes who thought you died two decades ago."

"A lot of people would have killed to have just one of those awards," said Calvino.

"That's the cosmic joke. Most people care too damn much about the wrong things in life. Kill for the wrong reasons. Love for the wrong reasons. And certainly die for reasons that rarely ever make any rational sense."

He had said many other things during that first meeting two years ago. Perhaps it was one of those moments when a man thinks aloud to himself in the presence of a stranger. Calvino remembered the twinkle of delight shining in the old man's eyes as he spoke. He said the night before he had dreamed about the bowling pins and woken in the middle of the night with a bar *ying* sleeping in his bed.

The metaphor had come full circle for him; he had reflected upon the nature of being in the world of Hollywood and had come away with the lesson of duality—that writers like him in Hollywood were both the bowlers and the pins at the end of the alley. It was why so many sought refuge in booze and drugs, went crazy or into deep depression because they knew that no matter how many times they had set up the pins someone would come along and knock them down, flatten them if they could, destroy them if they could, and eat the flesh and blood of their work.

Later, Calvino had done some background reading about Quentin Stuart; he was, after all, a public figure, a legend, so getting material was not difficult. Quentin had gone on record as saying he had left Hollywood as a protest against a corrupt, dying, and evil system. In truth, he hadn't so much retired to Bangkok as fled Hollywood for an Asian exile. He soon enough established himself on the scene, around the comfort zone—in the expat bars, shops, restaurants, and clubs in the City of Angels, where a semicircle of dancers nursed their lady drinks as they took turns trying to guess his age. Late fifties was the usual shot in the dark when asked about Quentin's age. These women had a knack for guessing the age of a *farang*. They had a knack for lying to please. But in the case of Quentin, they weren't lying, they were simply decades off the mark.

"Excuse me, Mr. Stuart, but I thought you wanted to discuss a job."

His eyes lit up. "I do. A show-business job, Mr. Calvino."

"Vincent."

He put an arm on Calvino's shoulder. "I want you to help me with a movie."

"I grew up in Brooklyn watching your films," said Calvino.

A fire came into the old man's eyes. "Those were different times," he said. "The creative and sexual infrastructure in America has been ruined, laid to waste in a way as thorough and complete as what our bombers did to Berlin and Tokyo during World War II. I am a refugee from that devastation. Japan and Germany had the Americans rebuild the destruction of their cities, their countries. Where is the Marshall Plan to rebuild sex and creativity from the ashes of America? Instead, I have the Stuart Plan. I want to send films back to America from here. Films a new generation will remember as their first vision of Asia."

Quentin had been doing his own research as it turned out. He had sold a Bangkok-based script and asked if Calvino would personally introduce him to Col. Prachai Chongwatana of the Royal Thai Police Force. "I want to offer Colonel Pratt the role as chief police adviser on a movie. It's going to be shot on location in Bangkok in about three months. What do you think? Would he be interested?"

Disappointed. What else could he think? What had he thought? That Quentin Stuart wanted him in the movies: yeah, it had crossed his mind. Why not? Of course, the assignment didn't stop there. Help a Hollywood legend gain access to the police for a fee. He refused to take money for introducing his friend.

"You are an honest man, and in a dishonest world you will be broke your entire life."

"Broke is different from broken."

"Okay, as for you, I want your help in meeting some of the underworld characters who stay in the shadows of Bangkok, I want to interview some real life characters for background. Some of them might be used as extras. Paid extras. I find an incentive helps bring people forward." Then Quentin paused, his smile coming off. "And, one more thing, I want you to check out the story of a young Thai woman that I am keeping."

Now it was Calvino's turn to smile.

"Let me see if I understand, you want access to *farang* gangsters and you want to know if your Thai girlfriend is a gangster as well?"

"We understand each other perfectly," said Quentin.

"The ying who was in your bed when you had the bowling pin dream?"

Quentin smiled. "Strike. The same one."

Clients almost always kept the real reason for the engagement last. A woman who worked in a massage parlor on Sukhumvit Road had been the real target of the investigation. Meeting Col. Pratt and local grifters was only the opening gambit.

"Which assignment has priority?"

"Find out about Tip," he said. "And, one more thing,

how long do you think that will take?"

Calvino didn't have a chance to answer Quentin Stuart's question before Samantha McNeal bounced into the study. Dressed in white tennis shorts and a tan top, she removed the sweatband from her forehead and let her blonde hair fall over her shoulders, as she stepped forward and planted a kiss on Quentin's unshaven cheek.

"Darling, you are back. This is Mr. Calvino. You know, the private eye I was telling you about? The one who is going to help us on the film?"

The way the old man cleared his throat, he knew that mentioning Tip was not a good idea. Calvino liked the way the third reason for his presence had been conveniently ignored, and Quentin liked the fact that Calvino was streetwise enough not to mention the Thai *ying* in the presence of this blonde goddess.

She held out her hand. "Please call me Sam. Everyone does. Always has and always will," she said.

"Hi, Sam," said Calvino, taking her hand.

"God, where are my manners?" Quentin's brow collapsed into a matrix of worry lines. "This is Samantha McNeal. In a previous life, Sam's father once acted as my agent in LA. And a damn good agent he was."

"Then you got too goddamn famous for dad," said Sam. There was the distinct impression that this wasn't the first time that she had delivered that line. Somehow the line didn't ring true. The expression on her face made her look a little too sad, as if some personal, hidden message was beneath the surface and unable to rise in the presence of a stranger.

"Sam's an ex-ballet dancer turned reporter," said Quentin. "And my dinner companion when the occasion requires."

"What he means is that when he can't take one of his bar *ying*s with a fourth grade education to the ambassador's residence, I get a phone call."

"Darling, that's not the way it is at all. I adore you. Ever since you were a child, I have made you a very special part of my life. Besides, most of the bar *ying*s have at least six grades of education. Who knows, one day it may be more difficult to get a job in a bar than a place at a university."

She ignored Quentin's speech. "I had a great game," she said, making a little forehand shot in his direction. "I beat Ben the first two sets. That pissed him off."

"I thought you had decided to let him win," said Quentin.

"I changed my mind after I caught him eyeing the ball girl."

"Victory as punishment. I like that," said Quentin. Calvino had the feeling that each of them used the other as some mirror to a connected past, a mirror that had been shattered, but one tiny piece remained, enough of a portal to allow them to remember what needed to be remembered and yet safe enough to allow them to forget what they had selectively chosen to bury. Sam had a dancer's legs, firm, taut, developed; and a dancer's breasts, small and delicate under the tennis whites. How she ended up in Bangkok was really none of his business. Why she stayed might have had something to do with the old man, his penthouse, her father, his v-shaped trophy collection.

Benjamin was an American-Japanese lawyer— Benjamin Nakamura, and about the only thing Asian about Ben was his surname. He was fourth generation

American, and second generation lawyer; the kind of all-American combination which made one wonder why he had decided one day to trade in his promising corporate in-house counsel job in New York City for a job in Bangkok. It was like an upcoming pitcher on the Yankees asking to be transferred to the minor leagues. Such a decision made people scratch their heads.

If he had wanted to discover his roots, he would have gone to Japan. Sometimes roots were not a place but an elusive web of desire he needed to work through. In Ben's case, root and desire combined. He worked as the go-between for a Japanese telecommunication company doing business in Bangkok.

Ben lived in a large, teak house with its own grounds. His bosses in Tokyo liked the traditional landscaping in the gardens; they often stayed for weeks at a time. But it was his luxury accommodations with a swimming pool and tennis courts that kept his bosses happy between massage parlor and business appointments.

About ten days after that first meeting with Quentin Stuart, Calvino discovered, after a couple of stakeouts, that the massage *ying* had an undisclosed Thai husband and two children. The children were living with Tip's mother in Korat. He remembered hearing the sound of a bowling ball hitting the fold in a perfect strike, the pins scattering, and nothing left standing. Nothing in the old man's emotions remained standing as he had delivered the news. Those deep blue eyes shed tears that Quentin did not bother to hide or to brush away. It was often that way with those who had contracted The Sickness. Terminal romantics who suffered the illusions of love, building castles and bridges out of nothing more substantial than the dream of turning an attractive peasant into the perfect Western wife.

Tip, with the responsibility of financing two kids and a husband who wouldn't work, did what she had to do; she had become a skilled emotional assassin, hunting her prey in the playground where those with The Sickness gathered. Before Quentin, there had been a half dozen others, and after him, there would be many, many more.

That was life. And life was had its fair share of illusion, and the ability to spot the tiny islands of reality had considerable value. Tip was like the screenwriter; she created the fictional world, and found a way to turn promises and words of love into gold. She wore her trophies for best performance as an actress around her neck and on her wrists. These were the Oscars of the night awarded by those with The Sickness in the Big Weird.

THREE

WHEN VINCENT CALVINO arrived for his second professional house call at Quentin Stuart's penthouse, he hardly recognized the screenwriter. In the Year of Dog, Quentin had been old without showing his age, but by the time the Year of the Rat had rolled around, it was as if the old man had had twenty, thirty years slam into him with the full force of a freight train hitting a school bus. His white hair, a tangled mess, curled over his ears, and a three-day growth of white beard covered his sunken, unshaven face. Shoulders stooped, he teetered on top of a bar stool, standing above a huge aquarium—all glass and chrome. This fish bowl was at least ten-feet long and five-feet high. Swimming deep within the aquarium waters, a couple of dozen enormous fish, with a lot of impressive tail action, fought each other to reach the waterline, sucking at the small brown pellets the old man dropped into their open mouths.

Quentin shuffled around the aquarium in a pair of old, worn-out Chinese slippers with the back of his heels crushing the back of each slipper. For a brief moment, he looked like Deng, the aging Chinese leader, the Party kept parked off-stage, the one no one ever saw, the man whose death everyone was waiting for. The old and sick discarded their nationality, ethnicity, and even their gender as they headed toward the ultimate equalizer of death. Quentin's face bore the look of desperation and futility, the expression, which the terminally ill can never fully disguise no matter what mask they try to wear. Death broke through in his eyes and in the corners of his shriveled mouth like a black hole that gorged itself on light beams.

"Each fish in this tank cost around five hundred dollars," Quentin said, as if he had merely paused in an ongoing conversation. He spoke with the timbre of an old man's voice, the one where the tone goes slightly shrill, the sound breaking up like a wave against a distant shore as the words left his dry throat. Stopping in mid- sentence, he coughed up phlegm black as midnight, and pulling a handkerchief from the pocket of his dressing gown. He touched it to his lips, made his deposit, examined it as if unable to believe it had been discharged from his own lungs, and then stuffed the handkerchief back into the pocket.

"About six months ago the new maid's husband arrived from Buriram. At least Lek said the man she brought to this house was her husband. As you taught me two years ago, never assume status. Never assume anything in Bangkok. I was in hospital getting a shot in the gut with one of those long needles you sometime trip across as you are running through a nightmare chased by monsters. So Mr. Daeng, the husband, goes straight to the aquarium, nets a fish, whacks it on the head, takes it into the kitchen, cleans it, cooks it in a frying pan with lots of garlic. Throws in some fish sauce. Does it up real well. You know the Thais can cook like no one else in the world. And I include the French in that as well. So, the inevitable happens. Lek returned from the market and her husband was proud. And why shouldn't he be? He has spent half a day cleaning and cooking the catch. They were planning to have dinner together. One very happy couple united at last. And she says, 'But darling, you shouldn't have gone to all the trouble. Bringing a fish all the way from upcountry. And keeping it so fresh. I can't believe I ever ate fish so fresh.' He says, 'It wasn't from home. I took one from there.' And he points to the fish tank. 'There are lots of fish. They were the right size for cooking. Keeping them in the house. God, these *farang*s are not so stupid after all.' She flipped out. Hit him on the head with his rice bowl. By the time I got home, both had fled the scene, leaving the head cook to tell me the story. Ten thousand baht worth of fish. In Isan, a peasant works a whole year in a rice field under a hot, boiling sun, sweating, growing old before his children's eyes to earn ten thousand baht. And when I get home, you know what I found?"

Calvino shook his head slowly wondering how much the old screenwriter had made up and how much of it had actually happened.

"One whole cooked fish lay in a serving plate, its dead eyes staring at the ceiling. Neither my maid nor her husband had touched the damn thing. They had vanished from the scene of the crime."

"And what did you do?" asked Calvino.

"I sat down and ate the fucking fish. Not to mix my metaphors but when God gives you a lemon, you make lemonade. But I didn't ask you here to talk about fish or lemons. But my story has a point of sorts. Cultural misunderstandings can sometimes turn out to be lethal. And not only for fish. I have learned a lot since we last met. Maybe not as much as you. But I am a lot wiser than last time you came through that door."

"Yeah, every year I think I know less," said Calvino. "I don't know if it's the lead in the air, or if I am starting to understand that the things I thought I figured out, I never figured out at all."

The old man slowly shook his head, his hooded eyes looked a bluish gray, and his shoulders were hunched beneath his dressing gown. He held out his hand, and Calvino shook it.

"A man who knows his limitations is a wise man. Vinny, come in and make yourself a drink. I no longer have my appetite. It is why I love to look at these fish eat. That is hunger. There's the life force. Hunger, the desire to consume, to feed, to snatch food out of the jaw of another fish. The desire to survive."

Calvino walked behind the wet bar, opened the door of the small fridge, took out a can of Diet Coke and pulled back the tab. He filled a glass half full, watching the old man feeding the fish. Was he putting on another show for him? Calvino asked himself. Or was this a show for himself?

"Everyone has their own way of dealing with grief, Vinny," said Quentin. "It's been nearly a week since Sam's father took her home. And I still can't believe she's gone."

"I heard she was going to be buried in LA," said Calvino.

"Putting her ashes in the ground in Bangkok was unthinkable for her family. The morning after the cremation, I went to Wat Thart Thong. Sam's ashes were laid out in the shape of a stick figure. About eighteen inches tall, with stick arms, legs, and body. That was all that was left. There was an ash head. And as I looked down, I saw a small boy mopping the marble floor below. Life went on. A cat walked near the wall, the sunlight catching its paws. Nothing had stopped. As nothing will stop when my ashes are laid out at the same place."

Calvino stood behind the bar, drinking his Diet Coke. On the bar counter was an old copy of the Bangkok Post, folded to the page containing the story and picture of Samantha McNeal. He glanced at the photograph; it was as he remembered her. The English language press did not print death-mask photographs—they left gruesome death shots to the Thai press.

"Underneath the newspaper you will find an envelope with your name on. Please open it," said Quentin.

Calvino lifted the lip of the envelope and removed a stack of glossy eight-by-ten prints. A series of morgue shots. These were the kind of horror shots that English language newspapers never ran, as a nod to the tourist authorities who formed the opinion years ago that a highly visible, public image of a young dead foreigner in Bangkok was bad publicity. Such photographs made the rounds on the news services and someone in Iowa City decided to cancel their trip to Bangkok and go to Manila instead. If the photographs were kept out of the press, it was as if the murder hadn't happened. Or it happened in such a private, secretive fashion that it was like a whisper lost in a sandstorm.

Calvino forced himself to look at the pictures, knowing the image he had of Sam as she had appeared in her tennis outfit that day two years earlier would be forever shattered. It couldn't be helped. Looking at pictures of the dead went with the job, even if the deceased was someone you had known and liked. He held his breath and looked at Quentin.

"Go on, have a look," said Quentin. "That's Sam in the morgue."

"I can see that."

"The poor kid. All I can say is that she didn't suffer. There are much worse ways to die."

He took another drink of Diet Coke and looked down at the photographs.

"Her father see these?" asked Calvino.

"No way. You don't show someone's father photographs like that. At least, not if the father's an American. It was bad enough seeing him crying over her ashes."

From the photographs, Samantha McNeal had an entry bullet hole on the right side of her head, which looked like a tiny black wormhole. But on the exit side, part of the skull had been blown off and she looked like a broken china doll. Her long blonde hair had cascaded to one side and the blood had clotted, making her hair look dark, stiff, and twisted—like a doll's hair caught in a fire. Calvino had seen many pictures of gunshot victims and each time he had an uneasy feeling that he had stumbled upon a private moment of the deceased— in that death mask was a blank screen, empty of voice and gesture. Empty of worry and care yet not devoid of the abiding sense that something important, urgent, had been left behind unfinished.

Violence had contorted Sam's face, making her look dour as if her lips had just pulled away from a glass of house wine. Looking around the scene of a violent death for forensic evidence was as close as any investigator ever came to interviewing the deceased. Who did this? And what was the purpose of doing it this way? Who was the messenger and what was written in the message? The bowler and the bowling pin in a flash had been united.

"How did you get these?" asked Calvino, looking up from the photographs and directly at the old man.

A cunning smile flashed across his face. "If you know the cost of a big fish, you know the price of just about anything else that you want to buy," he replied.

His expression turned serious, the eyes narrowed. "I was very close to her, Vinny. She was my best woman friend in Bangkok. We went everywhere together."

"I remember."

The way Quentin Stuart strung the words together made Calvino feel as if there was the full force of truth behind the declaration. Calvino reminded himself words were the stock-in-trade of a Hollywood writer. He used them to create an illusion of truth when, inside, the reality had been hollowed out. The lies were coiled inside the husk of truth waiting patiently for the chance to betray innocence.

"I remember she said, or you said, that Sam's father once acted as your agent in Hollywood." Calvino sifted through the photographs one more time.

"You have an excellent memory for detail."

"And she was your arm piece at official functions, the kind of event where you are expected to arrive with a respectable partner," continued Calvino.

"You have an amazingly accurate grasp of the fault lines cutting through a person's life." Quentin crossed the vast living room and eased himself down on a couch. Sprawling out on the couch would have been a more accurate description of how the old man had taken the weight off his feet. He collapsed for a moment, closing his eyes, resting his forearm over the bridge of his nose. "That sounds like a line out of a movie," said Calvino.

"It is out of a movie. One of my movies. *Outward Bound*. I wrote it in 1972. I've been looking for the character I created all those years ago, and maybe I have found him."

"You brought me here to talk about Sam," said Calvino. "Not about your old movies."

"I was talking about Sam. You were simply listening. And I was saying that Sam simply wasn't the type to kill herself."

"What type kills themselves?" Calvino found himself repeating what Pratt had said to him on the phone.

"You are right, I guess you can't tell, any more than you can say 'girl' in America for someone Sam's age," said Quentin Stuart after a couple of moments. "She had too much going for her, too much to live for. I just can't see her doing it."

"Sometimes people kill themselves out of a sudden depression or it's a sudden impulse. One of those rash acts that everyone regrets except the person doing it and that person is dead and, as far as we know, the dead don't have regrets—only unresolved grievances."

The old man smiled as his hand slipped into the dressing-gown pocket and emerged with a small notebook. "That's a good line. I can use that," said Quentin.

He uncapped a Mont Blanc pen and wrote for a moment, then snapped the notebook closed.

Calvino shook his head wondering if he ought to stay with the Diet Coke or go for something stronger. The interview was taking a long time and wasn't going anywhere he wanted to go with it. "I've had clients steal a lot of things from me but never my lines."

The old man reopened his notebook and made another note. He rose from the couch and crossed over to the bar, sitting down on one of the stools opposite to where Calvino stood. The morgue photographs were at his elbow and he laid his notebook over them and continued to write, filling the page, turning it and then writing a few more lines.

"I knew for a long time that Ben Nakamura had been cheating on her," said Quentin, looking up from his notebook.

"Cultivating faithfulness isn't one of the reasons foreigners choose to live in Bangkok," said Calvino. "What I am saying is, she had been around long enough to know the score in the scene. Boyfriend seeing another woman is not a surprise in this town. It would be a surprise if he didn't. On the other hand, *farang*s will kill themselves just because they are tired of living. And after Bangkok there is no other place to go but to the next life and hope it ain't Bangkok all over again."

Quentin closed his notebook and put down his pen. He was silent for a moment, looking off into space.

"Maybe she did kill herself. I haven't ruled out the possibility. I have lived long enough to know that no one can truly know another person. We can barely know ourselves. If she did kill herself, then I would like to know what drove her to do it."

"You mean who?"

"I mean who, what, why. We know where. Ben's house. You may conclude after your investigation that the only person who knew why she did it was Sam herself. I want to know as much as I can pay you to find out."

"So you've decided Sam was worth a few fish worth of investigation time. Maybe I should be even more direct. You knew Sam. A lot of people knew her. Why are you going to all the trouble and expense of looking into what the police have already decided was a suicide. I gotta say, it doesn't make a lot of sense. Unless you have something in the back of your mind that you haven't told me?" Calvino had the urge to walk out. There was absolutely nothing about the case he liked. The manner of death, the way the assignment was coming, the instructions, the lack of any coherent reason other than sentiment for why Quentin Stuart would get himself involved.

"Vinny, come on. I loved her. And I am willing to spring for a small school of fish and will throw in a tank as well if you can give me some peace of mind about Sam. I am dying myself. And when you know that the end isn't that far away, you try to do the right thing. I need some closure about what happened to Sam before my ashes are put together like a three-year-old making a stickman from ground up bone dust. Isn't that reason enough?"

This cooled Calvino down a little.

"You think Ben Nakamura had something to do with her death, something the police didn't find out or, if they found out, he used his money and influence to have it covered up?"

The old man appeared to gather his thoughts. His hands dug into the pockets of his dressing gown. He rattled some change in one pocket. "If I knew the answer to that, I wouldn't need you, now, would I?"

"No argument there, Mr. Stuart."

"Christ, if you don't stop calling me Mr. Stuart, I am going to fire you."

"I haven't decided whether to take the job," said Calvino. This time he made a point to leave off the Mr. Stuart. Up to two years ago, he had never talked to a Hollywood legend. He never knew anyone who had. They lived secluded lives, insulated by a payroll list of many people whose duty was to keep them away from outsiders. Now he was inside, and Quentin Stuart was asking him to take a case. He couldn't believe how the legends were as flawed as anyone and, close-up, they even had security gates thrown around their lives so no one could see that the legend inside the walls was pretty much like everyone on the outside.

Quentin extracted a wad of hundred dollar bills from the pocket of his gown, thick enough to roll across the bar counter. The money rolled to a stop under Calvino's hand, which was perched on its fingertips half covering one of Sam's death-mask photographs. Benjamin Franklin and Samantha McNeal had merged on the bar counter, and Calvino didn't like the combined image of money and glamor united in death. He could see that it was a lot of money and Quentin was waiting for his hand to clutch the roll. It was enough money to make any man's palm itch. And Calvino could see by the way Quentin had rolled his money across the table that the old man was accustomed to throwing money at hired retainers, at problems, at pain, at disappointment. At death.

"Mediate between me and Sam's soul. Please, Vincent. I need your help. Most of my life I have needed no one. Life at the end is pulling rope for a life preserver that is no longer there. Please mediate for me."

Calvino remembered reading about Quentin and he had used this word "mediate" before. It seemed odd in a Hollywood context, and even more out of place in connection with Sam who was already buried in Los Angeles.

"Quentin, I read that once you had to mediate between Paul Newman and Steve McQueen on the set of a film."

"What you read is true. Paul took me aside and said, 'Steve is doing that blue-eye thing in the scene, and I don't like it. Stop him.' A couple of minutes later Steve McQueen came over and whispered, 'Get Paul to stop blue-eyeing me in the scene. He's stealing the fucking scene, and I don't fucking like it.'

"McQueen didn't have much formal education. He was a street kid. A high school drop-out. He used a lot of profanity. But there were words he couldn't say but he was too embarrassed to admit it. He would get angry and throw up his hands and he would scream that the fucking line didn't work, and he wasn't gonna say it. Or he would scream that there was a blue-eye thing with Newman. 'Fix it,' he would rage.

"Then, I would get him alone after the public outburst. I'd shut the door, and say, 'Steve, talk to me.' And he would say, 'It's that ssh sound, Quentin. I can't say words with that fucking sound.' So I rewrote the script, put in words he could say, had a word with Paul, and we shot the scene with no problem. McQueen died from the slow dance with DNA replicating out of control. He went to

Mexico for all that phony treatment, wasted his time, his money, his hope on quacks. In the end, mediation with our destiny doesn't save any of us from the grave. But it may help us reach those who have gone before us."

He stopped the story, his watery blue eyes looking at the money, then looking at Calvino.

"Well, are you taking the money or not?"

"You're doing that blue-eye thing with me, aren't you?" The old man laughed.

"Of course, I am. Why shouldn't I? I am fucking dying. The daughter of a dear friend of mine is dead. Gone. I want to find out anything you can dig up that will shed light on how Sam ended up dead in Ben's house that night."

Calvino turned the wad of money over in his hand. Something told him that Quentin's motivation lacked some essential moment of truth-telling, that he was keeping something back. He looked at the money and peeled five C-notes off the wad and tossed the wad back into Quentin's lap. The old man looked down at the money, blinking, then up again at Calvino.

"Five hundred is an advance. If it comes to any more, I'll let you know."

"I don't get you, Calvino. You got no family, no wife, no connection other than one Thai policeman, and certainly no goddamn money. You live in a slum. I throw nine grand your way and you throw all of it back minus five hundred."

The sympathy he had felt drained away. "I don't have any of those things, you're right," said Calvino. "It's the price I pay for a certain kind of freedom. And it's a fair price. Not a good price, only just above the line fair. So I have this one thing which a lot of people don't."

"What's that if you don't mind my asking?"

"I charge for my service, but I can't be bought. I have already paid the price to be free. I don't need your nine grand to buy what I already have."

Quentin stuffed the wad of notes into his dressing gown pocket.

"In a place where everything is for sale, your attitude is an asset a lot of people would say is a liability," said Quentin, smiling, the kind of smile that suggested victory.

"But for me, it instills confidence. If you need anything else, please let me know."

"Don't worry, I'll let you know when I need anything else."

As the old man got off his stool, and walked back to the couch, Calvino remembered Sam McNeal dressed in her tennis whites, carrying her racket, smiling the triumphant smile of a winner who had come off the court with a victory. That smile wasn't in the picture; it was never on the lips of a person with a bullet hole in their head. In death, there was never any winner, only a body with that puzzled expression of the dead: one that seemed caught halfway between a struggle for breath and the startled realization that the last one had filled the lungs. Quentin waved him over to the couch.

"I know you want to go. But sit for just a few minutes more. The impulse to live is the strongest impulse we have." Quentin held a pillow over his chest. "I've entered that time of my life when I can still hold five cards, but I no longer have the strength to shuffle the deck. What I hold now is all that I will ever hold. The final hand. And I have been spending a lot of days and nights trying to read those cards, this last hand of mine. "One of those cards that I drew is the slow death card. The Joker in the pack. I can accept that. I can accept that I won't live forever. I'm already off the charts for life. I should have been dead years ago if you go by those insurance tables. But can those bastards in Hollywood accept my way, the way that I am dying? Not one of them. All I receive is fax after fax, one long hysterical reaction. They want to convert me into a victim. I am not going to give them that satisfaction. To die at my age doesn't make me a victim. Rather it is a kind of victory. Sam was robbed of that victory. Something isn't right about the way she died. I feel it. She was not the kind to put a loaded gun to her head and squeeze the trigger. The reason I asked you here is to find out how she came to be dead in Bangkok at the tender age of thirty-one." Calvino opened another can of ice-cold Diet Coke, moved around from the bar, passed the aquarium, and walked into the large open area. The floor covered with Persian carpets, antique armchairs and two long sofas. He eased himself into one of the antique chairs opposite Sam McNeal's photograph, smiling, alive, and happy was on the table. The old man slumped back with his eyes closed, breathing in a measured way— the Buddhist meditation way. He was controlling his breathing, spacing his inhaling and exhaling, his lips parted slightly. After a few minutes of silence, Quentin's blue eyes opened, so blue and clear you could hear the echo of a dolphin deep within.

"I don't take the pain medicine. And you know why? Because I want my body to acknowledge that this pain is not the final pain, this is only the start-up, the warm-up to the pain that lies ahead. But I didn't ask you here to talk about that kind of pain. I have one request. Find out what really happened to Samantha McNeal."

FOUR

A YOUNG THAI *ying* stood at the railing above them. Wearing tight red shorts and a tiny tank top, her nipples visible underneath, she balanced herself forward on her arms. Her frame was tiny—less than forty kilos—and the gold chains which hung from her throat caught the afternoon light, casting a glitter of light on the sliding glass doors below. Calvino wasn't certain if she had been quietly spying on them or watching the display of light and shadow cast by her gold on the wall of glass which led out to the balcony. For some time she had been standing above, watching them, the wad of money, the photographs of Sam in the morgue.

She had exhibited an incredible degree of patience, or was it something else, thought Calvino. Mix a little fear with a pitch of consideration—*kreng jai*—stir it with an astute calculation, she was figuring out how she fitted into the weave of the conversation taking place below. She would have known that Quentin was in a meeting and coming too close might be dangerous. So, like a child, she hung back, looking, waiting, hoping, playing, and day-dreaming in the golden light of the afternoon sun. Waiting to be noticed, waiting to be asked downstairs. *Ying*s from the comfort zone cultivated an ability to wait until the time was right—the time to strike, sure and swift, with a degree of accuracy that ensured success. Quentin spotted Calvino's eyes as they rested on the railing above his head.

"Darling, is that you up there?"

She responded with a loud giggle and this lit a hundred-watt smile on the old man's face.

"Come on down and meet Khun Vinny."

She leaped down the stairs, skipped passed the Khmer lions and jumped onto the sofa next to Quentin, kissing him on his unshaven cheek. She nestled her head on his chest for a moment, then looked up and *waied* Calvino, pressing the palms of her hands together and slowly lifting them so her fingers touched her chin.

"This man is a private eye," explained Quentin.

She looked puzzled until Calvino translated private eye into Thai, "*Nak suep*," he said. She nodded; a little cloud of doubt twisted her expression into one of disappointment registering at the edge of disapproval. If private eyes didn't have much status in America, they had even less status in the stringent hierarchy of Thai society.

Such an occupation fell somewhere between a private security guard and a traffic cop in one of those tight-fitting brown uniforms. Calvino had grown accustomed to the experience of being feared and looked down on at the same time by the Thais. It went with the territory.

"This is Luk Pla. Isn't she the most beautiful thing that you have ever seen?"

The moment of truth, thought Calvino. Luk Pla translated as "Baby Fish." He watched the tiny *ying* wrapping herself around the old man like an alien creature hatched out of some rusty old starship. It would take a blowtorch to break her grip. Not that anyone in the midst of yellow fever would ever try to break free. Was he going to confirm Quentin Stuart's assessment of a goddess in human form or tell him the truth: she was an ordinary peasant with slightly bucked teeth, who had cast a magical spell. The dilemma happened frequently with *farang*s in an advance stage of the Sickness. He watched her narrow cunning face and asked himself how much he wanted the job.

Quentin Stuart might have been dying but he also had a relapse of The Sickness, which had brought Calvino to his penthouse two years before. Most *farang*s who caught The Sickness never knew they had it; meaning, it was one of the few sicknesses where victims misdiagnosed their condition as one of good health, as liberating, a new lease on life. Calvino had seen the symptoms hundreds of times before. Truth was, there was no vaccination, no cure for The Sickness in the Big Weird. Once contracted, the sufferer had a life-long condition.

He thought for a moment and then decided on the middle path, the path most people sought to tread in Thailand, the one most people talked about all the time as the way to enlightenment, the way to civilized compromise, the one that avoided confrontation. The path easily named but rarely found, and if found, rarely walked.

"Beauty isn't an object solely for the eyes, it is an experience to be felt," said Calvino. "No one can know the image of the interior eye."

"Exactly, Vinny. It is one thing to buy a big fish for the aquarium, it is another to keep the small fish happy in the much larger aquarium of this apartment."

He squeezed Luk Pla, kissed her forehead, and slowly pulling her head back. He said, "You see, darling, Khun Vinny knows how we feel about each other." He turned and faced Calvino. "Now, as to business, I hope that you can start immediately, and I must excuse myself but I have work to do. There is one more thing. What do you think of the Chinese?"

"That there are a lot of them and they study the art of war from the cradle," said Calvino.

"Yes, but I feel that there is a larger metaphor for the Chinese. It used to be only writers were in the metaphor business. Now everyone is, including, I suspect, private eyes," said Quentin.

"A metaphor for what?" asked Calvino.

"You should ask her. Pauline Cheng's an ABC. An American-born Chinese. And *The Art of War* is her favorite book. Sam said it was Pauline's bible."

"I'll do that, Quentin. I'll ask her about the book." He decided not to disclose that he had already met Pauline Cheng the year before at a charity function. He knew that she liked American football and pizza so at least they had some safe, common, neutral ground to occupy during their short conversation. She had referred to herself as ABC, and Calvino remembered smiling to himself at the time.

As he left the room, Calvino turned for a final look at his old client with a new case. Quentin could not keep his hands off Luk Pla. Brushing her long, thin hair with a red rinse back off her shoulders, he rearranged it carefully into a thick wave on top of her head. He admired his handiwork, and no longer looked like a dying man, or a man obsessed by the ghost of Sam. She was already dead, he was heading to wherever the dead meet or don't meet soon enough, and Luk Pla was taking an edge off the bumps along that journey. Who could blame him? He had the image of Sam's ashes burnt deep into his consciousness. Who could blame her? She had the image of more gold dancing like fireflies in her eyes.

And, then, why did Sam McNeal kill herself? The answer, he was convinced, lay somewhere in the most difficult, inaccessible community in Bangkok: the single expat women's community. The society of mem-*farang*s would give the Masons a run for their money in terms of allowing outsiders inside the square. At least he had an idea of where to begin. A friend of Sam's, one that Quentin said she had been close to: an American-Chinese, Pauline Cheng, who also admired *The Art of War*.

FIVE

CALVINO'S GOLDEN RULE for a *farang* living among
the expat community had a broad-based consensus—
Don't shatter my illusions and I won't shatter yours. The
rule was necessary for time logged inside a playground
where much of the personal reality was constructed from
cigarette smoke and dark bar mirrors. The town catered
to *farang*s looking for co-conspirators in the illusion
maintenance business—not just those with a bad case of
The Sickness, but those who had plans to tap into the
wealth of an accelerating economy. Tap, tap. Hit that little
hammer all day and all night and wait for some response
at the other end. Listen, wait, hope, and feed into the
chain of illusion makers who lurked behind every bar,
every office, every corner.

In the case of Quentin Stuart, the illusion machine
was operated by Luk Pla, a young bar *ying*, who, at first
meeting, almost anyone who had been on the streets
recognized as possessing the classic combination required
for success on the scene: the face of an angel, the heart of

a gangster, and the hips of a hydraulic press. On her home territory, no one but no one was better at the art of war.

In Southeast Asia, wars were fought for people and not for land. For hundreds of years, the region had been underpopulated. The invaders—Thais, Mons, Khmers, Burmans, Malays—returned with slaves for their fields and women for their brothels. History hadn't changed all that much. Luk Pla's object was to capture a slave, and she had shown herself one very successful warrior.

Calvino had walked out of the penthouse, leaving behind that fat wad of hundred dollar bills, thinking how Quentin Stuart had stuffed the wad back into his pocket as if they were so much tissue. Why had he taken only five hundred dollars and tossed more than eight grand back? The answer was in the expression on Luk Pla's face as she had watched the money on the table; she was like a cat with infinite patience, staying low, studying, fully concentrated, sealed in a dedicated and focused coldness, knowing when to unleash claws and teeth in one powerful, explosive burst.

What the old man was buying from him was only marginally different from what he had bought from Luk Pla. What big money always bargained for: control, stability, the smooth masonry of life where all the razor sharp corners that ripped into the poor could be eliminated. Maybe his mortal illness had thrown a natural inclination into overdrive. Money, a lot of cash, was a parachute in the freefall into the void. The old man, with his death sentence, was tumbling down that shaft, clinging onto Luk Pla. The cruelest reality for the rich was that their money could not change the verdict of random chance, or provide life with meaning where there was none.

Calvino liked to think what separated him from Baby Fish was that he had taken only five C-notes, five one-hundred dollar bills, to cover his fee; but she would have taken the entire wad, stuffed it in her pocket, smiled, and asked for more cash a week later.

After he returned to his office off Sukhumvit Road, Calvino sat at his desk and opened *The Art of War*, and read: "Know your enemy and know yourself, victory will not be at risk; know both heaven and earth, and victory will be complete."

He was about to have Ratana, his secretary, put through a call to Pauline Cheng when the office telephone rang. Sitting behind her desk on the other side of the bamboo partition, Ratana answered. "One moment, please. Mr. Calvino is in a meeting. I will see if he can be disturbed." She put the caller on hold, pushed back from her desk, and walked around to where Calvino sat, hands behind his head, staring out the window.

"It's Mr. Stuart."

"I'll take the call," said Calvino, putting down the book and swinging his chair around and lifting up the telephone receiver. He waited until Ratana had returned to her desk before he spoke into the phone. It was Quentin's voice on the line.

"I'm having a few people around to my apartment for drinks tonight, including Pauline Cheng. I thought you might like to meet her. Why don't you drop in around, say, eight or so?" asked Quentin.

"You can bring your lady if you like." Before Calvino could respond, Quentin continued, "Do you know what Luk Pla told me after you left?"

"I have no idea? What did Baby Fish say?"

"She said that when she was a child living in her village she would lay on her back and watch the sun through the gaps in the tin roof, and she thought the sun belonged to Thailand. That is Thailand's sun, she would tell herself. Each and every country has its own sun. But is it like Thailand's sun? Is it bigger, brighter, and as hot as Thailand's sun? She didn't think so. She felt no country had a sun that came close to the beauty of the one she saw through her roof, the one belonging to her country.

"Only after she came to Bangkok did she find out there was only one sun for all the countries. Everyone shared the same sun. She said that losing her virginity had caused her less trouble than dealing with the notion that

Thais had no greater claim to the sun than a *farang* or an African. It was their sun, too. Then she told herself that she was just a stupid, ignorant village *ying* and everyone in the world except her and her friends and family in the village had always known the truth about the sun.

"The reason I am telling you this story is that it reminded me of something Sam said a week or so before she died. She was in a low mood, and I asked her what was wrong, and Sam said, 'I am suffering from a loss of uniqueness.'

"Pauline Cheng says that once a woman has lost that sense of special belongingness, she loses her self-respect, her self-esteem. I remember Sam saying, 'Quentin, do you have any idea how low I feel? Because I am lost, and I don't think that I can be found again.' I thought Sam's words might give you inspiration in your investigation."

"I take it Sam and Cheng were close friends?"

"They were inseparable. They knew each other before they came to Thailand."

In the background, Calvino heard Luk Pla laughing and kissing him, the *ying*-like giggles bursting with health, vitality, and youth. The old man started laughing, too. His voice was muffled and Calvino guessed that Quentin had covered the phone with his hand, "Tilac, I'm trying to talk to Khun Vinny. Stop putting your hand there. It feels too good. I can't think. I can't talk."

It was like listening to a dead man talk. Someone submerged below the sea, feet hooked on a coral reef, sucking at an empty oxygen line, the nitrogen entering the blood, making him giddy just as he lost consciousness. If victory came from knowing heaven and earth, as *The Art of War* suggested, Calvino wondered if Quentin had won such knowledge. One thing was for sure, Calvino was going to have a tough time flushing out any enemy inside a social gathering at Quentin's penthouse. Not long after Quentin Stuart had hung up the phone, Calvino decided to go ahead and place that call to Pauline Cheng and a few more calls for background information about Sam's best friend, the one who had taken away Sam's personal, private sun.

SIX

CALVINO STOOD OUTSIDE the door of Cheng's office as the late afternoon light slanted through the window blinds, throwing prison bar shadows over the floor and computer equipment. Inside the main room, Pratt sat forward in an office chair, concentrating on a large computer screen on the table a few inches away. From Calvino's vantage point outside, he could take in the entire room. The unguarded activity of a person in their natural environment, one where they felt safe, was worth more than a week of gum-shoeing around the city asking questions. People had an automatic way of pulling down the gates on their personal life, walling off their private city from strangers, hiding a secret life in the small routines of their normal unobserved day. Learning to read the normal actions and reactions was half the way to reading the person's character.

One dead giveaway came from observing a single woman working beside a married man in an office where they were entirely alone. What was their zone of separation? Knees, elbows, face—all had a proximity factor. Pauline wasn't playing knee games with Pratt. Her face was far enough away from his to be well within the safe zone. In other words, her body position read-out and attitude allowed an initial conclusion: no apparent sexual ambiguity at play.

The content of the moment suggested mutual intellectual stimulation. Was this the same pure intellect, which Pauline had used to demoralize Sam? The medium was the message, so Western conventional wisdom had it. In Thailand, ambiguity was the medium and the message: ambiguity allowed for the essential ingredient in all manners of the heart and mind—deniability. The medium didn't exist. The message didn't exist either. Or they both existed sometimes. In the Big Weird it was up to you as to how to mix the ingredients into the salad bowl of reality.

Luk Pla, like many bar *yings*, had put a high value on the art of observation before she entered the playground battlefields. At the penthouse, she had observed them from above. She had been watching for some time before Calvino had noticed her presence. He had looked up from his conversation with Quentin and saw her.

She had already had formed her opinion of Vincent Calvino, he thought. She definitely knew herself, she knew Quentin, and this new possible enemy on the scene, a private eye, well, she had him pegged, too.

Inside Cheng's office area, Calvino observed four computer terminals, with dozens of cords snaking along the floor, set up on two long, intersecting tables. On Pratt's immediate left was a slim, attractive Chinese woman wearing a T-shirt which had "MicroHard" in large letters and beneath it a picture of Bill Gates inside a red circle with a red line cutting through the circle. She wore cut-off jeans. Calvino guessed she was early thirties, though she could have passed for a much younger woman with her long black hair tied into a thick ponytail. She had the kind of face that men remembered: large eyes, oval face, full lips, high cheekbones. She possessed the kind of face that men saw in their dreams.

Even behind a computer screen, she projected a natural kind of confidence, coupled with the controlled gestures of a catwalk model or a TV personality. No one would have mistaken her for a local. The protest T-shirt.

Her lack of kreng jai was replaced by a casual familiarity that came when people worked as equals, without the artifice of someone younger deferring to someone older, or someone in a lesser position humbling themselves to someone in a higher position. She reached over and pulled the keyboard away from Pratt and began typing away. "This is the right way. You do it like this," she said. No one would have doubted that she was as much American as she was Chinese from that one gesture.

Calvino formed a general profile of Pauline Cheng. She was Chinese-American, and worked as an NGO, which was the shorthand expression for all non- governmental organizations, from the Red Cross to a whole load of other groups with other crosses to bear in developing Thailand. It was difficult to say if helping Colonel Pratt was part of her job description. The name of her NGO was "Advancement of Autonomy of Women Foundation" or AAW for short.

The headquarters was registered at the address of a small accounting firm on the island of Vanuatu, a spot of dirt off the coast of Australia, which not one in fifty million people knew was a tax haven for the super rich, including those who were hiding legitimate funds from tax authorities and others like drug-smugglers, gun runners, and crooked politicians who were stashing away illicit funds for a rainy day.

Calvino found out from his local sources that the AAW had funded AIDS-prevention programs in the North, a hotline for abused wives in Bangkok, and a health clinic for pregnant factory workers along the Eastern Seaboard. It spent heavy funds and, there was little question, from his sources, it was doing good work; one said, "Doing God's work."

One of his sources, an American named Nathan Gold but who everyone called Slugo, a computer nerd, said Cheng also operated something called WULF—Women's United Liberation Front—which was addressing ways to eliminate Asian porno from the Internet. "Censorship, Calvino. WULF is an anti-free speech organization. They are cyberspace bullies. They launch search and destroy missions on any provider who they think doesn't have politically correct views about women. And the WULF provider? You can't even log on unless you are a woman. Cheng's a fascist," Slugo had said.

Sitting next to Pratt, Cheng didn't look like a fascist. But as Pratt had said, people don't look like an idea, whether it is suicide or fascism. If it were that simple, international law enforcement would have rounded up every terrorist and criminal a long time ago. WULF operated on a computer bulletin board service and had attracted nearly a thousand women subscribers. Pratt obviously wasn't a member of WULF, but he was a Shakespeare scholar, as well as being a cop in the Royal Thai Police Force.

That morning he had told Calvino that he had booked an afternoon session so that Pauline could guide him through cyberspace among the websites for Shakespeare, logging him on to the best sites long enough for him to have a look, showing him how to download material to the home terminal. A laser printer silently printed page after page of images and data about the playwright who had been dead nearly four hundred years but whose spirit lived on as a virtual reality entity on a hundred websites. Pauline was a Mac-head; all the equipment was Apple, a member of Apple cult. A true believer in the hardware. As for software, she knew one of the most valuable pieces of software was to make powerful allies with police officials.

Calvino, having watched long enough to capture an unvarnished image of Cheng's character and just short of that extra moment which would have converted him into a voyeur, opened the sliding door of Pauline Cheng's office. It was like entering a church. She was the high priest performing a rite, and Pratt, who sat next to her, was like a new wide-eyed convert who had seen the light, felt the spirit.

She pulled back from the table, looking visibly upset. "You were spying on us," Pauline said.

"Pauline, I phoned earlier about an appointment. Remember we talked about pizza and football last year?"

"Vincent, she has me logged into a site in California. Come over and have a look at this. Have you ever seen anything like it? Shakespeare's complete works, analysis, articles, theories of authorship. Everything," said Pratt,

as he peered up from the screen.

"Even the indecent parts?" asked Calvino.

"Even a child can tell the difference between Shakespeare and a pornographer, Mr. Calvino," said Pauline Cheng.

He had hit not only the wrong note, he had stopped the whole orchestra. She was staring at him, hard. One of those dead center stares sharpshooters have when they look at a target thirty meters down the range. The woman who was now looking straight at him did not remotely reveal the same attitude as the woman he had observed a few moments earlier through the window. Like a ghost, that woman had vanished, swallowed up by her hostile reaction to the challenge his presence had interjected into the room.

"Earlier we were connected to a Shakespeare database in Ireland," said Pratt, choosing to ignore the beginning of a confrontation. He used the Thai technique of changing the conversation, and hoping the change would take hold.

Col. Pratt was the large golden bear, Shakespeare the pot of honey that never failed to attract his attention, drawing him deep into a forest, which resembled home. How he ended up as a member of the Royal Thai Police Force rather than occupying a university chair was one of those mysteries that even Manee, Pratt's wife, could not adequately answer. Pauline Cheng had been showing him the ropes, how to access the online chapel of William Shakespeare.

"Mr. Calvino, shut the door. I've got the air-con running," said Pauline. She immediately turned her attention back to the screen.

Calvino reached around and slid the glass door shut. He turned and looked around the large room. The ceiling was decorated with large paper Chinese red and green and yellow dragons with female faces, sloping down at odd angles, paper flames shooting from paper jaws. The room was like a concrete bunker with high ceilings, a perfect place for a WULF member to feel at home. Computer books, directories, and novels lined one wall. Papers and boxes were scattered on the floor. Scanners, printers, computers, phones and locked filing cabinets gave the room a security-one-level feeling, as if Cheng had modeled her headquarters along the lines of a military operational center. Calvino moved around the table and stood behind Pauline and Pratt. On the screen was a color painting of the bard.

"I doubt Shakespeare ever imagined that his face would end up on more T-shirts made in China than all his plays on the stages of England and America combined," Calvino said.

"Or that one day people in America would spend more on dog food and make-up than on abused children and women," said Pauline.

"Vincent, I had no idea you would arrive so early."

"Neither did I," said Pauline.

"The traffic on Sukhumvit Road was actually moving. Meaning there is a coup in the works, a public holiday, and half the population is upcountry, or I just got lucky," said Calvino. "I think I just got lucky."

Pauline looked as if she were staring through him. "An unpackaged male *farang* has trouble finding luck in any place other than Thailand."

"Pratt, you mind if I borrow your bulletproof vest?" Pratt swung around in his chair. "You've already taken the hit," he said.

"Thanks for your support, but I don't think it was intended to be fatal. More like a warning shot," said Calvino.

"I take it that you two know each other," said Pauline Cheng, a hint of disapproval in her voice. "Meaning that you planned this. And you, Lieutenant Colonel Pratt, really had no intention of searching for Shakespeare on the Internet."

"Pauline, you're reading too much into this. Pratt's my friend. When I spoke to you on the phone, you said nothing about him being here," said Calvino.

"And neither did you," said Pauline.

"I think we have started off on the wrong foot," said Calvino.

"Huh, you can't use foot metaphors in Thailand. Shows how much you know." Quentin was right about Pauline and metaphors, he thought. Foot first, war couldn't be far behind.

Pratt looked at Calvino, then at Pauline and shook his head. "Why is it, putting an American man and American woman together is like putting two cats in a bag?"

"You're getting the wrong idea. Pauline, didn't we meet last Christmas at a charity party for slum kids? We didn't fight, we didn't argue. We even had a conversation. We talked about the Dallas Cowboys."

Pauline Cheng, her elegant face held at an angle, smiled slightly.

"I have seen your name in cyberspace."

"I hope that people are saying nice things," said Calvino.

"That's what you think."

"We are all going to be dead soon enough. We should

say nice things about one another."

"Since you are here, perhaps, you might want to tell me what you wish to discuss this time, and I presume it isn't American football."

"Maybe you have seen the name Samantha McNeal in cyberspace," said Calvino.

"You've developed a sudden interest in the Internet . . ." started Pratt.

"As of yesterday," said Calvino.

"Do you two always finish each other's sentences in code?" asked Pauline Cheng.

"Scary, isn't it?" he asked.

"I have to finish some work first, if you two don't mind." She pulled a cigarette from a pack, lit it, folded her arms and rested back in her chair; head tilted back she let the smoke roll out of one very perfect nose, one that Calvino had already some evidence liked to find its way into other people's business. He watched her sitting behind her Mac computer, wondering how to bridge the gulf.

Pratt had his hand on the door and had begun to open it.

"What time is dinner on Sunday?" asked Calvino. "We changed it to seven," said Pratt.

Her head lifted up from the screen to watch the police officer walk out and close the door behind him. Calvino sat down in a chair, folded his arms.

"You have *guanxi*. Which is . . ."

"I know what *guanxi* is," said Calvino. "What you are saying is that it's strange for a white guy to have a personal relationship with a government official."

Her tone had registered a nine in the ten-point scale of disappointment. *Farang*s because they were *farang*—and like either sheep or fish, one American of Anglo-Saxon stock was indistinguishable grammatically from millions of people living in Europe—and like sheep and fish, they were not entitled to *guanxi*. This was the monopoly of the overseas Chinese who prided themselves on knowing the art of war. They had figured out that the art of *guanxi* led to quick victories in business arrangements; the Chinese knew how to sit for hours and talk of gardens and reform and drink tea, and talk of family and ancestors and of villages and of sacrifice.

A private means to channel money so that it stayed within circles of family, friends, and friends of friends. In truth, establishing the connection was far less than an art form, involving tact and cultural understanding, and much more than a strong, unspoken sense of shared understanding and trust based on their Chineseness: a trust that no non-Chinese could ever hope to achieve. Race was the trump card. Yet, there it was, in her face, a *farang* in a close personal relationship with a Thai. The assumed racial comparative advantage had fallen apart.

"Were you friends with Samantha McNeal?" asked Calvino.

She peered at him, then nodded, still off-balance.

"I have been hired to look into the circumstances of her death."

"What is there to look into? She killed herself."

"Why would she do that?"

Cheng's face broke into a bitter smile. "She was betrayed by a man."

"Ben Nakamura?"

She shrugged her shoulders.

"If you were a friend, whatever you think about me

doesn't matter. You aren't helping me. You are helping Sam. And her family."

Pauline Cheng thought about this, pretending that she had focused again on the keyboard.

"Who's your client, Vincent?" asked Cheng.

"A man who collects fish. Large expensive ones and small very, very dangerous ones."

"Quentin Stuart," she said. "It figures Quentin would be the one not to let her spirit rest."

"Why does it figure?"

"You are a white guy, figure it out yourself."

"America must have treated you real bad to build up so much resentment," said Calvino. "I got what I wanted."

He was ready to leave and she was ready to see him gone.

"An education and attitude," he said.

"An education and a sense of who I am and where I belong."

"And that the sun belongs to all of us," said Calvino.

"Whatever that means," she said.

"Bar girl wisdom, Miss Cheng."

SEVEN

AFTER DINNER, MANEE had gone upstairs to put the children to bed, and Calvino and Pratt sat outside in the garden. The night was clear and the heat of the day had cooled with an evening breeze, leaving a slight chill in the air. Pratt sipped his coffee. At his feet, two mongrel dogs lay with their head between their paws on the lawn, ears flicking as the smoke from the mosquito coils drifted past. Calvino sat in a lawn chair, stretching his arms forward, then back behind his head, staring at the huge, yellow moon. Once a month, Calvino was a guest for Sunday dinner. Manee had decided years before that he was part of the family, and no one disagreed with her assessment.

"You don't like her," said Pratt. "Who?"

"Pauline Cheng."

"She's okay. Besides, liking her isn't important," said Calvino.

"If you want her help, it might be useful if she at least thought you liked her."

Calvino looked over at his friend.

"She likes you. How do you explain that?" asked Calvino.

Pratt smiled. "Maybe she likes the uniform."

"Exactly what were you doing at her place?" "Surfing the Net. Looking for new Shakespeare sites."

"You could be the only Thai ever to serve on the police force who used William Shakespeare as a beard so you could get close to an American-Chinese. It is so complicated I don't think anyone would understand who hadn't lived here a zillion years and at least one lifetime over there."

"So you qualify?"

Now it was Calvino's turn to crack a smile.

"Hey, if I qualified, she would have liked me. You saw the daggers she was throwing at me."

"You threw a few knives yourself."

"You're right. I blew it with her. So I have to live with the fact Pauline doesn't like me. But you still haven't answered my question. What were you really doing at her computer terminal? And looking for Shakespeare is not an acceptable answer."

Pratt reached forward and flipped open the lid of his saxophone case, removing the tenor sax. He played one of those sad Charlie Parker pieces, the kind which make you think that there is no hope, that you are going to spend the rest of your days bowing and scraping and sitting at the back of the bus. Jazz expressed a basic simplicity of emotion. If people had enough jazz in their souls, the pendulum might finally swing to a sense of shared purpose of civilization where people belonged because they accommodated each other. People could stand alone, compare themselves with each other, but it would be without hatred, without envy and regret. It was a tall order, given the torment of the world.

Pratt stopped playing and rested the saxophone on his knee. "There are a lot of things about the world I no longer understand," he said.

Manee had come into the garden, and put her arms around her husband's neck. He didn't register any surprise. "Like what?" she asked.

"Sam came from a good family. From a world of money, cars, clothes. You name it she had it. Have you seen the house where she was found?"

Calvino nodded. "I've been over there."

"It is a heritage house. There aren't many left in the city. Three teak houses. All original timber and right next to a klong. It is like the way it used to be in Bangkok. The interior of that house was perfect. Antiques. Expensive silk cushions and carpets everywhere. Fresh-cut orchids. And with everything to live for, she put a gun to her head and pulled the trigger. Why does an American woman so far away from her family do such a thing? Most Thais would have traded places with her."

"You don't understand how strongly a woman can feel about life," said Manee. "How easy it is to die when a man has let her down. Women talk about it. Some actually go ahead, make the final statement. They've had enough. It is our way of leaving before the Third Act. Not because we are weak. Quite the opposite, because we are strong."

Pratt was looking up at his wife. He thought he understood everything about this woman; they had children, they had been together twenty years plus. And she was saying that, in the end, with this dead American woman, a woman she had never met, she had a greater understanding and feeling than he did. He thought about the way his wife had talked, a way he had not heard before, an unsettling, disturbing way. Even though Calvino was family, he wasn't so sure he liked this degree of disclosure in front of anyone.

"I met Sam McNeal a couple of years ago," said Calvino.

The confession took both his host and hostess by surprise.

"You dated her?" asked Manee.

He shook his head. "She was at Quentin's penthouse one day when we had a meeting and she came in wearing a white tennis outfit and carrying her racket."

"What did you think of her?" asked Pratt.

"Someone on top of the world. She had it together. If there was a problem in her life, she wasn't showing it. Bangkok is a tough place for Western women. Manee's right, who can tell when someone has the strength to see the play through to the end?"

"Censorship," said Pratt.

This caught Calvino and Manee off guard, and they exchanged a look of mutual bewilderment.

"You asked me why I was at Pauline Cheng's shop," said Pratt.

"It wasn't for Shakespeare," said Calvino.

"Not completely. We have a public relations problem and I was asked to see if I might be able to help out. People in government are looking for a way to tell their story. Some might say they want to control content. In this case, the content is out of control. There are people in America telling lies about Thailand. Saying we have

800,000 children sold into prostitution, launching boycotts of Thai products."

"That's plain stupid," said Calvino.

"Of course it's stupid, but it won't stop people who couldn't find Thailand on a map from believing such outright lies. The bigger the lie, the more people are willing to accept it as being true. That's the irony. Small lies are dismissed. Massive ones become conventional wisdom. It doesn't matter that New York City and Los Angeles have more child prostitutes than Thailand. We are attacked. Is it because we are Asian?"

Calvino leaned forward from his chair. "Pratt, you lived in New York. You know how many crazies there are in that one city. Everyone has an opinion and a gun, saying whatever they have to say to get attention, to separate themselves from the crowd. And when you pay them attention, threaten to censor their ravings, then they have won. Others think, hey, they were right all along, otherwise why the heavy-handed stuff?"

"How do you protect your dignity?" asked Manee.

"Fools have no dignity. And you can't stop fools
  from trying to make fools of others," said Calvino.

"You ignore them. Silence is the best answer to a fool."

"I have been given a mandate to find a better answer," said Pratt.

"Yeah?" Calvino said, sitting forward, looking over at Pratt and Manee.

"This morning I was having breakfast with Joy and reading *The Art of War*. Sun Tzu says something like the wise commander is good at using intelligent people as secret agents and that secret operations are essential in war."

"There is wisdom in his words," said Manee.

"And I was just wondering what kind of an agent Pauline might be."

"That's more than likely a secret," said Pratt, smiling.

EIGHT

LATER THAT EVENING as he worked the room, Calvino listened in on the bamboo telegraph among the people who had gathered in the penthouse. Quentin had succeeded in recreating the ultimate Hollywood party with expensive catering and rich, celebrity guests. The invitees included an assortment of people, mostly expats: a couple of ex-CIA officials, staff from the American Embassy, an arms dealer and a couple of other big business people, a couple of idle rich (one of whom was ex-CIA with an encyclopedic knowledge of F-14s, illustrating that categories of power, money, and influence usually overlapped), and a token visiting Hollywood producer of B-movies. Luk Pla and the servants were the only working-class people at the party.

When Calvino finished working the area, he had confirmed that expats had divided themselves up into small groups. This turned out to be convenient for his purposes since only one of the expat groups at the party interested him. This group was mainly American in their early thirties and they shared a common bond: they were all FOS, according to Quentin. Friends of Sam. It was evident to Calvino that the whole idea of the party had been designed to bring the FOS together under one roof so that he could look them over. The other guests fell into several tight groups that circulated among themselves; their members rarely ventured out to talk to other people huddled in their own groups unless it was to sneak a closer look at the huge aquarium.

One woman nicknamed Baby, who worked in an advertising agency, came to celebrate her twenty-fifth birthday and got the idea—probably from the guy who brought her—that Quentin had thrown the party for her. At one point, Baby staggered out of his study, carrying a champagne bottle in one hand and Quentin's Oscar in the other. One of the straps on her red party dress had slipped down over one sexy shoulder, leaving her right pink nipple exposed. Her smile had gone crooked. She held the Oscar over her head, swaying her hips from side to side, then did one of those end-zone dances that football players do after scoring a touchdown.

"I am a star," she said to no one in particular.

She wasn't a star for long. Her legs went rubbery and flew out from under her. She collapsed onto a Persian carpet, the champagne bottle flying in one direction and the Oscar cart-wheeling across the room, making a dull thud as it struck the teak floor. A man with a ponytail and an open-neck shirt helped the woman to her feet, but she went limp and he then carried her off to one of the upstairs bedrooms and that was the last anyone saw of the couple for the rest of the party.

She had wanted to be a star, thought Calvino, nursing a Mekhong and Coke. Why was it that everyone wanted to be a celebrity? There was no answer other than a usual mixture of fear and death, the wish for immortality, the desire for love and acceptance, and getting invited to very good parties.

Quentin's idea was to have all of Sam's friends come to the kind of party she had attended many times. Calvino was trying to imagine Sam at this party, who she would have come with, how she would have circulated among the crowd—or would she have spent most of her time with one or two people and ignored the rest? Calvino suddenly realized after the one meeting just how little he knew about Sam. His first order of business was to spend time talking with Ben Nakamura, to get him to talk about what had happened inside his house. His target may have sensed he was being watched and had checked out of the main party, disappearing alone onto the balcony.

Calvino stepped out on to the verandah, leaned his arms on the railing and looked down at the pool and grounds sixteen stories below. The large teardrop swimming pool was lit by a series of lights recessed into the bottom of the pool. Like a jewel fallen to earth, the pool gleamed against the darkness, overshadowing all else as an object far too blue, too small, too still to be real. And before him, the nightscape of Bangkok, dotted with long-necked cranes and high-rises as far as the eye could see, gave the appearance of haste, recklessness, and greed unleashed by forces who believed that money, however earned, was the only gateway to power.

There was nothing about the city that said they were wrong; they were living in a time and place where money could buy anything, including the sky. The sky had been colonized by fungi and bacteria multiplying, as they waited for a new batch of human beings who would be breathing them in as they moved into the modern offices and condos.

"You've been watching me all night," said Ben, having pulled down the white surgical mask from his nose and mouth. He coughed, leaned forward and spit over the edge of the balcony. In the old days, the dancers could instantly identify a resident *farang* after hearing him speak Thai; now they knew the resident *farang* from his chronic cough.

Calvino turned around. "Since you've been out here most of the night, that would have been difficult to do." He paused and looked at the mask. "I have read that those things only keep out about 50% of the stuff in the air."

"I know Quentin hired you to talk to me. And it wasn't about my health"

"He tell you that?"

"Not in so many words." "Are you feeling guilty?"

"Wouldn't you if someone you had dated blew her brains out in your house?"

He took a good look at Ben Nakamura, who had sprawled out on the padded recliner, his ankles hooked, one arm held behind his head. He automatically put the mask over his face, head tilted upward as if trying to make out the stars through the haze of pollution or the colony of bacteria searching out his lungs. Early thirties with gold-rimmed glasses, blue Oxford shirt with button-down collar, gray Armani slacks, and mobile phone, Ben had tailored himself to fit the image of the packaged *farang* class.

"That would depend on a lot of things."

"Like?" Ben asked, pulling down the mask. "If you were somehow responsible."

"I didn't kill her, if that's what you think."

It didn't matter that Ben had Asian features. His attitudes, gestures and voice were American. Calvino had found out from Pauline Cheng that Ben was employed by a Japanese company which had won a telecommunication concession for installing phone lines in Bangkok; it was an expat job that came with the whole package.

"There are a lot of ways of feeling responsible short of actually pulling the trigger of the gun," said Calvino.

"Sam loved going to Quentin's parties," Ben said.

"You know why? Because she was impressed by all the Hollywood bullshit, his old movie posters, the TV producers from out of town, and the media image of someone who had been a legend before she was born."

"I gather that they were close," said Calvino, half turning and looking back at Ben.

"She was his beard. You can't take a twenty-year-old Plaza hooker to the American Ambassador's Christmas party. The small talk wouldn't be about the hibachi burns on the upstairs bedroom floors. It would be about how the old man had lost his morals. Or you can't discuss with a hooker from upcountry the big picture questions like how it is that when women talk about sex it is exploring their sexuality and when men talk about sex it is sleaze or pornography."

"Maybe that's because when woman talk about sex they are talking about dedicating themselves to a person, and when men talk about sex they are focusing on the act. For the guy, the woman doesn't matter other than for performance value."

The provocation brought Ben to a seated position. "Whose side are you on?"

"Did you and Sam have fights over sex?"

Ben let the question hang for a moment, shifting his weight on the recliner and reaching for his drink. "The old man told you that I had something to do with her death, didn't he? Because I'm just another Jap as far as he's concerned. The Rape of Nanking was my doing. The hibachi burns on the Ambassador's bedroom floor. I'm personally responsible for it all."

"Are you third, fourth generation American?"

Ben sat up, a little anger showing in his face, just a flicker, but enough to establish that Calvino had hit some small emotional minefield. His surgical mask hung around his neck on a string.

"I'm second generation myself," said Calvino.

"I'm fourth generation," said Ben Nakamura, smiling as if he had won a small victory.

"Your grandparents ever talk about the time they spent in the camps out in Nevada?"

"What would you know about the camps?"

Calvino stood with his back to the railing, his suit jacket was buttoned and his silk tie in a Windsor knot snug to his throat. He sipped his Mekhong and Coke, swallowed slowly, not taking his eyes off the young Japanese-American. Ben was carrying a fourth generation king-sized chip on his shoulders and living in Bangkok had not cut down the heavyweight grudge. He had gone out of his way to find more reasons to feel wronged by the world.

"I don't know a lot about the relocation camps the Americans used for your grandparents. But I know a couple of things about the concentration camps the Nazis built. Not as much as my mother. She was an expert. She lost aunts, uncles, cousins, and her father. None of them came out alive after their stay at Dachau."

There was a Calvino's law that guaranteed that no matter how much personal pain had been suffered, sooner or later one inevitably crossed the path of another person whose pain dwarfed your own. No one had a monopoly on grief, misery, injustice, or hatred— there was sufficient supply to go around for everyone, everywhere, and at every time.

When Ben looked up, the smile was gone from his face.

"Sorry, man, sometimes I can be a total asshole. Just ignore me. I would ignore myself if I could."

"Sometimes a man hits a pothole so deep that he thinks he can't ever climb out. In my experience, anyone who admits that just maybe they got things wrong is halfway to the top of the hole."

Ben was lost in reflection for about a minute before he responded. He looked out at the night sky.

"This has been some pothole," said Ben. "For your information, Sam broke off with me a month before . . . you know, before she killed herself. And she spammed a two-screen-high flame, screaming in all capital letters that I was a yellow Trojan horse. I looked Asian but inside I was just like any other white American guy who had discovered his prick in the Plaza. She said I had led her on, lied to her. And she wrote about how she had found me in bed with two *yings* I checked off at Renoir, what we were doing in my bed at six in the morning, and on and on."

"Renoir, I know. The impressionist painter. He should have painted in this city. One thing I don't understand is, a spam. What's a spam two screens high?" The two *yings* in bed had been bought out of a swank semiprivate members' club off Sukhumvit. Ben had started off most likely as part of a large happy hour crowd drinking at the Renoir, that much he had followed. But "spam" and "flame" had Calvino thinking the packaged *farang*s had their harems, their own slang, as well as their offshore bank accounts.

"God, are you out of the loop."

"So draw me a picture."

"It's like this. A spam is like the cc you put on the bottom of a letter. But you send it to a zillion people. No one has a couple thousand friends. Sam sent emails to a huge number of people, all about her private grievance against me."

"Electronic hate mail?"

"Exactly," replied Ben. "It was like being trapped in the remake of the movie *Fatal Attraction* with an invited audience to watch the rabbit boiling. In the digital age, if you want to get your revenge on someone, you write long, emotional letters and post them to everyone you have ever met in the world who has an e-mail address. That's a lot of people. My friends, relatives, were on Sam's expanded cc list. She sent them to all the senior executives in my company. That included the big boss in Tokyo. Her flame wasn't a one-off exercise. She was making a career of it. Sam sent sixty or so flames, filled with rage and hate, telling me to go to hell, saying how I had set out to destroy her."

"So she savaged you in public. Before your peers, your employer, your family," said Calvino.

"You say that like I did something wrong," said Ben. "Wrong is one of those slippery words that I can never hold on to for long," said Calvino, noticing that Ben had finished his drink.

"The relationship had been going downhill before she caught me. More like a nosedive. The thing was, Sam wanted me to do this small favor for her friend," said Ben.

"What kind of favor?"

"She wanted me to convince my company to back the main contractors in our project. The main contractor did one of these mid-stream changes of course. They substituted Chinese components for American components used in the equipment. My company had to redo all their specs. Three, four months of work would have gone out the window. My company was already losing money in this deal. Finally, Tokyo said enough is enough. No more changes. My company let the main contractor know that we were pulling out of the project. Sam was convinced that I could change my boss's mind, and he could make the case in Tokyo."

"Could you?"

He shrugged his shoulders, swung himself around on the recliner.

"Maybe. But why should I get involved in this? I don't like dirty money or substandard equipment."

"So you said no. She pushed you. But you kept saying no."

"Exactly. How can you have a relationship with someone who is trying to use you?"

"Who was Sam's friend? The one behind all of this?"

"Pauline Cheng. Who else?" asked Ben.

"She's at Quentin's party tonight. You saw her in the sitting room huddled with her own personal group of women. Ask her what kind of kickback was in it for her."

"You didn't like being pushed," said Calvino.

"You swing anyone's door back far enough and it falls off the hinges."

"And the castle door fell on top of you?"

Ben clenched his jaw. "It's still falling. Who knows, it might end up on Pauline."

"You don't like her much," said Calvino.

"Like her? I don't even want to be in the same room with her," said Ben.

"That why you are camping out here with a mask?"

"Bad air is a better risk than a bad woman," said Ben. "They haven't invented a filter against the nasty impurities of the Pauline Chengs."

"How did you end up with sixty odd e-mails from Sam?" asked Calvino, looking out in the darkness. Then he looked directly at Ben. "That's seems like a lot of grief to pour out."

"You've got it. They only stopped after she died. She posted the last one the night she killed herself."

"You remember the time of that message?" Nakamura shook his head. "Not really." "Can you look it up?"

"You think I kept all those flames?"

Calvino studied his expression, a smile creeping across his face. "I think you kept every last one of them."

Looking past Ben through the sliding glass doors and into the sitting room where several dozen guests circulated, laughing, drinking, sharing stories, living the life sixteen stories above the hard surface of the earth, Calvino had a glimpse of their world. They occupied a world without hinged doors; all the doors glided open and shut. From the penthouse of Quentin Stuart to the NGO office of Pauline Cheng, all those doors of glass and chrome were anchored at the ceiling and the floor, solid structures without hinges. You pushed such a door hard enough, it didn't come off the hinges, it broke, shattered into pieces. That was more the way Calvino thought about Sam McNeal—as a penthouse verandah door which in one instant of madness had exploded into a million shards.

"Can I get a copy of Sam's e-mails?" asked Calvino. Nakamura shrugged, "Sure, why not?"

"Anyone else at the party who was on the spam?" This time Nakamura smiled.

"About the only person not on the list would have been Quentin, and that's because he's still in the technological bronze age. Can you believe he still uses a typewriter?"

Calvino still used a typewriter. Along with Quentin, their writing machinery had become a generational divide. He let go of the urge to fight for the right to stick with the Remington, and instead asked Ben, "Was she seeing anyone else that you know about?"

"She hung out. As far as I know there was no one special."

"Was Sam ever that special to you? Serious to the point of making future plans?"

That one had Nakamura going to the railing and looking down at the pool. He hunched up his shoulders as if a shiver had passed through his body.

"I miss her. I wish it had turned out different. But it turned out the way it did. One day you are safe, the next, the government takes all your property and puts you in a camp because you're a Jap, and you might be dangerous. Once that happens then you learn to accept that anything is possible. You can't be safe even in your own house or in your life. Your mother's people would know about that. So would your mother. And I expect you know the same thing. You got to take care of yourself. First and last. Because this might be your last day before they come to take you away. Like they did for that English broker in Singapore. And he didn't do anything but his fucking job."

"On the back of other people's money," said Calvino.

Calvino stayed outside on the verandah after Ben Nakamura left. Ben moved to a circle of three men about his own age, and not long after, he was smiling, then laughing. They were all having good fun watching Quentin Stuart's expensive fish, the ones in the aquarium and the ones in gold necklaces and bracelets circulating among the guests. Nakamura had been angry, then melancholy, and now he was laughing with his buddies. What Calvino couldn't quite figure out was why Sam McNeal had blown out her brains over someone like Nakamura.

He had a number of unanswered questions: Why was she checking on Ben at six in the morning? Was it another opportunity to sell Pauline's plan to change component parts to his boss's boss in Tokyo? Had she gone to his house for business and found Ben with two bimbos, and this was the reason she killed herself?

Calvino didn't figure Sam for the type to spin out because she had found Ben in bed with a chorus line of playmates on either side of her guy. She grew up with the Hollywood crowd. Finding a couple of hookers in a man's bed would not have shocked her. Upset her, made her angry, yes, all that was possible. Killing herself was a quantum leap beyond a flash of anger. The impact, he thought, would have been vastly greater on Nakamura, a man who seemed to be on the run from an invisible force, suspicious, looking over his shoulder, waiting for them to catch him. 'They' were in the shadows, tracking him.

Whoever 'they' were remained a mystery for Ben, an enigma, which he could not unravel until it was too late. Not that it mattered much because, sooner or later, they always tracked you down, hauled you away. It had nothing to do with the relocation camps his Japanese-American grandparents had been herded into; it had more to do with the fast times of living in Asia, the cutting of corners, making the sharp deals, walking the walk around all the corners where people stood with their hands out waiting for a pay-off. That morning the 'they' had been Sam McNeal. She had caught him in the act. This was the man who had stood on honor and dignity. He had refused to approach his employers. If Nakamura had turned a gun on himself, everyone would have understood. It was also a good enough reason to put a contract on Ben Nakamura. That was the way business was often done in Bangkok. Only it hadn't worked out that way. Not this time.

NINE

"CALVINO, COME INSIDE, you are missing out on the party," said Quentin, taking half a step out to the verandah. "There are other people besides Ben that you should meet. And I understand that you already spoke with Pauline this afternoon. You didn't tell me that you had planned to see her. That's against the rules. Next time check with me first."

"Rules, Mr. Stuart? Maybe you don't understand. When I run an investigation, sir, I run it without checking with anyone, including the client. If you want someone to ask for your permission or advice every time there is a lead to follow up, then you should find another investigator."

"Please don't take it that way. I want only you on this case. It's just that I don't like surprises."

"Waking up alive in the morning is a surprise for a lot of people in this city," said Calvino.

Quentin smiled and held out his hand, "You're absolutely right. You must be in charge. So we will leave it for now. Friends?"

Calvino watched the still boyish like smile that had been flashed at directors, producers and starlets, thinking he was inside a case, which had the classic blueprint of trouble. He looked at the old man's tired eyes, and shook his hand, "Friends."

Then Quentin pulled him inside the sitting room and across the floor to the bar area where half a dozen people sat on wooden stools at the bar. Ben Nakamura sat behind the bar, half turned away so as not to catch Calvino's eye. Interesting, thought Calvino.

"This is Reed Mitchell. He works in the aerospace industry," said Quentin. "When a doctor delivers a death sentence you want to keep on the good side of those working close to the face of God."

"Mr. Stuart must mean my boss," said Reed.

"Aerospace covers a lot of industries," said Calvino.

"If you narrow it down to communication satellites, then you win a prize," said Reed.

"We even do business with guys like Ben. Or at least we did until somehow our components got knocked out of the project. Not that I would put down anyone with such a wicked reputation as Ben as a reference on my resume."

Nakamura looked over at Reed but then quickly looked away without catching his eye. All the flames he had received from Sam McNeal had scorched Nakamura's social underbelly, and even to lightly joke about his reputation caused Ben enough discomfort for a thin line of sweat to pull a corkscrew in a long, crooked wet line running from his hairline to his chin. Nakamura and Mitchell: same business, same kind of monkey business.

What else had Nakamura been lying about, wondered Calvino.

Quentin pulled over an older man in his mid-fifties who looked out of place in a rumpled shirt unbuttoned to his navel. His pants were torn at the right knee in a way that suggested an accident rather than fashion. He wore a pair of cheap sunglasses and on the right side one lens was missing. His gray hair was uncut, curling over his ears, and his face was wrinkled, particularly around the eyes, shooting him the look of a double for the late poet W. H. Auden.

"And this is Osborn. He's a writer." Quentin Stuart disappeared down a flight of stairs to answer the phone.

Calvino watched him leave, a slow, painful walk, one stair at a time. When Calvino looked back up, Osborn was staring at him.

"I know what you're thinking. I look like a pirate. But that's how I am expected to appear. You see, Quentin invited me to give the party balance. So that people of all walks of life might be represented and rub their shoulders together as we all admire that wonderful aquarium," said Osborn with a richly textured public school accent.

"I was trying to explain that the clothes were actually new. But they became rumpled and sweaty from the bus ride to Quentin's party. I didn't have the right change for an air-con bus so I took one of those lime green buses."

"You took a bus in Bangkok?" asked one of the younger *farang*s. Calvino guessed that he was in his mid-twenties. He had the kind of green eyes and swept back blonde hair that would have made him popular on the playgrounds. Sitting one stool down opposite Nakamura, the *farang*'s lower jaw was dropped, as if the word bus had taken his breath away.

"Don't sound so surprised. You know those large vehicles, which come in a variety of colors: green, blue and white, red and white, and air-con. Those are called buses. Would you mind if I had another glass of wine?"

"Did you know Sam McNeal?" asked Calvino.

"Now, I know you are some kind of detective and you want to interrogate people so I will be kind to you and tell you that no, I did not have the pleasure of knowing the lady. But this gentlemen, Greg did."

"Reed, the name's Reed, Mr. Osborn. Not Greg."

"Sorry, sorry. I'm terrible about names especially ones that sound like river weeds. But you were saying how much you liked Sam and how sad she wasn't her lovely self at the party tonight because she had killed herself. How thoughtless of her. For her to deny you her attention this evening must be painful for you."

"This guy's a real card. Kind of like Benny Hill on a bad hair day," said Reed.

"I am certain that if Benny Hill were alive he would resent that remark. But he's also dead, and for all we know he may still resent it. But I will let it pass since it was uttered by an American engineer of telecommunication satellites that take pictures of Saddam Hussein using his relatives for target practice."

"See what I mean? Why are the English always so funny?"

"Americans somehow seem to bring out the humor in us. I have never found a satisfactory answer as to why.

Perhaps it's the funny way they use their vowels."

"You should see how we use our bowels if you think our vowels are funny," said Reed Mitchell, bringing some laughter from the bar crowd.

"A gentleman never talks about his bowels in public," said Osborn, looking Calvino up and down, with his one-lensed sunglasses.

"But an American can never be a gentleman," replied Reed.

"Quite," said Osborn, but his interest in Reed Mitchell had faded and he had begun to look bored. "A suit jacket isn't exactly suitable for the tropics, is it? Not since Somerset Maugham's days anyway."

Calvino looked him straight in the eye. "Let's say it's practical," said Calvino, ignoring Alan's pun. There was a game for intellectual turf being fought at the bar and he was waiting for one of the guests to take a mortal hit.

"What Mr. Calvino means is that he's carrying a . 8 in the holster under his left arm and if we don't co-operate he will start shooting us one at a time. Hopefully, he is patriotic enough to shoot the Brit first," said Reed Mitchell.

Quentin walked over to the bar and put an arm around Calvino's shoulder.

"So how are we getting along?" Quentin asked.

"Like a house on fire," said Reed Mitchell.

"It's difficult to know. Mr. Calvino doesn't seem to talk a lot," said Osborn.

"True, true," said Reed. "But with you Brits around how does anyone get a word in edgewise?"

"Mr. Mitchell has suggested that your detective use his gun on me. How very American."

Quentin Stuart laughed. "Osborn is not only a very witty writer, he's an aquarium designer," said Quentin with some pride, nodding at the huge aquarium a few feet away. "He designed this one."

"I am doing a much larger one for a bar in the Plaza. Lollipop Bar. Wonderful name. The owner plans to stock my latest creation with beautiful *yings*."

"And he's hiring you as lifeguard for the night shift," said Reed Mitchell, looking directly at Calvino.

"Not a bad idea," said Osborn. "I must suggest it to him. Please be careful not to think too much, you might get a headache."

TEN

WHILE REED AND osborn sparred to establish who had the most wit, Calvino moved off to the side to watch a small group of women who had huddled together on the sofas, with Pauline Cheng sitting in the center. The women, who were mostly Thai, snacked on satay chicken and sipped glasses of wine. They wore the middle-class office worker's standard issue uniform of the Big Weird: padded shoulders, tapered skirts or dresses which revealed their tiny waistlines and were short enough to reveal a lot of leg. This short silk dress brigade had perfect long hair, not a strand out of place, and one of those two-hours-before-a-mirror make-up jobs.

And when Calvino first saw them earlier in the night, they were telling each other what beautiful white skin the other had. No one examining such a group of women at a party could mistake them for anyone other than women who belonged to the Chinese-Thai elite. They didn't occupy the nose cone at the top of the social rocket, but climbing farther down, they belonged at the fuel-tank level, a rung still high above the vast majority of other women in Bangkok. They had the kind of *farang* boyfriends that gave them the added status—which was saying something, since *farang*s normally occupied a position just below the paint job on the rocket's tail fins.

But a packaged *farang* who had attached himself to a designer name, a name connected to huge mega-companies with international recognition was different.

He was in the pilot's seat and the women were more than happy to go flying with him. Pauline appeared to be doing most of the talking with the audience of Thai women smiling in an admiring way at the style, confidence and open ways of this woman who was Chinese on the outside but *mem-farang* inside.

He could only catch sentence fragments. "WULF empowers women . . . hope . . . men are fearful . . . Sam supported us . . . we are not objects . . . No man in this room understands . . ."

One of the other women interrupted Pauline Cheng, who in a voice loud enough to be heard across the room, said, "Bangkok is the death of relationships. Death of family. Death of friendship. Death of all normal social connections. Smoke up the chimney. Ashes, ashes, we all fall down."

What she was saying Calvino had heard before, the Big Weird had evolved a way of living that, among the expat community, was aberrant, mutant, filled with stillborn couplings without meaning, without direction, without a future. In other words, a community not all that different from the one living in the air they were breathing. The men who suffered from The Sickness coped best in such a hostile atmosphere; stumbling forward as if going back was no longer an option. The women who suffered wanted to flee. And there the battle was joined.

Pauline's conversation stopped. There was dead silence on the sofa as all eyes looked upward at a tall American, wearing a floral-pattern jacket and an open shirt, his hair gray-flecked, who stood with a Thai hooker near the top of the stairs. He must have come through the door just as Osborn was leaving. He looked like a college kid grown into middle-age, with his boyish smile, lantern jaw. As he smiled, he set his jaw into one of those slight overbites, looking vaguely like the old photographs of Franklin Delano Roosevelt in those pre- wheelchair years of the 19 0s. His companion looked childlike next to him, the top of her head coming to about the middle of his shoulder. She wore one of the smallest mini-dresses ever manufactured and a woolly rapper hat.

"Quentin, how are you?" the man shouted in a loud booming voice.

"Slugo, welcome."

Nathan Gold came down the stairs with both of his arms extended and, as he reached the bottom of the stairs, he stepped forward and gave Quentin a big Hollywood party hug. He winked at Calvino. Earlier that day they had spoken on the phone, and Nathan "Slugo" Gold had passed on some reliable information about Pauline Cheng.

"I'm sorry we are late but I had a terrible time pulling Ice off the computer."

She came up behind him, peered around and batted her eyelashes at Quentin. "Hi, I am Ice," she purred.

The old man broke into a smile and shook her hand. "And I am Quentin. This is my house. Please get yourself a drink and there is lots of food."

Everyone in the room watched as Ice skipped like a schoolgirl across the floor, stopping to trace her forefinger with one super long fingernail across the cool glass of the aquarium.

"I am about to launch Ice deep into cyberspace," said Slugo.

"I am ready to go surfing," said Reed.

"We will be up and running tomorrow," said Slugo, beaming, rocking back on his heels.

"Congratulations," said Quentin.

"If I can pull it off, Ice will be the first ever D interactive avatar in cyberspace. She is going to be a very big digital star. I mean just look at her pixels," he said, laughing, a boyish laugh, the bemused kind that one imagined he had not changed since the eighth grade.

Luk Pla, who had been looking like a bored, impatient kid at a grown-up party, sitting alone off to one side of the sofa, spinning her gold bracelets on her left wrist, looking off in a half-trance at the large oil painting of a Vietnamese fisherman on the wall, came to life. She ran over and embraced Ice. They spoke in Isan, giggling and touching each others' gold. Slugo shouted at them in Thai, and then finished off his sentence in Isan. He was completely fluent in Thai and Isan—one of the language savants that the Big Weird attracted was Calvino's assessment of Slugo.

Both women, with their lack of social grace, appeared much younger than the other women around Pauline Cheng, even though those couldn't have been more than four or five years older. They were from the peasant class, dark-skinned upcountry class that the others would have been embarrassed to speak to as an equal; after all, Luk

Pla had worked in a bar, and was being kept by the old man. She was the prototype Thai woman who would never get a visa to the UK and would never be told why. It wasn't just the Thai class system operating like a well-oiled machine; it was the worldwide class system.

Despite the expensive clothes, the jewelry, the make-up, Luk Pla and Ice could not disguise the fact that they belonged to the same class as the servants who scraped around on their knees, holding above their heads trays of finger food, speaking Isan amongst themselves, invisible people who were not acknowledged by the women who had come with the *farang* men around the bar. Until Ice had arrived, Luk Pla was the only one who had talked to them, acknowledged their existence, and this made them feel awkward, not knowing what to do, so they laughed and quickly moved across the room, putting distance between themselves and one of their own who had gone from kneeling to standing in elite company.

Luk Pla felt that she had been totally ignored, unable to talk to her own people, unaccepted by the other Thai women. She had been having a rotten time. Her face had come alive with joy as she saw Ice. The two *ying*s hugged each other again as the men watched. The party had started for Luk Pla. She had waited for Quentin to return and pay attention to her, but he had been busy with the guests. She had come out of social limbo.

"Baby Fish looked so lonely. Now look at her," said Calvino as he moved Quentin away from the bar.

Quentin looked across the room, looking for Luk Pla.

"She and Ice go way back," said Quentin. "I asked her what she is thinking when she stares out into space, and she says, darling, I am thinking about you."

Calvino and the old man joined Luk Pla, and Quentin gave her a playful hug, then leaned over and touched Pauline Cheng's arm.

"How is your drink, Pauline?"

As Pauline looked up, she saw Calvino next to the old man, but just as she was about to say something to the private eye, her attention was diverted by the presence of Slugo.

"Slugo the pornographer has arrived," said Pauline to the women around her, then she looked over at Slugo, "And Alpha Domo is one of the most disgusting projects ever in cyberspace."

"Why doesn't this woman like me?" asked Slugo, shrugging his shoulders and setting his square jaw, flexing the jaw muscles.

"Because you are using the Internet to create a new class of cyberserfs. Women as sexual objects."

Slugo laughed nervously. "God, this is a great party. I just arrived and already Pauline wants to start a fight with me. That's rather tacky. But okay, have it your way. One thing you might have overlooked is that working *ying*s like Ice don't have such a great life at the moment. What I am doing is empowering her far more than all of your WULF-like rhetoric which gets them nowhere. They don't even understand what you are talking about. All these *ying*s do for you is to provide you with the means to attract private donations. WULF means nothing to *ying*s like these. They would think it was a joke. And what really gets me, Pauline, is you don't like them. You don't talk to them, and you really don't care a rat's ass about them. But cyberserfs, I like that term, Pauline. Sometimes, despite yourself, you have a creative flair, in a kind of scary Pol

Pot fashion."

Pauline turned her back to him.

"Pig," she whispered under her breath.

"Pig? Why not a rat. It is the Year of the Rat. Being Chinese I would have thought at least you could get your animals right."

Slugo did not wait for her response and moved across to the bar. Ice had her nose and lips pressed against the outside of the aquarium. On the opposite side, Luk Pla did the same thing. They both laughed and slobbered on the glass, laughing themselves sick, until they dropped to their knees. Even the Welsh and Scottish oil executives and their wives had stopped talking and watched.

After a few minutes, Calvino sat down next to Pauline.

"Hi again. Sorry for showing up early today. We got off to a poor start. Can we try again?" asked Calvino.

"I was just explaining to Janet that a fortune teller said that in a previous life I had been raised around elephants near the Burmese border. Then I had been reborn in America because I had done much good in my last life, helping the elephants, and in this life I had returned to help Thailand again."

Quentin sat down on the other side of Pauline. "You believe in the supernatural?" asked Calvino.

"The supernatural is like a thief that sneaks up on you at night and logs onto your soul, leaving messages here and there. Like secrets, the ones lovers tell as lies to each other," she said.

"Did Sam believe in astrology?" asked Calvino. Quentin answered before Pauline had a chance.

"She loved astrology. She showed me her natal chart and said it was her destiny to never grow old."

Calvino caught sight of Osborn, who obviously had not left. He stood at the top of the stairs.

"Ice, you are magnificent. The party is so balanced socially that I can leave," Osborn shouted. Osborn gave a little wave and disappeared. The upstairs door opened and closed. Then Reed's voice came from the behind the bar, "Elvis has left the building. There will be no more encores."

As Calvino looked up he saw a table with three expat couples sitting around talking and drinking together. The *mem-farang* wives were staying close to their husbands who talked about the oil business and pipelines in Burma. Welsh and Scottish accents that no one could understand but themselves helped to maintain the isolation. They came with bottles of Johnnie Walker Black and were drunk enough to start singing Welsh ballads. They had arrived as a group to a Hollywood party; but this wasn't Hollywood, and, if the women were lucky, they would get themselves and their husbands out of town before they reeled in a Baby Fish.

Every time they looked around, Luk Pla was running up and kissing Quentin. Now Ice had arrived and had attracted the eyes of every man in the room. That was how The Sickness started—it was spread by *yings*. And *yings* like Ice and Luk Pla were like a flu-germ running around the room looking for a new host to light on. Elvis might have left the stage but his performance lived on. Keep the men drunk and singing and they might not come down with the bug. Just maybe, they realized, despite the hardship of postings to Ho Chi Minh City, Perth, Aberdeen, Saudi, that the lesson was families thrived on hardship, it brought them together. Bangkok brought them the big easy, and that was an altogether different lesson they were just beginning to learn.

ELEVEN

IF QUENTIN HAD trouble with the idea of dying, he did not show it at the party. With the all the posturing, envy, backstabbing in full operation, Quentin might have found the perfect way to come to terms with his own death—surrounding himself with distractions powerful enough to allow the mind to forget the inevitable end was near. If that was his game, why had he kept probing into Sam's death? Such activity could only cause him to remember that his doctors had given him less than a year to live.

Writers lived by a different set of values, where curiosity was elevated above love, where constructing an original scene had more meaning than building a family, and where the world of words and images had more of a connection with human nature than real blood and real tears. As Quentin had walked him to the door the night before, he put a hand on Calvino's shoulder and asked, "What misery of Sam's soul coalesced to the point of self-destruction?"

All morning, Calvino had been asking himself that same question and not finding anything remotely satisfactory for an answer. Cases like Quentin's were a tedious task of arranging evidence without knowing for sure what to look for, and this was like trying to realign the freckles on the shoulders and back of a redhead. It took considerable concentration. Then the phone rang; it was Quentin Stuart on the other end.

"Good morning, Vincent."

Quentin's call came as no surprise, and neither did his gentle questioning as to how much Calvino had learned during the course of the evening that might be useful in his investigation. He had asked the same question at the door, and over the phone Calvino gave him the same answer.

"It's too early to know what was useful and what wasn't," said Calvino.

"I loved Pauline's description of your contradictory Cancerian nature, possessing a strong sense of working to prevent injustice being at war with a natural crablike selfishness. The hero who celebrates the antihero and who is neither."

"Who else did you deconstruct the evening with, Quentin?"

"I'm hearing that hard edge in your voice, Vincent."

The old man was right; there was no point in taking any of Pauline's jabs personally. He had climbed into the ring, so he had to expect to be hit.

"Cheng didn't like Slugo all that much either," said Calvino.

"It turned into a pissing contest between two computer nerds. It's like locking two writers in the same room; you might as well put two cats in a bag and shake it. And another writer is the reason I am calling. But, first, let me get your reaction to Osborn. Psychologically, I think the man is brilliant. But talk about difficult. God, I have never met a more difficult man in my life. I want to expand your assignment. Just slightly. I want you to do some checking up on Alan's background. He doesn't really fit into the usual crowd as you will have gathered from last night. But I don't hold that against him. Actually, it endears him to me.

"He sees right through their bullshit and pretense, and they hate him for it. But if he is going to write the definitive Quentin Stuart biography, I want to make certain that he's qualified for the job. That's the Capricorn in me. Some years ago he wrote a lovely book of short stories called *The Visitations*. It was published in England and had some very good reviews. The stories are vignettes about prisoners serving time in Bedford prison. On the strength of that book alone I have no doubt that Alan's a literary genius."

"A literary genius throws away a writing career in England to build fish tanks in Bangkok?" asked Calvino. "Why would he do that?"

"Precisely my question. Of course, as to your compensation, I don't expect you to do this added work for free. I propose giving you another thousand dollars as an additional advance. Whatever expenses you have, just keep a record, and if your time runs over a thousand, let me know and I will pay you. Cash."

"Cash is not what I am thinking about," said Calvino.

"What's on your mind, Vincent?"

"My mind is like one rider on two horses. And I am

thinking to myself, 'What's his priority? Sam McNeal's death or a due diligence investigation in Osborn's background?' I don't mind counting freckles as long as I know whose back I am supposed to find the freckles on. And I still don't have an answer."

"They have equal priority," said Quentin Stuart.

"One rider on the back of two horses. Forget about the freckles. It's a mixed metaphor."

"One writer and one dead woman I am starting to think is another mixed metaphor."

"This conversation isn't helping. Please get started," said Quentin Stuart. His voice had gone into heavy studio mode: meaning, I want this now.

Calvino found himself saying into the phone with the broken connection. "Who knows, there might be a connection?" Expat Bangkok was a small fractured community: the packaged *farang*s with all the perks and status and the unpackaged *farang* underclass, those with Thai wives from good backgrounds, those with Thai girlfriends from the nightlife world, the gays, the corporate types, the journalists, the English teachers, the ex-soldiers, drifters and grifters—they lived within their narrow circles rarely venturing beyond the borders of their private lives into the domain of other expats.

Quentin's party was a microcosm of the different *farang* lives assembled in his sitting room with the same care that he had stocked his aquarium. When Osborn turned up at Quentin's party, he found himself surrounded by other guests like Ben Nakamura, Reed Mitchell, Pauline Cheng and the half dozen others like them. He stood out from the crowd and he was as foreign to them as any Thai tuk-tuk driver fresh in from the country. Lives like

Alan's were as incomprehensible as they were disturbing to the packaged *farang* crowd, which clung onto the hometown values of the West. The latest trend had been for some of the unpackaged *farang*s to go home, finding jobs that would return them as packaged *farang*s; a kind of economic laundry, dry-cleaning and pressing the new man and sending him back all clean on an expensive hanger.

Quentin Stuart got away with playing the iconoclast, the man who reviled Hollywood as empty, sterile, deadly; a legendary figure was granted the right to play outsider after he had enjoyed all the spoils of an insider for forty years. But guys like Osborn had never been inside anything other than a prison, and then only to write about their experience. Even in England, Osborn had chosen the outsiders as the subject of his book. He was the kind of man who sought his literary characters as time servers in an English prison and who built aquariums for rich bar owners in the Plaza. Calvino had a gut feeling that a woman like Sam McNeal had a history of strong attractions to outsiders: Ben Nakamura and Quentin Stuart fitted the pattern. He felt that if he dug deep enough he just might find Osborn's steadfast idealism, a fish out of water who built fish tanks for the rich, had connections to Sam's world.

TWELVE

RATANA SAT IN Calvino's office watching her boss as he struggled to understand the nature of social relationships in Thailand. It was a Rubik's Cube that most foreigners went crazy trying to solve. Even for the Thais, the effort was considerable and not always correct.

Ratana gave her spin on how the puzzle had shifted. In the 90s, the question in Bangkok was no longer whether you were on someone's wavelength, but whether you were listed on their expanded cc-list. People talked about bandwidth not wavelength. The Big Weird smart talk with guys like Slugo at the head of the class was about cash and knowledge; thoughts could be converted into digital information and transmitted over telephone wires around the world.

After Quentin Stuart's party, Calvino had renewed respect for his secretary's deep insight into the inner workings of Bangkok's expats. At the same time, Ratana was not immune to the notion that meeting a handsome young Japanese-American could lead to something.

Calvino had described Ben in some detail, and Ratana pretended not to be interested as she took in his every word.

Her first glimpse of Ben Nakamura was as he was getting out of his new silver-gray BMW outside of Calvino's building. It would be difficult to sell Ben as being Chinese, and Ratana came from a strict Chinese family where dating a non-Chinese would have caused an uproar. It wasn't that difficult to read her initial reaction to Ben. He fit the picture that Calvino had painted. Looking down at him as he was getting out of his car, she was playing it real cool, pretending she didn't know whether the perfect hunk below was her boss's appointment in contrast to the usual gangster-stroke-investors in real property, meaning someone headed for an appointment with the Finnish real estate developers on the ground floor. She knew this man in his tailored suit would continue walking up the staircase until he reached the offices of Vincent Calvino, private investigator. Nakamura, after walking up the two flights of stairs, opened the door to Calvino's office. Ratana noticed that, up close, his tailored suit was Armani and his smooth good looks turned her lips curving upward into a light bulb flash of a smile.

"I have an appointment with Mr. Calvino. My name is Ben Nakamura," he said, holding out his business card.

She listened to this as if he had recited a profound theorem.

"Would you like coffee or tea, Mr. Nakamura?"

"Mineral water," said Nakamura.

She showed him into Calvino's office and excused herself so that she could run over to Villa market and buy him a bottle of mineral water with her own money. She slowed at Nakamura's BMW, caught sight of herself in the rearview mirror; she smiled, winked, as if she liked looking at herself reflected in a BMW.

"Here's a print-out of the e-mails we talked about last night," said Nakamura. He set a manila envelope on Calvino's desk. It had "Vincent Calvino, Private and Confidential" written on the front.

Calvino opened the envelope, removing a computer floppy diskette and a print-out of the sixty-three e-mails Ben had received from Sam McNeal. He flipped through some of the messages. Ben sat erect in the wooden chair as if he were at a court martial and Calvino were the judge who was about to hand down a verdict. He said nothing, letting Calvino read through the letters. Most were less than a page long. If he could have measured the force and speed of her anger, then by the end of the messages, Calvino would have gauged this emotion in terms of light years. A white heat of anger underscored the latter messages, as if something had broken inside her and what rained out was no longer in control.

"Did you reply to these messages?" asked Calvino.

Ben nodded.

"I tried to reason with her. But it didn't work. Then I stopped responding."

"But she kept on sending letters."

"Not saying anything seemed to make her even more mad. And she included my boss's boss in Tokyo on the spam. She was doing a good job of ruining my career."

"What did your boss say about the e-mail?"

Ben Nakamura showed no emotion, looking straight ahead.

"He said she was unstable."

"Meaning?"

"I had allowed myself to get involved with someone who could cause trouble."

"Not to mention the embarrassment." "Of course, there was that."

"All because you wouldn't help her to convince your company that the switch to the Chinese component procurement was in their interest?" asked Calvino, sitting back in his chair.

"I go back and forth about the Chinese company. Sometimes I think it was her forcing this business deal which was none of her business. Sometimes I think, it wasn't the Chinese components that caused our personal life to crash."

"Crash?"

"Like a plane that lost altitude and power. Once she saw the power had cut out, well, that made for a scene. She wanted something more, how can I put this, more permanent."

"A commitment."

"Yeah, I guess you could call it that."

Ratana came in with a glass of mineral water, which Ben took off the tray. The boyish smile had vanished from his face which looked drawn, worried. Ratana stood for a moment, thinking he might acknowledge her. But he didn't, so she retreated to her office.

"Did Sam ever talk much about her ballet dancing?" asked Calvino.

"Once or twice. Women like talking about the past. That was especially true if they had worked as a model or dancer. It was usually a time when they had some physical advantage over other women. Men noticed them. And they ignored other women. You know, once anyone gets that much attention it is difficult to break the addiction."

"Addiction?" asked Calvino, thinking that Ben could have been talking about himself as much as about Sam.

"You know, being in the limelight is like taking a drug. Sam mainlined on her five years as a ballet dancer in LA. Then it was over. It's like a baseball player who one day is starring in the major leagues, and the next week is in the 'burbs selling secondhand cars on commission. It's a long fall until you hit the bottom of that barrel."

Calvino remembered the first time they met and how she had talked about the importance of control over the body and breathing for a dancer's career. She had said that a ballet dancer was perfectly in tune with each breath, each muscle, each movement, and it was in the coordination that beauty and elegance arose for all to see. The ability to control her body had been her attraction to ballet, not that her body attracted attention, so Ben had gotten that part wrong.

Then, why, Calvino wondered, had there been nothing in their meeting that suggested such uncon- trolled rage lay boiling just beneath the surface. Such a transformation did not make sense to him. But if life held one universal lesson it was that judging another person's reaction to private pain was at best a lucky guess, and that pain anointed some sufferers with majesty and grace while the catastrophe of pain robbed others of their dignity and drove them to acts of destruction and despair. Her death appeared to have been an accident of her pain; she turned her pain into a ceremony of self-inflicted destruction.

The ultimate revenge on the body which can no longer be controlled. Kill it.

Calvino scrolled through the list of name on the cc: most of the names meant nothing to him, but a number of the names at Quentin Stuart's party were also on the cc-list, including Osborn's. A man who could only afford to take a bus to a party but had a computer and Internet account was an interesting contradiction, thought Calvino. But it was her last e-mail, the one sent on the day of her death, which caught his attention. At the top was the date and time. He reread the time and date a couple of times. Sam McNeal had been found dead at about half past three in the morning. Her last e- mail had been recorded as having been sent at 5: a.m. A dead ballet dancer had sent a message an hour and a half after her death?

"Do you believe in the existence of the human soul? So that after death, there is some essence of the person that remains?" Calvino asked.

Nakamura had been expecting a lot of questions, but this wasn't one of them.

"Yeah, I guess if you don't believe in the soul, what is the alternative?"

"Seems Sam sent her last e-mail an hour and half after she died. Or the alternative is someone who didn't know that she was dead sent it, thinking that she was alive."

Nakamura spilled mineral water down the front of his white Italian shirt.

"Why didn't I notice that?" Nakamura asked, clenching his jaw.

"Do you have any idea who she was with that night?"

He shrugged his shoulders. "I have no idea." Nakamura answered a little too fast; he seemed off balance, his mind perhaps still shifting through the time sequences on the e-mail. "She was found dead in the sitting room of your house," said Calvino. "What time did you come back home?"

"I can't remember. But it was late," said Ben. Calvino didn't like the evasive answer. "Where were you earlier? You know, before it got late."

Ben sighed as if he had gone all through the same questions before. "At a private members' club. Cezanne. It's just around the corner from your office."

"Are you a member or were you a guest?" "I'm a member," he replied.

"Any other of Sam's friends members?" Calvino handed him the top e-mail and a pen.

"Go through the spam, put a check after any name you think might be a member or who has spent time at Cezanne."

"Was Sam at the club earlier?"

Nakamura nodded and played with the pen, looking down the list of about twenty names.

"You're asking me to rat on my friends?"

"I am asking you about club membership or hangers-on. I am looking for someone who can establish that you were at Cezanne on that night. Since you stayed at the club after Sam left. It is a routine check."

Calvino watched as Ben thought about this fine distinction. "If it makes you feel any better, no one is going to know how I acquired this information. It could have come from someone at Cezanne, from the police investigation or from Quentin after he looked at the spam."

That assurance did the trick, and Nakamura checked off five names: Quentin Stuart, Reed Mitchell, Pauline Cheng, Andrew Williams, and Slugo. Calvino examined the names.

"Andrew Williams, I don't remember him at Quentin's party the other night?"

"He was there. One of the oil crowd. The one who was reciting poetry at two in the morning. He stayed upstairs with his wife, Karen. The Welsh woman with red hair who wore a blue dress."

Calvino remembered seeing three *farang* couples who sat around the upstairs dining-room table, drinking Quentin's wine after their Johnnie Walker ran out, keeping to themselves, singing and dancing. Partying a little too hard to overlook. He remembered Williams was the one who had the red-haired wife. The packaged *farang*s often arrived with a wife as part of the baggage. They stayed within their own social circles, and made a point of not mixing with *farang*s who were either single or had Asian girlfriends or wives.

It was not all that strange that someone like Andrew Williams was a member of Cezanne. Packaged *farang*s were known to lead double lives, and a private club offered them the two basic requirements for a double life: anonymity and the opportunity to meet the right multiplier. And someone like Pauline Cheng loved to play the spoiler, sitting at a table, watching them, knowing their names, the names of their wives and girlfriends.

"What was with Pauline Cheng and Slugo at the party last night?" asked Calvino.

"The usual. A turf war over who ends up controlling the sexual agenda on the Net."

"You ever do battle with Pauline?"

"Everyone ends up doing battle with her. She likes to quote the old Chinese saying that the marketplace is a battlefield. She reads the *The Art of War* for pleasure." Nakamura was staring at Calvino's copy of the book on his desk as he finished speaking.

"You sound a little bitter."

"I think she turned Sam against me."

"You wouldn't get your company behind the Chinese parts deal because you thought the parts were defective. Only the Chinese parts were going through whether you helped or not. The decision had been made. All you had to do was smooth things over with your boss, right?"

He looked shaken as he nodded, then took the glass and sipped some water. "I explained it to Sam like this. Take a Boeing 747 with all the latest radar and computer equipment in the cockpit, and all the bolts manufactured by some guy and his family out of a shophouse factory. Some of the bolts hold together but a number of other bolts disintegrate after two hundred air miles. All that world-class computer equipment isn't going to stop those Third World bolts from popping out and the plane dropping out of the sky. I told her that's what Pauline wants my company to agree to. And my company believes in quality. We don't fly planes that are going to fall out of the sky in five years."

"What did she say?"

"After she talked to Pauline, she said, 'Your company doesn't make planes. No one is going to fall out of the sky.'"

"Why didn't you tell me about Reed?" asked Calvino.

"Because my decision had nothing to do with him. Otherwise, you would get the wrong idea."

After Ben Nakamura left, Ratana came in and removed the glass of mineral water. He had barely touched it. She caught Calvino's eye, the one which watched disapprovingly. "His last girlfriend killed herself," said Calvino.

That piece of information had no impact. "I can take care of myself," she said.

It was an exact quote from one of Sam McNeal's e-mails; hearing it from Ratana's lips made him shiver, the kind of cold that comes from hearing a voice from the grave, not in a tone of regret, but the provocative, sure voice of one who had never come out second-best in a relationship game.

As Ratana eased out of his office, he read Sam's e-mails in the sequence in which they had been sent. "Maybe I was bored, and needed too much attention. But I wanted you on my side, Ben. I needed you there. Whatever shortcut I had to take to make that happen, I would take it. I don't know why you couldn't understand the one thing I needed from you. I wanted to be wanted by you. You had wanted me, and I knew how that felt. Then when you no longer wanted me, how do you think that made me feel? Can you know what it is not to be wanted? Probably not, you have all the women wanting you, you have all the wanted desires the rest of us have the luxury of coming across once in a lifetime. It has made you careless and callous, Ben. To be wanted too much by so many is just as bad as not being wanted at all. Can't we meet and work this out? Can't we find a middle ground where our souls can find peace?"

The question of the human soul existed in the realm of maybes, which could never have been explored. Other maybes abounded, which could turn into either a yes or no based on objective evidence. In Thailand, there was no distinction between the objective and subjective maybes; they were one and the same.

What the letters to Ben indicated was that Sam had undergone some kind of expat identity crisis and the rupture of her relationship with Ben Nakamura was part of the catalyst that had broken her line of emotional support. Before she knew it, she was falling into a state of despair so profound that only a bullet could stop the fall.

The question of who had pulled the trigger that night had been complicated by another mystery: who had been lurking in cyberspace at the time of Sam's death, sending out messages in her name? The messages of someone wounded. Someone stranded, rejected, slipping into depression—convenient messages that established a motive for suicide. Timing was everything. Dead people don't send e-mail.

The Big Weird

THIRTEEN

AFTER ELEVEN THAT evening Calvino turned up at one of the upstairs Plaza bars, one of the single shophouse bars with a small stage, a dozen topless *yings* wearing Hawaiian skirts. The stage was only large enough for three to dance at one time. The music came from one of those ancient tapes which had not been updated since "Ring My Bell" had been released as a single. The bar was dark and had the smell of a gym locker room on a hot afternoon after the big game. The mamasan was squatting on a low stool behind the bar and she looked like Vietnam War vintage ex-bar girl.

Calvino counted three *farang*s in the bar, the kind of customers who came to nurse their personal sorrows and to watch slightly overweight topless peasants hang on a chrome pole and shuffle their feet. At the far end, Slugo sat on a stool, elbows propped back on the bar, his grinning face concentrated on the stage. Calvino sat down on the stool next to him and ordered a Mekhong and Coke.

"Ice lets you out on your own?" asked Calvino.

Slugo giggled.

"What kind of relationship do you think I have with her?"

"Flexible."

"I like that. It's a good word. But the relationship is mainly business. Ice is the center of my Alpha Domo Project." Slugo turned and picked up his orange juice and sipped through a straw before putting the glass back on the bar counter.

"Isn't the girl on the right, number 47, lovely? I could make her a star. She doesn't know it. But I could change her life just like that." He snapped his fingers.

"Like you plan to change Ice's?"

Slugo grinned. "Like Quentin changed Luk Pla's destiny. Don't tell me you have never changed the life of a bar girl, Calvino?"

"Never for the better," said Calvino.

"Didn't you see the sign on the door? No honesty allowed in this bar. You can keep your knives and guns, but don't go dragging that dangerous honesty into this place," Slugo broke out laughing at his own joke.

"I am interested in your Alpha Domo Project."

"A couple of days ago, my guess is that you didn't even know what a spam was. But I take it as a compliment. Okay, how can I explain this so you will understand it? Let's say the first, biggest revolution happened since Patpong, Soi Cowboy, Nana Plaza, all the way from Klong Toey to the Golden Mile. The next revolution occurs decades later and it is to take the bars into virtual reality with D interactive avatars. No sick days, no police payoffs, no drunks who won't pay their bills, no disappearing upcountry with their boyfriends. I mean a perfect bar.

It runs as a twenty-four-hour-a-day business machine. A license to print money," Slugo said, as number 47 stepped off the stage, walked across the floor, and sat on his lap. She cupped her mouth around Slugo's ear and whispered, "Buy me cola." He gestured to the mamasan, who was also doubling as the counter *ying*, to bring a cola. Then looked over at Calvino.

"Educate me," said Calvino. "Tell me more about how the Alpha Domo Project is going to make you a fortune and Ice a star."

With a bar *ying* on his lap, Slugo began, "The old world has been dying out since I was a student at Harvard. It was obvious then, anyone who can't see the writing on the wall now is living in a submarine under the North Pole. Quentin and all those Hollywood legends are dying off fast. No one can believe they are actually leaving us. Their lives are closer to Plato and Socrates than to yours or mine. Or at least to mine. The big departure is happening now. This isn't some small evolutionary step; it is a revolutionary one. We are busting every threshold those guys have believed for two thousand years would never be breached; they believed in an eternal system of small changes to the way we amuse ourselves.

"I am talking about something totally new, a new species of entertainment. A new species. One day, historians will look back and write that Ice, this little nothing bar *ying* from Isan was the first real, full personality to go into cyberspace and that Ice was the Eve of the new world. Alpha Domo created the New Eden. This time the first person in Eden isn't a man. It's a woman. She is giving birth to the new order of women. It is her destiny to be your mother, my mother, and mother of everyone who comes after us. She is so simple-minded that she can't see it; her bar *ying* greed and paranoia stops her. How can I explain it to her?, 'No more flesh, blood, bone; no more cancer and nasty, ugly deaths. Ice is the new medium.'

"I can't even begin to discuss the implications with her because she wouldn't understand. Pauline hates me because the new order is being born from a mother who she didn't create and who isn't Chinese. A mother created by a man. Can you imagine how pissed off she is that the new Eve is Thai and not Chinese? I asked her once, 'Pauline, What is wrong with sex for god sakes? And what is wrong with a sex worker being the handmaiden for this new world?'

"Nothing, of course, is the obvious, intelligent answer. But Pauline is on her own wavelength. No one can get through to her. Certainly not me. I have concluded that Pauline thinks that if the Chinese can't control the change I am talking about, if the Chinese cannot be the mother and father, then it has to be destroyed.

"Pauline is also so incredibly bright. But she's living in the past. Holding on for dear life like one of those decaying old emperors who have always run China; half ga-ga on bear paw soup and toasted gallbladders but still giving orders. She might know something about computers, but she can never transcend her mission which is to put ancestor worship and the imperial past above everything else. I wish her luck. But she doesn't stand a chance. We are entering an era where no one will have an ancestor."

"Pauline doesn't like the morality of Alpha Domo," said Calvino.

Slugo laughed so hard that his bar *ying* lost her balance and fell onto the floor. She didn't bounce; she didn't smile.

"Calvino, there is no morality in cyberspace. That's what Pauline and people can't accept. It is like Mars or Venus. Cyberspace is an amoral world that we plug into; the digital world has zero morals. Every digit is moral- free. It's nothing more than a sequence of zeroes and ones. Our destiny is in the right sequence for those two numbers together. No wonder Pauline's pissed off."

Calvino swung around on the stool and faced the stage, resting his arms back on the bar.

"What do you know about Pauline's connection with a Chinese firm that's selling components to a telecom project in Thailand?"

Number 19 had climbed onto Slugo's lap, straddling him, wrapping her legs around his waist, and her arms around him, leaning forward to kiss his ear.

"You don't really expect me to talk about Chinese components in a Plaza go-go bar?" asked Slugo.

"Why not? It's your office. Besides, you are an expert on the Internet and since you and Pauline have some disagreements, I thought you might have done some cyberspace investigations into such matters."

"You think I am a snoop?"

"You are a wise man. Just in case you might need some material on Pauline's godfathers in China."

"Godfather," said Slugo.

"I just loved the movie." Another *ying* stumbled out of the toilet smoking. She stuck her tongue out at a *farang* passing her. He wore a surgical mask, and pulled in close to Slugo.

"This is my wife," said the masked man, his eyes bloodshot and crazed. "You are fondling my wife, asshole."

Slugo smiled, his lower jaw jutting forward.

"Sir, this is a bar, and these are communal wives." Then he turned to number 19 and asked her in Thai, "Are you married to this man?"

"No like him," she said, her lower lip extended into a pout. "He's a cheap Charlie. And look like ghost."

"Well, I guess that qualifies as a barroom divorce. Sorry, maybe you ought to find another wife," said Slugo.

The man was hyperventilating behind his mask. He looked at Slugo, then at Calvino, and brought up his fist and shook it in Slugo's face.

"You'd better watch your back, mister," he said. "I will remember you, and people I remember wish I hadn't."

"That sounds vaguely like a threat?"

"Take it however you want."

As the man stormed off, Slugo shrugged his shoulders, leaning to one side, he said, "Remember the days when F&B used to stand for Food and Beverages? Or for a while it was shorthand for fuck and beer money, required for a night in the playground. Now F&B means fungi and bacteria and I think it is causing somethinglike the mad cow disease in some of the lower classes of expats. People never used to be this crazy in the Plaza. Or it is just me?"

The *ying* with wild eyes and high expectations of scoring a lady's drink sat on the stool next to Calvino. She sat staring at herself in the mirror and muttering into her glass.

"Buy me cola," she whined.

Calvino gestured for the bartender to bring the *ying* a Coke.

"And what if I have information about Pauline, why would I give it to you? I mean we are friends and I like you but hard information is not easy to come by," said Slugo.

The lady drink arrived and the sullen bar *ying* on Calvino's right raised her glass to touch Calvino's, he turned and raised his glass, and she leaned over and offered to toast Slugo and number 19. Then she took her drink, jumped off the stool, and went on stage, doing one of those sleepwalking shuffles as she leaned against the chrome pole, staring at herself in the mirror.

"I said, Calvino, why should I give you any more information about Pauline? I mean you phoned me today. I helped you out. Isn't that enough?"

"You decide if it's enough," said Calvino. "What does that mean?"

"One night you walk out of a bar, your house, or you are on the street. And before you know it, you are in the shit. Some guy with a surgical mask pulls a gun, a knife. It happens so fast you can't believe you aren't in a dream. You defend yourself and, if you are lucky, you survive and he doesn't. But whatever happens, you have to explain it to the cops. They're not interested. They slam on handcuffs and push you into the back of a van, and all that is going through your head is what did I do and how do I make this nightmare stop. A Third World arrest, an hour later you are inside a Third World jail. You ever see one of the holding cells? You get one phone call if you are real lucky and slip someone five hundred baht. Who are you going to phone, Slugo? Who is going to be there for you at that moment? Say, it's two in the morning. Your rich parents? Ice? Someone from cyberspace? Who are you gonna phone. Where do you log on?"

"I guess I'd phone you," said Slugo, looking up with a serious expression on his face. He caught the guy staring at him in the mirror. "I mean that guy did threaten me," Slugo said as if talking to himself, weighing up the odds. Number 19 was no longer bouncing on his lap, and he wasn't tickling her any more. "Trying to figure out connections between Chinese and overseas Chinese companies is like trying to sort out a bowl of noodles after an earthquake. But one rather interesting connection is the one between Pauline's Foundation and several mainland Chinese companies. One of the companies makes component parts for the telecommunication industry. This company, Muo Dun Company, it turns out, was a subcontractor for the Chinese Long March rocket program. Specifically, the Long March -B rocket. The name translates as Spear/Shield Company." "Didn't a -B rocket blow up in China not long ago?" asked Calvino.

"It sure did. The rocket blasted off, no problem, only it didn't stay in the sky all that long, as it came down in the middle of a populated area, blowing up a couple of thousand people. The Chinese immediately clamped down on information concerning casualties. That's no surprise. But there was no way they could stop the information from leaking onto the Net. The Chinese think that if you can manufacture fireworks for a commie festival you can launch a satellite into outer space. As they found out, it doesn't work that way. Pauline runs another amateur operation. Her NGO is in bed with the same dubious mainland characters who haven't done all that well getting the Long March -B rocket to stay in the air for longer than ten minutes. There was an American satellite as payload on that rocket as well," said Slugo; his bar ying, having crawled off his lap, was now on the stage shuffling against a chrome pole.

"Does Pauline know that you have this information?" asked Calvino.

Slugo tilted back his head and roared with laughter. "Are you kidding? She might have me killed by one of those thousand-baht hitmen who live in the Klong Toey slums."

"A thousand baht. Inflation is driving up all prices in the Big Weird," said Calvino. "Thanks for the information, Slugo."

"If I ever have to make that call, Calvino, make certain you are home, okay?"

Calvino lifted off the bar stool. "Don't worry, Slugo, I'll be there."

"And none of this information ever came from me, remember?"

Calvino gave him the thumbs up and walked out of the bar; not far behind was the strange *farang* wearing the surgical mask, the one who had threatened Slugo.

FOURTEEN

WALKING INTO THE Plaza early in the afternoon, Calvino had been thinking about the possible connection between the Chinese Long March -B rockets and Slugo's D avatars launched into cyberspace. Rockets and avatars had appeared on the same screen in the Big Weird, and as he passed the empty bars, he toyed with the question of whether Sam had been a casualty of the full collision when the forces hit. There was little doubt that Pauline Cheng had targeted Alpha Domo for obliteration, hoping to rescue a new generation, which would, if Slugo had his way, lose its virginity in cyberspace. At the same time, she was up to her arched eyebrows in doomed Chinese rockets.

He shaded his eyes against the blazing sun and looked around in the brilliant light. The air was stifling, filled with dust; it was oppressive and exhausting to be outside that time of day. The nighttime Plaza and daytime Plaza were like twin sisters separated at birth. One had survived, prospered, while the other one had withered.

The afternoon Plaza had the same queasy gut feeling that came whenever the cops had asked him to identify someone, sometimes dead, sometimes alive—the target of an investigation or a client who had been targeted. The dead ones always looked the same shade of death when laid out on a mortuary table.

A person gone blue, cold, gone to ice. Ice, he thought. Slugo had hit the right note with that nickname, and Ice had never looked back. At Quentin's party, Calvino had heard a Thai whisper, *kang-hok khuen wor.* That translates roughly as a toad that had climbed onto a royal carriage. Someone who had gone beyond her station in life as Osborn would have said. Ice was just the start of an assembly line for Slugo. Who else would he create for his digital Garden of Eden? Number 47? She had played the lap dance game but that was only an audition. Going into Eden required a quantum leap from the stage, from the lap, from the memory and into a realm that even Calvino wasn't certain that he fully understood.

An old man who looked like God hired him to investigate these creationists, not to worry about the new Gardens of Eden mushrooming in Bangkok, but to find an explanation of why one young woman had killed herself. Sam. Had Sam lived, what would she have made of Alan's aquarium world? It was a question no one would ever know the answer to. Souls didn't have mirrors; they had no surface on which to reflect an image.

Calvino stood at the base of the horseshoe, which formed the three-tier levels of the Plaza, and on his left was a glitzy bar. The outside had an unlit neon sign with the word "Lollipop" on it. The front of the bar looked like a candy house decorated with garish splashes of yellow and red plastic titles. The Plaza was nearly empty. While a few gray-haired *farang*s nursed beers at a nearby outside bar, Lollipop Bar itself was devoid of movement. Inside, the stools were turned upside down on the bar counter. At the far end, squatting on the floor with a cigarette in the corner of his mouth, Osborn broke off his conversation with two Thai workmen, as he saw Calvino walking down the aisle.

"Mr. Calvino, have you found your villain? Or is this excursion part of your never-ending search for love in all the wrong places?"

Calvino's eyes were on a long gaping hole in a wall; at the edge of the hole, workmen were mixing cement; others were positioning rockery in place. The construction site curved around one wall, and then snaked along the line of another wall forming a shape roughly like the letter "Z." On the lower edge of the cement wall someone had written in large white chalk letters: Lazy, you no work you. The glass was partially in place, the rest of the aquarium was open, unfinished. The surface was covered in a thick debris: nails, bits of wire, plastic pipe, wood chips, crumpled newspapers, rat shit, small mounds of dust, tools, brooms, several pair of worn-out sandals, and a red bra hooked around one of the support posts. Osborn stood nearby supervising a worker who was helping with the construction of the waterfall.

"The aquarium is huge," said Calvino. The roughed-out form looked like the cross section of a space, which was a combination of a Viet Cong tunnel and a New York City sewer.

Osborn pulled up a bar stool, planted one foot onto the black cushion, and climbed on top of the bunker-like structure. "Let me give you a tour."

Calvino followed him down the passage. "Mermaidium is what I call it," said Osborn as he stopped, looking out at the bar area.

"You see, there will be no fish. It works like this. A dozen *ying*s will swim in an underwater grotto, and stand under this waterfall. Look at the craftsmanship in these fake ancient stonewalls. And over there, I will place a splendid pirate's treasure chest."

Osborn pointed at a concrete hole where the chest would go and then ran his hand along the stone face of the waterfall, smiling. He lit a cigarette, crouched down, and exhaled smoke inside the unfinished aquarium.

"They will become performers, working below the surface, turning and twisting, and diving to the bottom of this magic kingdom, eyes opened, eyes closed. Like marine life. Dolphins with breasts. The interior lights shifting from red, to orange, then to green and to blue, washing them in a rainbow of colors. Disney couldn't have done it any better. The Mermaidium takes the sex business underwater. My dream is to one day build a fifty-meter Olympic swimming-pool-sized Mermaidium in which every lane will be the fast lane. Every *ying*, seventy of them, performing an underwater ballet.

"The Mermaidium will be a chain like the Planet Hollywood restaurants. Sex, like food, requires a commercial theme. Customers expect a theme that makes them feel part of the show. Food is no longer enough. Sex is no longer enough. Your entertainment experience inside the place of consumption is everything. Boredom is death. How could anyone ever be bored gazing at the Mermaidium? Impossible! Poetry, dance, and naked *ying*s in a watery paradise."

"A man's paradise has a way of turning into a woman's nightmare," said Calvino.

Like Slugo, Osborn had found in the Big Weird his own personal vision to create a commercial, money-spinning Garden of Eden. Bangkok's creative forces seemed to be moving in the same direction. Brain cells, awash in all that pollution, were misfiring, causing these apocalyptic projects. Alpha Domo. Mermaidium. WULF. The men jumped down from near the point where the pirate's chest was going to be placed, and walked over to the bar. Calvino looked back at the Mermaidium, looking inside where they had been standing, and tried to imagine supple bodies submerged, peering out at half-smashed punters sipping beers and throwing coins, laughing as they dived dolphin like to the bottom of the tank. One side wet; one side dry. How long would that imbalance last? Not long, thought Calvino.

The innocence of Eden never lasted. Sooner or later, the Eve inside Alan's Mermaidium would splash back at the Adams on the other side. Sooner or later she would find water was her weapon, her hands the delivery system and water would go over the top of the glass. It was human nature that whenever faced with a wall, one would find a way of escape.

A couple of Thai workers had taken Calvino's arrival as cover to slip away along the opposite side of the bar and out the door.

"Now there go my workers. They are hungry again," said Osborn. "We live in a region where cooking is at a significantly more advanced state than the rule of law. Which proves that, for the vast majority of citizens, what people eat commands far more importance than the occasional execution of an innocent man."

"Or the untimely death of a young woman," said Calvino.

"Precisely. Now what further interrogations do you wish to carry out? And I hope that you don't mind if I continue to work while I answer your questions? I am running behind schedule. The Mermaidium was set to open last week, but as you can see it is not finished."

"Why do you want to write Quentin's biography?"

"You mean, am I in it for the art, or for the money?"

"The first alternative hadn't occurred to me." Osborn pivoted around and acknowledged Calvino with a half-crooked smile.

"You may be smarter than you look. Let me enlighten you about the connection of art and money. It was a lesson I learned as a boy. I had a relative who made a fortune in the art business. He was a terrible painter. I mean he really couldn't paint worth a damn. To his credit he knew that he had this fundamental flaw. But he was a good businessman. One day, he was in one of those old junk shops in Norfolk and discovered a bin of quite old oil paintings, which were either landscapes or of the seashore. Just scenery. There were no personages in any of these paintings. They had no commercial value, and very little artistic merit. He would buy them for a pound, which was worth more than the piece, and then he would painstakingly paint in a series of tiny fishermen along the shore. I mean extremely small yet visible. Suddenly he transformed the one-pound oil into a piece of art that he easily flogged for ten guineas. He became quite rich doing this. Then he expanded by putting in tiny windmills when he discovered that the Dutch were coming for their holidays."

"Tiny fishermen?"

"Yes, it was a scam. But he made very good money. And here I am in Bangkok doing fish tanks rather than tiny fishermen and a biography of a dear old man who doesn't have that much time left and who just happens to be the greatest screenwriter America ever produced. My role is to place the personages in his seascape. Also, I plan to put tiny windmills at the bottom of each page of the book. As a small tribute to my ancestor."

With someone like Osborn it was difficult to know how much of the stories he had made up, had heard from others and passed along as his own, or whether they were a way that he kept himself amused in a hot, closed-in bar in the late afternoon, trying to finish an aquarium. Osborn reached into a bag and produced a copy of *The Visitations* and tossed it to Calvino.

"I've only written one other book," he said.

Calvino concentrated on the cover, which was a painting of sea and shore. Tiny fishermen dotted the coastline. He assumed the cover was one of the paintings done by Osborn's relative, and that he had an in-joke with his friends about how he had scammed the publishers to use the scammed painting. A scam within a scam, and depending on how one viewed the contents of the book, it might have been a triple bagger scam.

"Nice cover," said Calvino.

"Don't judge a book by its cover, Mr. Calvino. You must really read it."

"I will, don't worry. I plan to."

"Without moving your lips."

"Tell me, do your lips ever stop moving?" asked Calvino, looking up from the book. "Only when I read."

"You should read more often," said Calvino.

As Calvino opened the book, he stopped and looked across at Osborn, who was not paying him the slightest bit of attention. He measured the cantilevered rock formation in the center of the Mermaidium. His brow was furrowed and he stopped to take the cigarette out of his mouth and contemplate the interior of his creation.

"How is it that someone who lives in apparent poverty has access to the Internet?" asked Calvino.

"You find TVs in cardboard shacks in Asia and Africa. Why not a computer? They cost about the same as a TV. Mine is secondhand, and I managed to get a student rate for my Internet account. I lied and told them I was a mature student. A very mature student." Osborn smiled as he said the word "student," as if the scam had given him considerable pleasure.

"You got a lot of e-mail from Sam before she died," said Calvino. "Letters she sent to Ben and you were on the spam."

"Yes, that's very true. She was obsessed by Ben. A case of fatal attraction you might call it. Except, rather than being shot in the bathtub, she shot herself in the head. Not a Hollywood ending, but then, no one would ever confuse Bangkok for Hollywood, would they, Mr. Calvino?"

"Did you ever go to bed with her?"

Osborn feigned a hurt, pained expression.

"Please don't use euphemisms, Mr. Calvino. If you want to know if I fucked her, then ask me."

"Exactly, did you fuck her?"

Osborn flicked the ash off his cigarette. "A gentleman never discloses such information. Especially when the lady in question is dead."

"Meaning you did."

"You can draw whatever conclusion you wish but I refuse to acknowledge the accuracy of that conclusion one way or the other. But you must feel some sympathy for poor Ben. Think of it. Coming home and walking into the mess. As my mother once said of one of my girlfriends, 'If one hadn't been enough for her, an entire regiment would hardly suffice.' You know, Mr. Calvino, one should really listen more closely to one's mother."

"I'll keep that in mind. Now tell me, how much is Quentin paying you to write the biography?" An edge had come into his voice; he was thinking of Calvino's law: Money and doubt should never be used in the same sentence. Especially when it was your money.

"I would hope substantially more than he is paying you to ask me these silly questions," said Osborn. Noticing the change in Calvino's demeanor, he smiled. "Alan, Alan, how can we be friends with all this hostility you've got bottled up. Tiny fishermen, and tiny windmills. Your mother's stories about the past. But we are talking about some very big fish tanks and you are swimming with some very expensive, dangerous fish. I am trying to say I am on your side, Al. So you can cut down on the English bullshit humor. I don't care one way or another if you had sex with Sam McNeal. What matters is whether you might be able to help me puzzle together some tiny reasons, which I can paint into the landscape of her death. Some personages would be even better. That's what I am being paid to do. No one is saying Sam didn't off herself. There's no evidence her death was anything other than suicide. So you can relax. I am not accusing you of murder. I came around because I wanted to ask you for your help. Al, help me."

Taking another cigarette from his packet, Osborn broke into a broad smile, threw his head back and laughed. "Why didn't you just ask me from the very beginning?"

"I never would have heard your story about the tiny fishermen."

"It's a true story. I swear it."

"Tell me some true stories about Sam McNeal that you can swear to."

"Oh, there are many, but I do have a favorite. The best was when Quentin caught Sam in bed with Luk Pla. They were stark naked, looking like a two-headed beast trying to climb a slippery wall. He said it was quite amusing. It seems that Sam had gone to shower after a tennis match and when she came out, Luk Pla was standing naked outside. One thing led to another. He was quite amused by the incident."

"Were Sam and Nakamura still an item when that incident happened?"

"I guess they were. Though I don't think that Ben would have minded. Sam said that he was two people. Very uptight about everything but strangely this excluded sex. He was according to her a very kinky boy in sexual matters. It seems that Ben left her for a bar *ying* named Ice. Can you imagine a teenage hooker named Ice? Not nam khaeng, which is the Thai expression for ice, but the

American rapper named Ice. She wears one of the rapper woolly hats, too."

"She was at Quentin's party with an American named Slugo," said Calvino.

When Osborn nodded, his double chin elongated his face. "Yes, that did raise an eyebrow. A bar *ying* named Ice, who is a first-class butterfly as well. Are there no ethics left in the playground?"

Slugo and Ice had avoided Ben Nakamura, and he made no effort to join any group that included them. Quentin's party dealt Nakamura one humiliation after another. Questioned about the death of one ex-girlfriend, to find another ex-girlfriend arriving on the arm of a *farang*. If one defined major loss of face, it had to be this: Ice floating around Quentin's penthouse and everyone knowing that this is the *ying* that Ben had dumped Sam for and now she had thrown him over for a computer nerd who was turning her into a porno cyberstar.

"Did Sam know about Ice?"

"Of course she did. Sam quite liked women, and Ice liked any creature who would pay her. The three of them spent several weekends together. The funny thing is that I think they could handle it much better than Nakamura. He suffers from a certain rigidity in his opinions and specializes in narrow thinking. Very American, and very Japanese at the same time. A little like a Ford worker who drives a Honda to the factory with an American flag on the windscreen. Ice is a smart girl. She could see that Nakamura had plans which would disrupt her most productive years on the game."

"Ben was that serious about her?"

"Serious? I think he wanted her to move into his house. And he lives in a palace. But she turned him down."

"Instead she moved into Slugo's Alpha Domo project," said Calvino, shaking his head.

"A woman's taste in men rarely coincides with what a man thinks such taste ought to be. But, yes, much to everyone's surprise, Slugo turned out to be the highest bidder and walked off with the prize."

Ice was like a visitor from the not too distant future, time traveler who had been called back to the Big Weird, stepping out of a time machine, landing naked on the stage of a Plaza bar. Ice coming up alongside a target, dressed in oversized gold hoop earrings, rapper hat and a knowingly come-on smile, promising the kind of commercial transaction which came with a warranty: use as directed and you can break free from the galaxy of lies, conventions and half-truths of your pre-Galileo social universe.

Earth was no longer the center of our universe; marriage was no longer the center of relationships in the Big Weird. And there was one significant message she delivered: no one had to live on the marriage planet. Ice winked, and before he knew it, the target was hitchhiking across space and time into a new universe. By her very presence, Ice promised a man what a man wanted more than anything else—freedom at a fair price. She had worked her magic with Ben, then with Slugo, and doubtlessly hundreds of men before they came along, and hundreds more would come after them.

What did Ice know about relationships? Was it more or less than someone like Sam McNeal, thought Calvino. He tried to imagine what impact Ice would have had on Nakamura. He was something of a first: a john who was much younger than she had ever gone with. He would have watched her straddling Sam with horror and excitement; and Nakamura struck Calvino as someone who deeply cared what other people thought about him.

In Bangkok, the future had already arrived; no one cared deeply, no one who survived cared about the judgments of others. The city was the black hole which swallowed moral judgments like light going down the deep throat of a black hole, one with solar system-sized earrings and a laughter of cosmic wind that mixed snow and ice into a wall with no address. It just was always there, waiting to smash the present against the past.

FIFTEEN

THE CEZANNE CLUB'S happy hour ran until 9.00 p.m. and behind the main bar a half dozen college-age women—with less than half of the formal education—dressed in white silk blouses with small red bow ties and short skirts, leaned forward smiling as they nursed lady drinks. The customers were two middle-class looking *farang*s still in their office white shirts and neckties. The bar had a few other patrons, but the ratio of bar staff was five to one. Calvino sat at the bar. The two men had the sports pages of the two daily newspapers spread out on the bar, and were studying them closely.

"The *Post* runs the shot of the runner from Kenya breaking the tape to win the marathon. And what does *The Nation* run? A picture of the German woman who trails in eighteen minutes behind the guy from Kenya." The other *farang* looked at the two images of victory. "You're right. That kind of reporting sends an editorial message, doesn't it? Magic suspended and fined, then a picture of the German woman winning the marathon."

"That's the point, she didn't have the best time. She didn't win the marathon. She won the woman's division. The Kenyan, who won, has already had a shower, drunk a beer, done the crossword puzzle by the time she breaks the tape," replied his friend.

"And he's thinking how did I, a marathon winner from Kenya, end up in as a footnote in a Thai newspaper story about a Nordic female runner."

"As Bernard Trink says, 'TIT'—This is Thailand." They both shook their heads, sighed and raised their glasses in a toast.

"To the winning woman," one said.

"To the Kenyan," said the other.

A waitress appeared a moment later. She had long, straight black hair and smiled at Calvino.

"What would you like to drink, sir?" she asked Calvino. Having snapped the word "sir" as if she were ex-military.

"Mekhong and Coke," said Calvino. This was not the kind of entertainment establishment where the patrons drank Mekhong, and the waitress laughed.

"You joke me, yes?"

Calvino nodded his head, "I joke you, no."

He slipped a photograph out of his jacket pocket and laid it on the bar. The waitress cocked her head to the side, picked up the photograph.

"Your wife?" she asked.

"No, a member of the Cezanne Club. Her name was Samantha McNeal."

She glanced at Sam's photograph.

"She have accident with gun at Khun Ben's house. Very bad thing to kill yourself, you reborn a *soi* dog," she paused.

She looked troubled, her long, red nails tapping against the edge of the counter. "One girl see her ghost. And her ghost is very unhappy. No good."

Calvino noticed the waitress was wearing a cross around her neck. It had become the fashion to wear a crucifix as costume jewelry, so it was not necessarily a symbol of belief in Christianity. But there was something in the way the waitress fingered the cross that caused Calvino to think it held some significance.

"Are you a Catholic?" The waitress nodded.

"Do you believe in ghosts?" asked Calvino.

It was a question he had asked before, and, sooner or later, he felt that he would receive the unexpected answer.

She shook her head. "No, Catholic people don't believe. Ghosts, they think stupid."

He waited for a beat. "But are you afraid of ghosts?"

She nodded.

"Sometimes, afraid."

Fear was always more deep-seated than faith. That was the expected answer; the one certainty was that this answer never seemed to change over time.

"I understand that Sam was in the bar earlier that night. You remember seeing her? Who was she with? Or maybe she was alone?" Pratt had gone through the inventory of her things. There was no cash in her wallet; no jewelry on her body. But a receipt from the Cezanne Club had been in her handbag. It had the date of her death at the top.

"I see her with Chinese woman. They not stay a long time. But I don't want to talk about Khun Sam no more. You talk too serious. It is more fun to joke," she said, smiling and giving his hand a squeeze.

145

"Yeah, talking about the dead is not joking." "I don't like." She pulled back her hand.

Not many people did.

"That Chinese woman, do you remember her name?" Calvino slid a five hundred baht note across the counter until it touched the *ying*'s fingers which had stopped tapping as her eyes watched the journey towards her hand.

"Khun Paulee."

"Khun Pauline?"

She nodded and Calvino let go of his end of the note. Like the belief in ghosts, the hot desire for instant cash was another constant to be relied upon.

According to the police record, Sam McNeal had died after closing time. The police had been enforcing one of the periodic crackdowns, meaning that the bars and clubs had to close at two, and during operational hours the dancers were required to wear their bras and panties or the bar faced being closed down and the license revoked. He had reached the end with the waitress. She put a small bamboo tray filled with peanuts on the counter, smiled, and left for a *farang* in a suit and tie, his mobile phone placed on the bar like a six-shooter in one of the old Western movies. They were romantic that way. They liked cowboy towns in the old West, especially the bars, where the men hung out after a cattle drive and the women who served them had a chance of escape.

SIXTEEN

BEN NAKAMURA SAT on the top step of narrow stairs, which led down to a *klong*. He had a glass in his hand and a half-empty bottle of Johnnie Walker Black balanced on the step. A long-tailed boat sped past, churning up the black water into an oily mist. The waves surged and broke against the bottom steps. Ben sat with his back to his compound. The compound was large—three buildings with a flagstone-covered courtyard. In the center was a large traditional teak house and there were two smaller structures, one on each side of the main house. Calvino had let himself in through the gate and slowly walked to where Ben Nakamura was sitting.

His footsteps had been masked by the drone of ferry moving at speed along on the *klong*. He stood a couple of feet away, watching Ben pour another round of Black Label into his glass. A man who poured more than two fingers at a time either had a drinking problem or had personal problems, which were leading him to develop a drinking problem. He waited until Ben took a long drink from the freshly poured glass before saying anything. The lights were on in the main house, and from what Calvino could see from the outside looking in, staring at a polluted *klong* with the mosquitoes buzzing overhead or sitting inside in luxury would not have been a hard choice to make. Ben had, for some reason, decided to inflict the fetid stench of the klong on himself.

"I thought Colonel Pratt would be here by now," said Calvino. "Guess he must have got himself caught up in heavy traffic."

Ben looked over his shoulder. "He's inside."

Now it was Calvino's turned to be surprised. "Yeah? Doing what?"

Ben shrugged and raised his glass. "Looking around, I guess."

"Why are you sitting out here?"

"You might not understand this. But I never knew anyone who died before. I had never seen a dead body before except on TV. Sam wasn't just someone I knew. At the funeral, her father slapped me across the face. He was so angry. Can't really blame him, can I? After all, I had a relationship with her. She died inside my house," he raised his glass towards the house, and for the first time Calvino could see that he was a little bit drunk, slurring some of his words. "So I am trying to do some major forgetting. But how can I forget when the police are inside my house? Examining everything. Looking at my stuff. The stains are still there. You can't get it out. It just stays and stays. If you don't know what happened, then you don't even see it. But once you know, then you can't take your eyes off the stains. The police won't let me throw out the carpet. I have to keep it inside. Can you believe that bullshit?"

"How long has Colonel Pratt been inside?"

"Half an hour or so. He's just sitting in the chair. It's weird. He's weird. You're weird," said Nakamura.

"Ben, if you're the plumb line for normal, we would all be in trouble," said Calvino, walking away from Nakamura and towards the main house.

"You got that right," said Ben.

Calvino turned around as he reached the door. "Getting drunk isn't going to let you forget."

"I know that. But Johnnie dulls the weirdness. You know what the Lao *yings* call Johnnie?"

Calvino said, "*Bak* Johnnie *yang.*"

"That's it. Another asshole who walks through your life, through your head, through your dreams."

It was the kind of speech that called for no response. Calvino closed the door behind him and took off his shoes. There was no maid to come with a glass of water. The only sound was the drone of a TV at the far end of the room. Gunfire sound effects. Then the sound was killed. The room looked empty, but he knew that the tall chair with its back turned to the door contained a man.

"Pratt?"

There was a pause. "Over here," Pratt said, looking around from an overstuffed chair.

Calvino nodded.

"Some place."

The central downstairs room was a vast open space, lavishly furnished with antique furniture, hand-woven carpets, collectibles from the graveyards of surrounding countries. Calvino stopped for a moment and looked

149

around the room, trying to locate the stains of brains and blood which continued to haunt Ben. He walked towards the far end of the room, where the seating arrangement indicated a home-style karaoke room had been created. He knelt down beside Pratt's chair and touched the carpet.

"Bloodstain," said Calvino.

"It happened about right where you are standing."

A few feet away, curtains were drawn over a small bank of windows, and Calvino saw more bloodstains. A pattern of blotches had left a mark like one of those ink-spot tests that shrinks use to determine how much sexual innuendo could be drawn from an abstract pattern. Calvino made out a half-moon image toward the bottom of the curtains.

"She must have been watching the TV for the spray to have hit the curtains at that angle," said Pratt.

"Watching what?" asked Calvino.

There were a couple of sofas, glass-topped coffee tables, a 25-inch-screen Sony TV hinged to the wall above the bar, giving the faint impression of a hospital suite minus the conventional bed.

Samantha McNeal must have been seated close enough for the single round, which entered and exited her skull, to spray blood and brains on the curtains, but far enough away that the curtains didn't take the full force of the head blasting into fragments. Calvino stood up and walked over to the bar. As he sat down, he turned and faced Pratt seated in the overstuffed tall-backed chair. The image on the TV was frozen. His walkie-talkie squawking with gravelly Thai voices lay on the coffee table next to the remote control.

"Ben's sitting beside the *klong*. He's drunk. He's worried you are going to arrest him."

"Did he tell you that?"

"No, but he has this high level of paranoia. I saw it the other night at Quentin's party."

" 'The grief is fine, full, perfect, that I taste, and violenteth in a sense as strong as that which causeth it; how can I moderate it?' " Pratt quoted *Troilus and Cressida*. It was one of his favorite plays.

"Sam's father slapped him around at the funeral. Made a big scene.. Ben's lost enough face that not all the Johnnie Walker Black in the world is going to put it back together again," said Calvino

Pratt turned back towards the TV screen. He wasn't interested in Ben's face problems.

"Vincent, do you remember this part?" asked Pratt, as he pressed the pause button on the remote control, which froze the frame on the screen.

On the Sony was an image Calvino had not seen in years and never on video. This was not the usual karaoke—no bouncing ball over the lyrics, no half-naked women in the frame, and no one was singing. The images of two men at a table with scarves tied around their forehead flickered. One of the men held a revolver to his temple, his elbow held out at a right angle to his body.

"*The Deer Hunter.* I remember when the people from Hollywood were filming in Soi Cowboy."

"We were there together for a couple of nights during the filming," said Pratt.

"The director wanted you to play an extra but you said no," said Calvino.

"All of that seems like another lifetime ago," said Pratt. "Sometimes I regret having said no. I could watch this film and see myself and remember the self that was. Now all I can do is just remember."

"Why are you watching *The Deer Hunter* in Ben Nakamura's house?" asked Calvino.

Pratt hit the play button on the remote control and the sound of the revolver exploded on the screen and the actor holding the gun fell off the chair and onto the floor.

"That's a question I would have liked to asked Samantha McNeal. I am guessing that this was the last film she ever saw. The cassette of the movie was loaded in the VCR when they found her. The video was paused at one of the Russian roulette scenes. And when they found her, she had a scarf tied around her forehead just like in the movie."

"She grew up in Hollywood. Her parents were part of the business. Who knows what was inside her head? Maybe the film, in some strange way, was her inspiration," said Calvino.

Pratt shook his head. "I don't think so. If I had to bet, I would say that there were others in this room that night, and others were playing the same game, only Sam was the one who lost."

"She invited an audience to her suicide?"

"Maybe an audience invited her," said Pratt.

Calvino eased himself down on the sofa and, together with Pratt, sat and watched *The Deer Hunter*. Neither said anything as they watched the Russian roulette sequences. Calvino thought about one of Sam's early e-mails to Nakamura.

Today I watched my breath. I sat quietly in my chair, noticing each breath—inhale, the beat, and exhale. The practice never fails to convince me how messy I can be with myself, with others. Watching your breath isn't easy. It requires discipline, control. You must stay in touch with a process. Focused. When my mind starts to wander to a certain man named Ben, I go back to watching my breath. My mind surrenders itself to big questions like Did I Fail To Do The Right Thing? I return without an answer to my breathing, feeling my lungs fill and empty. Breathing is not something I do out of choice. It is something I must do. The world depresses me so much that I sometimes don't have the strength to leave my bed in the morning. I lie staring at the ceiling, counting the inhales and exhales, thinking about the Universe and God and Magic and the Star signs. Sometimes I think about the last movie deal my dad got for Quentin Stuart and the irreversibility of choice. Breathing is not choice. Risking your next breath is a choice. That increases the heartbeat, makes your breath speed up, which makes you know that you are really alive. Dad was able to get Quentin work on The Deer Hunter. He reworked the Russian roulette scenes until those scenes of death worked like a smooth, long kiss in the deep, black night. Then he cut dad loose, and dad had to let go.

Pratt pushed the reverse button and waited a couple of beats. The brains splattered once again. Calvino looked over at the curtains, shaking his head about the time the VCR shifted to pause mode.

"Sam's e-mails that you gave me were an interesting read," said Pratt.

"I was just thinking about all that stuff she wrote about breathing. Given the air quality in Bangkok, I can understand the obsession. But she carried it a bit too far."

Pratt hit the play button on the VCR and the handgun exploded.

"What I meant to say, Vincent, is that Sam's e-mails weren't written by the same person," he said, turning his head away from the screen and looking directly at Calvino.

"How do you know that?"

"There is this software program. I read about it on a Shakespeare website. This American who was working in Oxford used the program to prove that Shakespeare wrote a poem called "A Funeral Elegy" that he found in the library."

"Is this a joke?"

"It's serious, Vincent. The program picks up word order, sequence, the grammar of the writer. And this American, who calls himself a literary detective, was able to demonstrate that Shakespeare was the author of the poem."

"What's this have to do with Sam's e-mail?"

"I put together a database of all her earlier letters. They came from her apartment. She had written a lot of letters before she got an Internet account. And I indexed all of the words in her letters. Words like 'gentle,' 'maximize,' 'retrospective,' 'disqualify' . . ."

"Tennis?"

"That was one of the words. Her expressions were part of her. Like her thumbprint, they identified her. And my best guess is that Sam McNeal didn't write about thirty of the letters to Ben."

"Then who did?"

Pratt turned the VCR back on.

"The software doesn't tell you that."

"We don't know?" asked Calvino. "I don't know."

"My guess is that Ben Nakamura may have more

cause to drink than I thought."

Pratt got up from his chair and walked towards the door. He opened it and looked outside. "He's still sitting out there, staring at the *klong*," said Pratt.

"I don't think he will come inside the house until after we leave."

"We should go before he falls into the *klong* and drowns."

"You're worried how that would look in the newspapers," said Calvino.

"One funeral eulogy is enough for this house."

Pratt walked ahead to the gate. Calvino waited until he had left before returning to where Ben was seated. Calvino noticed there was less whiskey in the Black Label bottle. Ben sat back on his elbows, staring at the klong. He squatted beside Ben.

"You ever kill anyone?" Nakamura asked. "I have," said Calvino.

"How did you feel when it happened?"

Ben was staring at him, waiting for an answer. "Lucky that it wasn't me."

"Not powerful?"

Calvino shook his head. "No. There's no power in death or killing. The power is with the living. And you need courage to accept the whole horror show, which crept into the lives of the living. What you don't do is run."

"When are the police going to let me change the curtains and the carpet?"

"It shouldn't be much longer."

"I hate being in that house now. The servants all quit. They're afraid of Sam's ghost. So I am basically fucked."

"I notice you're not wearing your surgical mask tonight. Is the air that much better by the klong?"

"I didn't know you were concerned about my health," said Ben.

Calvino smiled and tossed a small stone into the klong. There was a splash and then silence. "What do you know about the Chinese Long March -B rockets?"

Ben turned his head and looked at Calvino. "I wouldn't want to be an astronaut sitting on top of a -B," he said.

"What about Pauline, you think she would fly in one of those Chinese tin cans?"

He went silent as he refilled his glass. "I think Pauline would try and sell Chinese tin cans as hubcaps to Rolls Royce if she thought she could pull it off."

"But she didn't pull it off with your boys in Tokyo, did she?" asked Calvino.

"No, she didn't."

"Are you going to be okay?" asked Calvino. "Quentin's party was the first time everyone was in the same room since the funeral."

"It took guts for you to go," said Calvino. "But it's going to take more guts for you to let go of what happened."

Calvino left Ben sitting in the dim light beside a klong that could have passed as a toxic waste dump. Nothing he could say or do was going to stop Ben from feeling sorry for himself and punishing himself. He was a man with no place to go but deeper into his own sorrow and the bottle, which he used to chart a course in that unhappy place. Not even his grand house could provide the safety and comfort that he wanted. He was alone and he was, in a very large sense, defeated.

SEVENTEEN

DARK CLOUDS MOVED fast across the sky, gathering, parting. A bright shaft of light streamed through a narrow opening before the clouds closed the hole. The sky raged with motion, and out of that whirl of tumbling clouds, a single black bird appeared, circling overhead as Vincent Calvino walked barefoot alone down a long, white beach. He felt the warm sand under his feet. The sun broke through again and he shielded his face with his right hand against the blinding light and watched as the bird came closer to the earth. The bird was a moving black object in the sky like a jet leaving a vapor trail. The bird might have belonged to any species or it might even have been a large bat, he thought, watching its flight.

As the bird flew closer in a direct path towards him, Calvino felt afraid. He had a strong feeling that somehow this creature had locked in on him, as if it had been pre-programmed to find him, as if it were a heat- seeking missile. A liquid discharged from the wingspan, yellow and green leaving long trails in the sky. Not long after he started watching, he looked around at the empty beach, feelings of aloneness broke over him like giant waves of sorrow. In the foreground were sand, sea and behind him tropical trees, the fronds silent, motionless. The place seemed frozen in time. As he looked back, the bird was close enough for him to identify it as a black swan, one with a wingspan that touched the edges of the sky and like a giant cloud, the bird's body cast shadows that stretched across the water, skirting the horizon. Its mouth was wide open, its tongue gaping from the beak. The creature was screaming. It stared at him with red eyes burnt from suffering. The black swan dived at him, pulling up inches from where he crouched in the sand.

It circled back towards the sea, and as Calvino rose back to his feet, wiping the sand from his hands, he saw for the first time that the great swan was wounded. It tried circling back but lost altitude and it was falling, falling towards the sea, not flying but tumbling to green water uncontrolled, without direction except downward. There was nothing to break the fall of the swan and as it crashed head first, the sea boiled blood red and the wind shook the fronds of the tropical trees as if a sudden storm had hit the beach.

A chill in the air made him shudder and he closed his eyes against the sand blowing in the wind. Opening them again, he saw her, Sam, coming out of the sea. Dressed in black and as she walked through the coral and rocks, the feathers which covered her, smooth like duck feathers, were falling away from her body, leaving a black trail. She walked with her hands extended, her polished fingernails catching the rays of the sun as they reached out to Calvino.

"Vinny, I have been waiting for you so long. I need you to help me. Will you?"

"Help you do what, Sam?" he asked, his fingertips touching hers.

She leaned forward and kissed him on the lips.

"No power games, promise?" she asked him, pulling back, squeezing his hands.

Her hands felt cold as if she had been under sea for a very long time. Her white, perfect teeth bit gently into her lower lip. She gave him a coy, little girl look.

"Promise," whispered Calvino. "Please don't be angry with me."

"Why did you do it, Sam?"

"I was so tired of everything and everyone. The pressures of the group were more than I could stand. I got restless and tired of being with them. Tired of all the competition. Of having the men judge my body. Why are men so intolerant? So critical. How does a woman break free in Bangkok? I asked Pauline. She said, 'If you are a woman. You don't. Not unless a woman has faith in magic. Only fools seek understanding detached from intuition. Most men are made fools because they believe only in rationality. That was a mistake. Ben's mistake. Reed's mistake. Is it your mistake, Vinny? Don't dismiss the magician when she comes. Don't dismiss the wolf when she creeps up on you during the night.' "

She was starting to merge with another form. The form became another woman whose face was obscured by a cloak.

"What is it like where you are?" he asked her.

"Solitude inside a dream that you dream forever," she whispered.

Then, she merged with the other form, and Sam vanished before his eyes. He ran along the beach calling after her. But she was gone and there was no bringing her back. He pitched forward onto the sand, balanced on his knees, looking at the sky. The distant horizon shimmered with small black birds. These tiny black swans circled high above the seashore. Hundreds of them and after a while the flock was so thick that it blotted out the bloated red sun. They flew silently above a seascape of windmills and beyond the windmills were fishermen, solitary figures in rubber boots and old hats. The fishermen were hooking the tiny birds, casting their fishing rods into the sky. Bringing down the birds, one after another, putting the dead carcasses into bamboo baskets. Calvino ran down the beach, shouting at them to stop, but either they didn't hear or they didn't care, and the faster he ran the smaller the fishermen became until they, the sea, the sky, and the birds disappeared.

Outside his bedroom he heard someone banging hard on the front door of his apartment. Joy nudged his arm with her cold, wet nose. Calvino opened one eye and stared straight into brown liquid eyes of his German Shepherd. Joy sat on the floor, her paws on his bed, her chin on her paws. The pounding from outside continued as he rolled out of bed. He walked across his apartment and opened the door. He found Quentin Stuart standing in the hallway with tears filling his blue eyes.

"Did I wake you?" asked Quentin.

"No, I always look this good in the morning," said Calvino, showing Quentin into his apartment.

"She's left me, Vinny. I don't know what to do. Or who to turn to. You've got to help me. Please, may I come in?"

Calvino stepped back and gestured. "You better come inside. There are very large rats which use the stairs behind you."

Several minutes later, Quentin spilled out the story of how Luk Pla had gone out for a pack of cigarettes three days earlier and still had not returned. He was beside himself with grief and worry, driving himself crazy with all the possible explanations for her disappearance—road accident, kidnapping, suicide, insanity, illness, new lover, old lover. As a screenwriter, the old man had gone through all dramas and his emotional health had certainly suffered in the process. Quentin had lost one important thing: his control over the situation. Calvino had seen the same horror-struck look before on the face of *farang*s who believed they were immune to both death and betrayal. Quentin's face, at that moment, was like that of any other *farang* in the Big Weird who suddenly realized betrayal was more common than death. They mostly took it hard, with disbelief or denial. Who? Me? Suffer the loss of the woman who promised she loved me? With Quentin, as he came into Calvino's apartment, it wasn't clear. What was worse, his cells dividing out of control or the emotional lack of control The Sickness had caused.

The old man took off his shoes and shuffled across Calvino's sitting room. His moist, red eyes surveyed the slum conditions—the broken floor tiles, ancient bamboo furniture with faded, torn cushions, clapped- out fridge in the far corner, and large map of Brooklyn on one wall and stacks of the Bangkok Post in a corner. The apartment had the look of a space untouched by the hand of a woman, except a maid whose duties did not include housekeeping. The old man blinked away tears as he stared at the poverty. He was beyond consolation. As Quentin sat slumped into a chair, he immediately leaned forward, placing his face into his cupped hands, and wept.

Calvino walked over to the fridge, took out a plastic water jug, poured a glass of cold water and brought it over to Quentin. He sat in the chair opposite and waited until Quentin had composed himself. The old man took a sip of the water, then leaned back in the chair. Joy sat a few inches away watching Quentin's every move.

"Does that dog bite?"

Calvino glanced at Joy and smiled. "Once she ripped out the throat of a man." He paused, patting Joy on the head. "But that was a long time ago. But, no, she doesn't bite. Unless, of course, you piss her off."

"Sometimes you sound very Thai," said Quentin. "You think that she could sit a little farther away?"

Calvino spoke to Joy in Thai, and the dog got up and moved to the entrance of the bedroom, sitting down, ears erect, watching Quentin.

Joy and the old man faced off for a few seconds until Quentin felt comfortable enough to relieve himself of the troubles that had plagued him, sending him running to Calvino's door at that ungodly hour of the morning. "She's never been away from my side for more than a couple of hours. I can't even remember what she said before she left this time. I was working when she came into my office. But I am reasonably certain she said that she was going out for cigarettes. Or she might have said something about going to see a friend. Christ, it could have been both. I don't recall. I was rewriting a scene and not really focusing on what she was saying. This much I know: she said nothing to indicate that she would not come back. It has been several days and she hasn't even phoned. She may be in trouble. All I know is that I must find her. You must help me find her, Vinny. Please, help me."

"If she's gone to ground, she may be difficult to find."

"Why would she want to hide from me?"

That was the question those with The Sickness often asked when their latest woman had fled the scene. It was the shock, the realization they really knew almost nothing about the woman they had invested all that emotion in. Her family name, the name of her village, or her house number.

"Do you have Luk Pla's house registration?"

"What's it look like?"

"It's an official Thai document. Every Thai is registered as an occupant of some house somewhere in Thailand. Chances are high Luk Pla is registered at her mother and father's house. If she has run, the chances are good that she ran home. Did you ever ask her for her house registration?"

Quentin Stuart shook his head. "She was my girlfriend. I wasn't hiring her for a job."

Calvino's law of service-worker girlfriends: Go through the hiring formalities, and a thumbprint isn't romantic but certainly helps in establishing identity.

"What about a copy of her personal ID card. It's plastic, has a photo of the person."

"No, I am afraid not. I have none of her official documents. What man keeps a dossier on his wife?"

Calvino left the question unanswered, leaving it hanging high in the air where he had dreamed of the black birds and Sam. After a moment, the answer was obvious enough to Quentin. Without the documents, how did one ever know from where those birds came and where they were going next?

"I know that Luk Pla is from Isan," said Quentin, after a minute.

"That's a big region and she's a very small fish." Quentin's eyes welled up with tears, spilling out of the sides.

"So I fucked up," he sobbed. "I know that I should have been more careful. Asked her exactly where she was from. She told me the name of her village. But I really didn't understand. I pretended I did so she wouldn't realize how bad my Thai is. I should have made her write it all down. I should have taken copies of her documents. Maybe I should have put a tattoo on her: In case found, return to Quentin Stuart. Reward guaranteed. But I just loved her, and thought she loved me. We were so incredibly happy. I gave her everything. And she made me so happy."

And he gave her nothing more than any other *farang*. Giving only delayed the inevitable.

"What about her friends?"

"Ice is her best, best friend."

"I met Ice at your party," said Calvino.

"She was the punked-out one who used to go with Ben and now goes with Slugo."

"Why don't you want to check with Ice first. Save yourself some expense," said Calvino.

Quentin Stuart shook his head. "I want you to talk to Ice. She will talk to you and you can understand her Thai. Find the name of Luk Pla's village. Find out anything you can. Just bring Luk Pla back."

"I'll talk to Ice." Calvino rubbed his cheek, feeling the stubble of a beard. His hair was uncombed and he was wearing a faded Saigon Beer T-shirt and white shorts. He looked like no one anyone would talk to. But Quentin was a desperate man and, at that precise moment, he overlooked Calvino's lack of grooming and tailoring. The private eye was the only person in Bangkok who, in Quentin's mind, could return his Baby Fish.

"Can you start soon? Like now?" the old man pleaded.

"Quentin, it's seven in the morning. Ice won't be up for another six or seven hours. Assuming she has even gone to bed yet. She has the working hours of a bat and the sex life of a rabbit."

Quentin blew his nose on a piece of tissue, then he wadded it, put it back into his pocket, and pulled out his notebook and wrote a couple of lines. Calvino could read the word "bat" upside down in Quentin's clean, neat style of writing. After he finished, Quentin looked up and smiled at Calvino.

"I have full confidence in you, Vinny. I know that if anyone in Bangkok can find Baby Fish, it's you."

Clients were like this in Bangkok: they engaged Calvino for one case, and before long, more and more of their personal life, as it started to unravel, was assigned over for investigation by him. If he found Luk Pla—no easy task—he would bring her back (that part was easy), but she would likely run again, and again. An old pattern was at work; the *ying* waited until the gold on her neck and wrist reached a certain weight. Then it was as if the *ying* had a built-in scale and one morning an alarm bell silently rang in her head and a little voice whispered, "You have enough. You can go. You can do whatever you want." Enough usually meant sufficient gold and cash to buy a holiday upcountry with a Thai boyfriend, and after everything was exhausted, she would filter back, calling daily, pleading for her *farang* husband to take her back. The *ying* knew that The Sickness was her friend, and that sooner or later, the *farang* would take her back into his life because she had become indispensable, and before long she would have rebuilt her supply of gold. And the cycle would start all over again.

EIGHTTEEN

THREE IN THE afternoon Calvino tracked down Ice at a cybercafe on Silom Road—a weird place to find a bar *ying* in the late afternoon on a working day, but Ice had established a private spot at a table in the back of the cybercafe. Computer terminals were set up on a table inside the old Aztec Restaurant, which, like the Indian tribe it had been named after, had gone out of business. The cybercafe premises were squeezed between the Standard and Chartered Bank and the Dusit Thani Hotel complex. The rich who lived in Bangkok spent a lot of time in banks and hotels so the location was inspired.

Calvino walked halfway down the restaurant before he stopped and pulled up a chair next to Ice who was bent over a keyboard, working away with intense concentration. She wore a black baseball cap backwards, fire-engine red lipstick and matching nail polish, her body clad in a black bike racer's tube, leaving her thin arms and legs protruding. She had an evil tattoo of a human skull on her left forearm. The skull had a smoking cigarette clutched in its teeth with a wisp of smoke rising up her arm. Quentin had said something about putting a tattoo on Baby Fish. If he told him about Ice's tattoo, he would remove that small notebook from his pocket and write down a description of the tattoo. Some things are better just seen. Better as an image. Some things were beyond the capacity of words and Ice's flesh art was one of those things.

Ice was online and Calvino sat back and watched. He didn't want to interrupt her quite yet. Ice was an interesting name, he thought; ice was one stage in physical transformation: gas, liquid, solid. Every stage had a charm, a challenge, a redeeming feature, a problem, a promise. The final solid stage was ice, though. The Big Weird, smack in the middle of the tropics, was one huge sheet of ice, and the *ying* he was watching did not move a muscle, her right hand on the mouse, her eyes glued to the screen. Now and then her small tongue licked her upper lip.

Slugo had told him that not only had Ice completed high school (a rare accomplishment for an upcountry *ying*), she had dumped her husband and eighteen-month- old baby because the two of them bored her to tears, guaranteed her a life of poverty. Ice figured that she had what it took to make it in Bangkok and no kid and no old man who drove a five-year-old Isuzu truck was going to keep Ice from reaching her full potential. What she hadn't counted on was that random chance would intervene and Slugo would select her as the new Eve for his brainstorm: Alpha Domo. She quickly established her presence as a cyberforce, a cyberpersonality. People on the Net flamed her as one of the Super Net Naughties, and she was starting to like the fact that she was someone in the world and not just another *ying* in the Big Weird.

Ice had made her share of cyberenemies, cyberfriends, and cyberalliances. Her new career in cyberspace had threatened to become a full-time job, and she was, despite her dress and gear, working more and more in conditions like any other office *ying*. Only she wasn't an office *ying*. Office *ying*s didn't get death threats. And they weren't famous on the Internet, either, Ice told herself. And, like in the real world, in addition to the death threats, the hate mail, there were digital crackdowns going on in cyberspace. Programs had been written with killer viruses and put out in cyberspace to find and eliminate her.

"Ice is tough," Slugo had said. "No one is going to blow her out of the water without one big fucking fight."

Since the crackdown on the Plaza bars, according to Slugo, Ice had eased into the idea of actually wearing clothes in public and she was no longer instinctively reaching out for the chrome pole for balance, as a frame of reference to circle the customers in the crowd. During this window of time, Slugo had seized the opportunity to import Ice into cyberspace. No license or passport required.

The bars had become dead, dull shophouse rooms with too many cops watching. The attraction of hanging out with the cops, peering out from her chrome pole at the vast number of empty stools, had caused Ice to remember how bored she had felt with her husband and baby. Wearing clothes at night felt strange, she couldn't show it, she couldn't use it. If the truth were told, like using a keyboard, clothes at night had this unnatural feeling. Ice hated working in clothes. Slugo thought what

171

she missed most was twisting and turning, both hands clutched around the chrome pole, looking at herself in the mirrors and watching herself swinging from a chrome bar, knowing that her perfect body was super hot, super cool. Ice on fire.

The first night Slugo had bought her out and sat her in front of a computer terminal, Ice had been staring into the mirror for fifteen solid minutes without blinking, without moving, and what she saw was her body covered, and she bared her teeth like a she-wolf and howled with laughter.

By the second night, rather than saying, "Buy me cola" she had shifted to "give me keyboard." Ice had gone through a rapid transition from gas to liquid, and finally she had congealed into ice behind a computer screen.

Calvino had watched long enough and it was time to make contact.

"You remember me, Ice? I was at Quentin's party and you were with Slugo," said Calvino. She was with Slugo without being with him, and Slugo had not seemed that evening to register the difference between being with and being without Ice.

She pointed at her name carved in English on the edge of the table. Ice. She had laid her fake Swiss Army knife on the table as a warning to the yuppies and university students not to fuck with her space because she was one mean Plaza idol of foreign men, and any idle chatter around her table would ignite a flash point felt right around the room, the block, the city, the whole fucking country.

"Who the fuck are you?"

"Calvino. Vinny. Remember, we talked at Quentin's party?"

"Don't know any Vinny," she said, glancing up from the screen. "Did I fuck you?"

Flame out. She couldn't locate his name in her memory bank and her eyes refused to leave the screen to look at his face.

"Not that I remember."

"My memory is fucked up most of the time," she said.

"So I hear you were the Big Thing in the Plaza," said Calvino. "And now look at you, in the middle of a Plaza crackdown, you've become the Ice Queen of cyberspace."

"Who say?" she asked. "Luk Pla."

"That little bitch Goddess got more gold than brains." It was as if Ice had repeated word-for-word Slugo's assessment of Luk Pla.

Calvino was thinking how Ice had started using phrases and slang that no bar *ying* would ever use. She was reinventing herself, picking up new lingo from Slugo and on her solo voyages through cyberspace, and, in the process, she was becoming all attitude.

"Quentin Stuart is looking for her."

"Yeah, so why do I care? Tell him to put an ad in the Lost and Found."

Another Slugo expression, Calvino thought. "Quentin says you are best friends." She didn't respond.

"So what are you doing in a cybercafe, Ice?"

"Same, same as bar. Lap-dancing with customer. Slugo call it surfing. Fuck off. I have new customer, I do business, okay?" She asked, slipping back into bar-talk.

This wasn't an ill-mannered kiss-off of the bars. This was a bar *ying* in overdrive, in her daytime space, a place where she never worked. Hitting on a bar *ying* in her sacred daytime non-working hours was sticking the nose into the gears, nothing but sparks, drive belts flying off, conveyors changing speed and crashing into flames. And it didn't do much for the nose.

"Looks like you are working," said Calvino. "Am working. Just not working my piece." "Piece?"

"Down here it glows in the neon. It give you electric burns. Love and hate. But Ice never melt."

"Tell me about yourself, Ice. Who are you? What upcountry berg are you from? You got an old man besides Slugo, or is he your only squeeze? How long have you worked at the Plaza? How long have you hung out with Luk Pla? How many times did you and the *mem-farang* Sam McNeal go three-mouth kissing with Nakamura?" With a *ying* like Ice, sometimes it was good just to get everything all laid out at one time, a kind of buffet, and let her decide what she was going to nibble on.

"I am from LA," she said.

"Meaning Roi Et," said Calvino.

His reply stopped her in her tracks. He knew the most recent street slang; where Roi Et became LA, and he could tell from her expression that it would be a little easier now.

"Three-mouth kissing is no good," she said, rewarding him with a smile.

"And after he pay me, I say, okay, where's taxi fare? He say fuck off. I say you a cheap Jappo Charlie."

Calvino already knew the basic outline of her story: Ice had worked at the Plaza for two years. When she arrived from Roi Et she was a shy, twenty-year-old who knew nothing of the life of a commercial sex employee. A year later, Ice had mastered bar English and the dead-eyed stare of a betrayed heroine. She met an American nicknamed Slugo. He was a Harvard-educated computer scientist. Slugo taught her that Java wasn't just coffee; it wasn't just Indonesia; it was fucking software.

Slugo ran around Asia with his fully loaded laptop, which he jacked into the phone socket in his five-star hotel rooms. He was either at the bar or online with a bar *ying*. He had been searching for the perfect Eve for his Alpha Domo, and he found Ice, who would become his model for a D avatar. Ice had memorized in the first month all the sound effects of high drama she had learned by heart from the porno films which ran nonstop on the bar TV sets.

At Quentin's party he had heard Slugo's version. At the cybercafe, Ice gave her own version. Slugo was no first-time fool. He had learnt the trick of watching her face as it bounced off the mirrors on the walls, reflecting on the ceiling mirror. Ice was a thousand fragments in the mirrors and each ice icon was totally engrossed by the screensaver which was two elephants having intercourse. He rolled her off and pulled her by the hand to the computer screen, logged on to the Net, and took her through the Web, stopping at porno ports, docking there long enough to watch the scene run by amateurs. Long enough to show Ice the possibilities before moving onto the next one, and the next. Ice traded one short-time session in Slugo's hotel for two hours of instruction on how to use this machine. The trick not only taught her how to use the Internet, but showed up all the sites where men were looking to meeting Asian women.

Slugo got her an account on a local provider and assigned her a special handle that no Internet surfer would ever forget—ice@naughty.com. The English words caused Ice to laugh and dance around the room with joy. She had her professional reputation billed as an ice princess who looked ultra-cool on short-time hotel sheets. She danced and danced, then got drunk with Slugo and rode him halfway through the night as he navigated the mouse over the curvature of her back. That night Ice got hooked on the Net because she saw the possibilities of making enough money from the technology that she would never have to deal with another flesh and blood *farang*. A bar *ying*'s dream machine. What else did anyone in Asia think technology was for but a license to print money?

Slugo's genius was not in discovering The Sickness, but the discovery of a potential cyberspace haven for all those who suffered from it. Ice tapped into the huge international reservoir of *farang*s who were offshore and suffering from The Sickness. Ice was sent deep into cyberspace as the keeper of the cure, the Madonna, Eve, Sarah Bernhardt, Charlotte Bronte; she came to minister to those who had caught it. She logged on daily with a dozen boyfriends around the globe and they sent her money.

The funds poured in through faxed credit card numbers, telexed funds, bank drafts, and cash inside couriered teddy bears. Ice thought the Net was about the best that had ever happened to a working *ying*.

With the help of Slugo, who exacted a heavy sexual barter price in exchange for transferring his technical expertise, she created her own avatar—a cross between her tattoo, her photograph on her official government name card, and Slugo's aerobics instructor in Hawaii. The finished product had all the right moves and grooves to torque The Sickness, until the man suffering ached from the top of his head to the bottom of his toes. Slugo was negotiating with a toy company in Hong Kong to create an Ice doll—one of those high-priced texture like real skin inflatables. Ice was hot in cyberspace and she knew it.

"Got to work. A husband's online," Ice said.

"Show time," said Calvino, looking over her shoulder.

"Don't talk. It hurts my concentration," Ice said, using a phrase she had obviously borrowed from Slugo.

Calvino watched as she participated in a live, real-time chat with one of her cyberspace husbands. She lit a cigarette and watched the screen fill up with his words. Her avatar, the very image of Ice, pranced across the screen, stretched, yawned, winked and smiled. The naked avatar swung around a chrome pole, then the pole became a spear which the avatar hurled across the screen, and it came back as a white dove, landing on her wrist; she kissed the dove and, in a flash, it was a chrome pole again.

Ice, my darling, I miss you, appeared on screen. The guy had blue balls watching Ice's avatar bumping and grinding against the chrome pole. Neon lights flashed and cyber mirrors reflected Ice's avatar from a hundred angles.

Ice miss you too, and think about you every night.

In the upper right-hand of the screen, Ice's avatar appeared, lips pursed on the cheek of the man. His was just a photograph, allowing Ice's avatar to suggestively dance around him.

That's me. That's me and you together. Hank's message appeared on the screen.

Ice turned to Calvino, "Slugo morph in all photos. He make my avatar from thousands of pictures. Good job, huh?"

"Great job, kid."

Where is my husband Hank? I wish he is here? Maybe he not miss me. Is he a butterfly or is he thinking about his little wife, Ice?

That question pushed The Sickness button every time. Hank was sitting behind a computer terminal twelve thousand miles away and he was suffering, sweating, wanting, out of his head with desire, his throat thick, the palms of his hands wet and sticky on the keyboard.

You miss me? Oh, God. I want to trust you, believe in you, our relationship is soooo important to Hank. I don't ever want any other wife. Just Ice.

Her wasp-waisted avatar twisted around a chrome poll, the rib cage pulled in, showing bones, the stomach all but disappeared, and then a tiny bikini materialized on the avatar which had in bold gold letters the word: ICE.

Your wife must have money to pay the rent. Very big problem for Ice. Mother is old and sick. Little brother he need money for schoolbooks. And older brother crash his motorcycle and break his head. He's in hospital. Ice have to pay. But have no money. Maybe you can help, Hank?

A man with The Sickness paid the rent faster than a hospital bill. He paid all the bills.

Ice, how much you need? The question was written across the screen just below his sad-faced image.

Just a little. Three-hundred dollars. I don't want my husband have problem. Ice have little problem. You not want your Ice melt. Her face pulled a deep, sad look to match his own.

I'll transfer the money today. I love you, Ice.

I love you, too, Hank. Not check. Electronic transfer much better. Love you, Ice. Her avatar had a smiley face and fluttering eyelashes.

Ice's avatar blew her digital john a kiss with one hand, then blew him a kiss with both hands, her avatar had its knees bent together in a half genuflect. This Slugo had been real good at showing her the ropes for making money in cyberspace. Whatever Ice had paid him by way of trade was about the best transaction she had pulled off in a very long time.

Ice looked pleased with herself, showing off her online skills in front of Calvino. He was someone who could appreciate Ice's transformation in such a short period of time. She had gone from being just another ice cube in the glass to an unstoppable glacier raising mountains of money.

"Luk Pla's run away," said Calvino. "Quentin Stuart's toy fish. Your friend. At Quentin's party, you were like sisters, remember?"

Ice smiled knowingly. "She's not toy fish. She's a gangster fish."

"I wasn't asking for a character reference. I know she's a gangster. Quentin knows that she's a gangster. I would be a thousand baht grateful if you let me know where I can find her."

"A thousand baht for that little bitch?"

"Two thousand," said Calvino.

"If I remember, I'll ask around," Ice said, stretching

and yawning. The problem with the Internet is that it made two thousand baht for a little information hardly worth the effort. Calvino was thinking how much the avatar and Ice were like identical twins: the screen personality and the off-screen personality. Show-biz clients like Quentin Stuart, and show-biz Net queens like Ice had merged, knew the same gangsters, hung out in the same places, used the same lines, and likely had the same agents. Same hair, same moves, same lips, and the same attitude towards the bottom line.

She was looking at the screen. "Gotta go, Justin just log on. And I can't remember if Slugo morph in his picture."

Slugo dragged a chair behind him and pulled it next to Calvino, "Of course I morph in his picture," he said to Ice, then turned to Calvino, "What are you doing here, Calvino?"

"Surfing with Ice."

"I saw your name in cyberspace the other night. "Attached to what?"

"Hate mail. Apparently you've already made yourself a batch of cyberenemies. In fact, you've got the WULF pack tearing you apart in cyberspace like a dog pack ripping into a bunny rabbit. I've copied some stuff their members have written. It's appalling. You must've pissed off Pauline or one of her friends. Don't take it personally, they attack me all the time. I've had so many flames I could supply enough light for every city in the world."

"Was Pauline involved?"

"Who knows? None of them are dumb enough to get caught using their real names. But there is a group of some very sensitive women in this city. I can understand it. In the States, women hold the balance of power in sexual matters. No one questions that they are used to having a total monopoly. The power lets them set the terms on all the fun stuff: sex, foreplay, afterplay, even the sexual vocabulary that can be used. Like all monopolists they abuse their power. Tough, strict, exact, no bargaining terms. Then they come over here and find the complete opposite. Men hold the power over sex. Men set the terms, and the terms are loose, vague, open-ended. It blows their minds. Most of them can't stand it and leave. The ones that stay are getting rid of all that anger inside of WULF. Bad for them, good for us. As a man, given the choice, where would you choose to live?" Slugo broke out into giggles.

"You're a smart Harvard guy, Slugo. But like a lot of smart guys you are overlooking the obvious," said Calvino.

"Which is?"

"You're taking a woman's pragmatism for lack of control. In the Big Weird pragmatism is the wild card. The one a woman knows how to play better than any man."

As Slugo was about to reply, Ice screamed. "My avatar die. Murdered. Look. Fucking dead. Slugo, do something. Help me!"

There was a message on the screen in large, bold letters which read:

They took away our dignity in the Opium Wars in the 1840s. Britain forced drugs on us. In the 1990s, it is the Porno War and Americans are forcing us to consume a new opium: Pornography. Each time the West has tried to destroy us with a poison and each time we have fought back and won back our dignity. We will fight back until we win. Keep Pornograph out

of cyberspace . . . or else.
    WULF

"See what I mean?" said Slugo, taking over the keyboard and executing a number of commands. He looked up at the computer screen as he talked. "They have zero tolerance. WULF wants to destroy Alpha Domo. That's always been the trouble of the leftists; they are destroyers and not builders. One day Alpha Domo will be listed on the Big Board in New York and I will be so rich that even Ice will be impressed."

"Am I dead?" asked Ice.

"No, sweetheart, you're not dead. You are just digitally sleeping until Slugo can wake you up and put you back on your pole," said Slugo, breaking out into laughter.

NINETEEN

CALVINO OPENED HIS copy of Osborn's *The Visitations* as he sat in the back of a taxi stalled on Rama IV Road. He flipped through the pages; inside he found short stories. Each story centered around the prison lives of lifers, burglars, embezzlers, murderers; there were stories of broken dreams and broken homes and broken, defeated lives. According to the preface, Osborn had been a prison visitor and his experiences during his visits to the prison became the material for *The Visitations*. The man who had signed on to write Quentin's biography had written: *What had begun as a humane exercise had degenerated into a literary one. Humanity rarely survives ego, and ego feeds on money and recognition.*

Osborn talked about an age in which humanity standing alone counted for nothing. This had been the theme of this story—Who came to see the lifers? The answer was—very old people: mothers and fathers in their seventies and eighties, wrinkled, gnarled, their eyes swollen with tears; the walking dead came to visit the imprisoned dead. The other family members of lifers had long ago vanished into the acid bath of divorce and forgetting. There were no longer wives or even girlfriends, brothers, sisters, nephews, cousins—all abandoned them over time. These men were alone except for the old people who had given them birth. And once they were gone, then on visiting day, there would only be visitors, the small band of do-gooders who would come into their lives briefly, and then they, too, one day would vanish, leaving them in silence, leaving them utterly alone.

Quentin Stuart was like a lifer, thought Calvino. Calvino looked out the window at street vendors selling watches, shirts, deep-fried spiders from their sidewalk stalls. The deaf and mute vendors communicating prices, complaints, gossip with sign language while stopping now and then to eat from a bowl of noodles. He thought about the prisoners confined in their cells without any means of communication.

What humanity was left inside a man who had shed all contact with the outside world? Boredom was pain's best friend, Calvino recalled Quentin Stuart saying on the phone. A man could endure pain, imprisonment, torment of the soul so long as he was stimulated in the mind and heart by those who mattered to him. Removing them removed hope, and without hope, it was steel meshed against steel, and either madness or death followed the descent into such despair.

The robbers and embezzlers, though, had families, which arrived en masse; these were the men who had a lifeline anchored to hope. The gap between the two camps of men was so vast as to put them into different species. All that was left for the lifer was drift time. That pocket of time when nothing moved; there was no struggle, no appointment, no obligation, a narrow tunnel under the bridge of time, where the clock simply stopped but the heart kept pumping blood.

Calvino thought about Quentin's fish tank and the one in the Plaza and Osborn's ancestor who had painted the tiny fishermen into the shoreline of very bad nineteenth century art. And then there was the little thrill that Slugo had received by announcing that Calvino's name was floating in cyberspace. Cyberspace had become a place of strong emotions, of passion. It was a battlefield to find and destroy Ice's avatar, and it was also a place for the message that WULF had left behind as a warning. There was a war going on in Southeast Asia and he suddenly had found himself in the middle of the action. Sam McNeal had already gone home in a small bronze urn. The question was, who would be next to follow?

TWENTY

AFTER LUNCH, LATE one afternoon a few days later, Calvino got a telephone call in his office from Ice that Luk Pla was hanging out at the Plaza with a Thai motorcycle taxi driver named Somchai.

"Gotta run, I'm back online," she said. He could hear Slugo giggling in the background. "My avatar has never looked sexier."

"Thanks, Ice. I won't forget the favor."

"Don't forget about two thousand baht you owe me," she replied. "I just love *farang* who give me the blues."

He got into a taxi in front of Washington Square and twenty minutes later, the taxi turned left into Soi Nana. Calvino paid the driver, got out, and immediately spotted Luk Pla, right where Ice said she would be, squatting, knees apart, on one of those low-level plastic stools used by street vendors on the pavement across from the Nana Hotel. Luk Pla's fingers hovered like the claw in one of those arcade "try-your-luck" vending machines, only there were no cuddly toys to be clutched. She picked at a plate of fried grasshoppers, taking one between her forefinger and thumb, then, dipping the head into the sauce, taking a small bite that severed head and shoulders, and a second larger bite that dispatched the rest of the insect. She was chewing on a grasshopper head when Calvino sat down at the table. Enough chemicals had been used to kill the grasshoppers to ensure that downstream in the food-chain, Luk Pla would win the grand prize of being able to glow in the dark, but she didn't care. She liked the taste of the chemically laced grasshoppers; deep fried, they reminded her of the village, her mother, relatives, and made her homesick, even though all the things she missed were the very things that drove her right up the mud and bamboo walls of her hut and onto the bus for the bright lights and big money of Bangkok.

"How you doing, Luk Pla?" asked Calvino.

"Quentin send you?" she asked without missing a beat, a grasshopper leg wedged in the corner of her mouth.

"He's wondering if you are in some kind of trouble." She took another fried grasshopper from the plate where dozens of grasshopper corpses were jumbled together, giving the vague appearance of victims of the usual road crash when an upcountry bus collided head on with a ten-wheeler driven by a barefoot cowboy who was high from having eaten too much ya ba—amphetamines.

"No trouble," said Luk Pla. "I am happy. Why he want to bother with me?"

She washed down the grasshopper with a sip of Coke. "He is worried because he hasn't heard from you. He thinks he might have done something wrong to make you upset. Like squeezing the tube of toothpaste from the top rather than the bottom. You know, the kind of stuff that makes for domestic unhappiness."

"*Mai khaw jai*—I don't understand," she said. "Quentin wants you back."

Luk Pla shrugged and picked out another grasshopper. Her Thai boyfriend rode up on his motorcycle, parked it at the curb, walked over and sat down at the table. He immediately helped himself to a fried grasshopper. He ate with his mouth open, the grasshopper legs and antenna roiling in his saliva. Grasshopper body parts washing over his teeth and tongue.

"I said, he wants you to come back," said Calvino. "All is forgiven. No hard feelings."

"Bangkok have many *ying*s. He find another beautiful *ying*. No problem for him. Now I stay with Somchai," she said. "Cannot go back."

So it wasn't the wrong end of the toothpaste after all. "Quentin will pay you forty thousand each month you stay with him," said Calvino.

She yawned. But Somchai's face clouded over as he swallowed hard.

"She go back to him," said Somchai. "I think no problem for her."

Luk Pla eyed him with great suspicion, as she watched him taking another grasshopper. "I don't want to go back to him. I want to stay with you," she said, hitting his arm with her tiny fist.

"You go," Somchai insisted, clenching his fists on the table edge, talking and eating at the same time. "He's old man. Never mind. One, two years. We have big money."

It was there on the pavement, eating grasshoppers, that Luk Pla discovered Somchai had the heart of a crooked accountant and the appetite of a racehorse. Her face registered no shock. A sigh of resignation came from her lips as she licked her fingers.

"He is old," she said like a runaway slave, thinking the master had only a short time to go before he died ... before she would have her freedom.

A motorcycle shot out of the parking lot of the Nana Hotel and squealed to a halt at the curb. Earl Luce removed his large, black bubble-like helmet and put it under one arm. He pulled a Leica out of his shoulder bag and snapped several frames. Suddenly he looked up from the viewfinder.

"Shit, I thought that was you, Calvino. Eating grasshoppers. I didn't know New Yorkers ate fried insects."

"Only on Wall Street," said Calvino.

Luce raised the camera and resumed shooting. "I'm going to make you famous one day," he said.

Calvino plucked one of the grasshoppers from Luk Pla's plate and held it up.

"God, that's great. Now, just eat the fucking thing," said Luce.

"It's full of chemicals," said Calvino.

"We are all gonna die, man. Chemical overload is as good as any way to check out," said Luce, shooting the scene. Now Luk Pla was playing to the camera, tilting her head back, and dropping a large grasshopper into her open mouth.

"*National Geographic,* eat your fucking heart out," shouted Earl Luce. "You're looking good." He paused and kept on shooting and talking at athe same time, "I just finished a shoot at an animal hospital. An autopsy of half a dozen dogs. Each one had inky black lungs like a two-pack-a-day smoker. The vet said dogs are dying of lung cancer all over the city. It's from the pollution. I got some great fucking shots of black lungs. And the vet said we are breathing the same shit into our lungs. Miners used to take a canary into the pit; if it died, they got out. From what I saw, it may be time to get the hell out of the mine."

Earl, an Australian who had yet to turn thirty, was already a local cult figure. The James Dean of the Big Weird roadways. He specialized in photographing violence of the night on the mean streets of Bangkok. His collection of photographs included *farang*s who had been splattered, punctured, burnt, flattened, butchered, drowned, or poisoned. One victim had been half dissolved in acid. Earl had the look of someone who had walked out of the ashes of a nuclear explosion— sporting a set of death camp hollowed-out cheeks, the AIDS hospice pencil-thin arms and neck; he had shaved the word "shit" where his hair would otherwise have parted. A long black ringlet of hair curled over his forehead, but otherwise his head was shaved like a monk's. He wore a black fishnet top, army combat fatigues that had dozens of huge pockets, and a pair of sandals made from old tire treads.

He got off his bike and sat down at the table.

"So what are you doing at the Plaza in the afternoon? And don't tell me it isn't connected with sex," said Earl.

"I am on the job, Earl."

"You are always on the fucking job. Why don't you have some fun?"

"How about a lift back on your bike?" asked Calvino.

"Hey, you're not gonna leave all that great food on the plate, are you?"

Calvino gestured with his hands. "Help yourself, Earl. You look like you could use a little protein in your diet."

Earl Luce lived so close to the edge that when he looked down at his sandals he could see the great black void between his toes. On the back of Earl's chopper, Calvino reached back and held onto the back of the saddle as Earl gathered speed, aiming to keep his bike in the narrow channel between the hundreds of stalled cars. The challenge was to go as fast as possible and retain kneecaps and elbows intact as they passed inches away from the mirrors mounted on the cars like reflective weather vanes against the storms. At the Asoke and Sukhumvit Road intersection, Earl stopped for the red light. One of those Bangkok lights that felt like it would last ten minutes.

"Having fun yet?" Earl asked.

Calvino leaned forward. "I'm going to go to every wat in the city and make merit for having survived."

"You look kind of green," said Earl.

Calvino swallowed hard, looking at the red traffic light. "You ever come across an American named Sam McNeal?"

"The chick who blew her brains out. Yeah, I photographed the body. I was hanging out with the body snatchers the night she pulled the trigger. What a fucking mess. The black-and-white shots came out incredibly well."

"I am working on the case," said Calvino.

"Why are you working on a fucking suicide case?" As the light changed, "That's what I am trying to figure out myself."

The motorcycle hit 100 kilometers an hour before Calvino had finished his sentence. Calvino was no longer certain that he was having fun riding on the back of Luce's death machine.

TWENTY-ONE

AFTER LUK PLA had returned to the tank, so to speak, Quentin had invited Calvino to his penthouse for lunch. He arrived to find that Osborn had also been invited. Following lunch, they went down the stairs to the living area. Quentin, Luk Pla, and Osborn went ahead. Calvino stopped and had a closer look at the aquarium. The huge fish swam from one end to the other, doing endless laps, sometimes adjusting their depth, but most of the time the fish, like Osborn's lifers in his book of short stories, were alone, going nowhere, simply going through the motions, waiting for death.

Calvino had read that medical people put aquariums in old people's homes; it kept the elderly engaged in life, kept them from growing too alone, kept their spirits up, and they lived longer—all because of the fish. That was the theory. Calvino started to wonder if watching the fish had given the elderly the sense of confidence that they were not alone. The fish were like their parents; they would never leave them. Yes, they might die, but the staff would replace them with new fish, an endless cycle, as if the supply of fresh parents to visit them in their solitude would never end. The old were like the lifers in Alan Osborn's *The Visitations*—the fish, the visitors. Calvino wondered if Osborn had made the same connection.

Quentin had already opened the sliding doors to the verandah, and then he took hold of Luk Pla's hand and led her outside. Osborn stood a couple of feet away, both hands on the railing. Luk Pla leaned against Quentin, who stood with his back towards the railing, looking down at the swimming pool. Luk Pla then pulled him over to the thickly padded recliner and they lay down together as Calvino came outside, closing the sliding doors behind him.

"Fame is very simple," said Quentin Stuart. Luk Pla, in short shorts and a blue tube top, had curled up in the crook of his arm. The visible signs of The Sickness were not evident; he was temporarily in remission. "Having fame means that other people envy you because strange men praise you and strange women want to sleep with you."

Osborn pulled a small black notebook from his pocket and uncapped a pen. He wrote down what Quentin had said, then looked up, and said, "And immortality means you are left with the praise when envy no longer matters."

"Immortality means no one gives a damn about who your friends were," said Quentin. "In Hollywood no one has friends. The town works like Thai political parties. Marriages of convenience arranged to accumulate vast amounts of money and property, but friendship in such circumstances is about as likely as a singing lizard walking on its hind legs."

Osborn tentatively had given Quentin's biography the working title of *Guns and Testosterone*. That was Quentin's formula title for a highly commercial Hollywood film. *Farang*s with The Sickness were diagnosed as testosterone junkies. The irony in Quentin's case was that his testosterone had become like a loaded gun pointed at every vital organ, cocked and ready to fire; his doctors had disarmed him of the hormone which had become no longer connected with sex but was gasoline feeding the fire that was destroying him.

Calvino had left them outside for about ten minutes. He needed to clear his head. He went downstairs to Quentin's study and had another look at the photograph of the young Quentin Stuart at the writers' strike in the 60s, the one with him carrying the picket sign in front of his Benz and the white poodle with its paws on the steering wheel. He picked up the framed photograph, went back upstairs and out onto the verandah.

"Vincent, what do you have there?" asked Quentin, squinting as he looked into the sun.

"I finally recognized what the dog has around its neck," said Calvino. "It's not a necklace."

Quentin Stuart broke into a broad smile. "No, it's not. But what is it?"

"It's a merkin," said Calvino.

"Not another Americanism," sighed Osborn. "A merkin is a pubic wig."

Osborn pulled a face, lowering his chin, staring straight at him. "Mr. Calvino, sometimes you surprise even me with the span of your knowledge."

"The set-up was a joke," said Quentin Stuart. "Have you ever seen a merkin on a poodle before? And in the middle of a writers' strike? Never. That photograph was picked up by the wire services and not one person at the time identified the mystery object around La-La's neck."

"La-La?" asked Osborn.

"The poodle in the fucking photo. I loved that dog," said Quentin Stuart. "If I am going too fast, please let me know and I can slow down."

Osborn puffed out his cheeks in frustration and raised his hands over his head.

"I am a failure. No wonder we lost the colonies. What can I say?"

"It's not what you say that I am interested in, Mr. Osborn. It's what you can write," said Quentin. "And I am not talking short stories or restaurant guides."

Luk Pla tongued his ear. He started to laugh. Squeezing his eyes shut, he pretended to brush her away with one hand and held her tight to his face with the other. Osborn looked over to catch Calvino's reaction, and found that the detective was studying the photograph and looking through the sliding doors at the fish tank.

Osborn went inside to use the toilet.

Quentin waited until he shut the door before he spoke to Calvino.

"Fame attracts a certain kind of opportunist," said Quentin.

"Of course Osborn wants a piece of the action," said Calvino, watching Luk Pla, leaning against the old man's neck, her eyes half closed, her lips pursed. She looked like a vampire, he thought.

"I am not a complete fool. He will get his money. That's not what I am talking about. There are other things in his background that make me uneasy."

"Have you found anything in his background to put you at ease?"

The old man stared hard at him.

"I am not asking that you return a verdict of not guilty. I am not even asking whether he did it. What I am asking is whether he will follow through and write the goddamn book, or is he wasting my time."

TWENTY-TWO

THE NEXT DAY Calvino took a motorcycle taxi to Soi Nana. He walked into the Lollipop Bar, and saw Osborn covered in sweat, working in the back.

Calvino glanced at his wristwatch. It was 2:7 p.m. He turned to his left and walked along the side of the bar. At Osborn's eye level, two plastic blue pipes came out of the water; a constant dripping of water was the only sound in the bar. Osborn knelt down, his back to the door, as he measured with a tape. He was contemplating the width of the trough where the glass would be inserted.

"Water is difficult to contain. The nature of water is to seek the weak point. Exploit the weakness of the structure. To escape the confines that held it. The nature of water is not that different from the nature of the *ying*s working the Plaza," said Osborn, talking to himself and measuring.

He leaned back, stretched his arms and back, and announced to himself, in a loud, clear voice as if he were talking to an audience, that the width of the glass along the perimeter of the Mermaidium would be exactly 27 mm, and this dimension, in his humble opinion, would be sufficient to keep approximately twenty tons of water from crashing through and drowning the *ying*s and patrons so overcome by The Sickness that they would drown without even trying to swim to high ground.

At 2: 8 p.m. a *farang*, an American in his mid-thirties, light brown hair, about 5'11," well-built like a weight lifter, appeared in a cheap pair of flip-flops, baggy trousers, and sweat-stained shirt. The man looked as if he had gone over an emotional edge; his anger had made him blind with rage, and as he came through the door, he stopped and looked at Osborn. He never thought to look across the bar at Calvino. Perhaps Calvino had been half-hidden in the shadows, or perhaps the anger had created so much adrenaline as to blur his peripheral vision—the reason wasn't clear, but the *farang*, who had obviously come to settle a score, had not seen him on the other side. Or, if by chance he had seen him, it wouldn't have mattered. The man had the look of someone wanting blood.

Halfway down the dance floor, Calvino watched as the *farang* pulled a long-bladed kitchen knife from inside his shirt. Osborn's attacker took a few more steps and Calvino lifted himself up onto the dance floor and rolled across, taking out his . 8 Police Special. After a couple of more steps, the *farang* was close enough for Osborn to feel a killer's breath on his neck. Osborn tilted his head, hearing the slip-slap of the sandals, his mind, still concentrated on the execution of his work of art, stalled out.

He had no reaction to the assault; he didn't even blink. It was then that Calvino brought down the butt end of his gun and, with economy of movement, hit the would-be assailant on the side of the head. He dropped like a rock in deep water. Osborn looked at the man who sprawled at his feet, then looked up at Calvino, a crooked smile on his face. Calvino kicked the knife across the floor, pushed back his jacket and pushed his . 8 Police Special back onto the shoulder holster. "Mr. Calvino, how very nice to see you."

Calvino bent down on one knee and rolled the man over on his back.

"You know him?"

"Oh, him. I remember that one. John is his name."

"Who is he? And why does he want to kill you?"

"He is just a disgruntled bar owner, afraid that

what I am doing might be a success. He boasted to all bar owners in the Plaza that I would never finish the pool. Oh, yes, one more thing, he claimed special expertise in building pools, and that he had the idea first, and that I had stolen it from him. All of which is rather doubtful. Pitiful might be a better description of a man who has never had an original idea in his life. And his Thai wife has an uncle in the local police force and that seems to be his major asset. He became jealous that I might finish on schedule. He did warn me that if I didn't stop, he would have his revenge. He put it slightly more crudely. He said, 'Go away from the Plaza, or you will have big trouble.' Whenever a *farang* starts sounding like a Thai gangster, you know that he has gone native. John says I will have big trouble, what he really means is that he will try and get his wife to kill me because he doesn't have the stomach for it. Thank you, Vincent, for making his job rather more difficult than he bargained for."

"Where's your phone?" asked Calvino.

"Don't phone the police. They may send his wife's uncle around and that will only make matters worse."

"I know someone on the force," said Calvino.

"Yes, I am sure you know someone. But it won't help. Let me handle this the Plaza way."

"What is the Plaza way?"

"Privatized corruption, I guess you could call it."

He paused, looking at the man on the floor, sprawled out, bleeding from the head. "I can handle this."

"He came close to sticking that knife in you," said Calvino.

Osborn shrugged. "If he had succeeded, then I would not have objected to you handling it. But since he failed, I think that I better handle it."

A couple of minutes later the *farang* named John regained consciousness, staggered to his feet. Blood from the wound on his head covered his face and soaked through his shirt. He shook his finger at Osborn—a most atypical *farang* gesture.

"I can have you killed for five baht," John said, rubbing his head and looking at the blood on his hand. For a moment, his face turned pale and it looked like he might faint.

"And I can have you killed for four baht," said Alan. "So why don't we compromise and not have each other killed."

"You are an evil, bad man. What you are doing is no good for the Plaza."

Osborn reached into his pocket for money and peeled a one-thousand-baht note off the top and handed it to the man who had tried to kill him. He did this with no overt sign of emotion.

John looked down at the money. One of his hands was caked with blood. He looked at his hand, then again at Osborn. "I will kill you."

"Yes, well, don't count on it. Why don't you take this money and go have your head treated at the clinic. Who knows, you may be able to use it one day for something productive."

The *farang* stared hard at the money, bile mixed with blood in his mouth, and to say this was a look of hate would have neutralized the excess emotion that had made this man's bloodied face a mask of pure, unavoidable, violent loathing. Osborn put the grayish blue note on the bar counter. They stared at each other for a full minute until the third-rate hit man wannabe grasped the note, turned, and left.

After the *farang* left, stuffing the thousand-baht note into his shirt pocket, Osborn lit a cigarette and returned to his work as if nothing had happened, or as If what had happened was of little or no consequence. "The man's a loser."

"Losers are more dangerous than winners in Bangkok." "And in which category would you place yourself?" asked Osborn.

"Ask the man who just walked out of your bar." Osborn raised an eyebrow, then turned back to the aquarium site.

"You see that pipe up at the top?" He pointed. "The one that is leaking. It comes from the toilet. I must really have the plumber put this right or the tank will fill with vile liquids, spoiling the entire effect. I doubt you came around to talk about my plumbing problems, Mr. Calvino."

There was something about Quentin's life that kept coming back to Calvino. He was a man who needed to make films; he had no real life independent from filmmaking. It was his blood, his guts, his intellect, his love. Sam's death, and how she had died, were somehow starting to come back to that original concept. Quentin the screenwriter.

"Quentin Stuart's working on a film. Are you involved in this project?" asked Calvino.

Osborn's smile broke into laughter, and he was a man who rarely laughed. It was the kind of social gesture that Calvino suspected Osborn rarely made. Laughing aloud would have been undignified in Alan's circles in London.

"Of course, he's working on a film. The man has been working on films for nearly forty years. There is not a day or night that passes when he is not plotting a script or plotting to get a script produced."

"Could he have been writing a film with Sam McNeal?"

Osborn frowned at the suggestion. "I can't imagine why he would require the services of a non-professional."

Osborn was playing it tough, playing it smart. Calvino shifted gears.

"Quentin did some work on *The Deer Hunter* script," said Calvino.

"He was what you Americans like to call a script doctor. No doubt like other American doctors, your script doctors are devoted to expensive non-necessary operations. In Quentin's case, he was one among many on The Deer Hunter."

"But he didn't get a screen credit," said Calvino. The ultimate way of breaking a writer's face in Hollywood was to deny him a screen credit.

"That is correct," said Osborn. "That must have bothered him."

"You should be asking him that question."

Calvino was about to leave when Osborn came up to him, putting a hand on his shoulder. "Thanks for the help back there. I once had a job at the crazy house where the Thais hide some of their mad. It's over at Thonburi. I thought it might be, with a little effort, turned into *The Visitations, Part II*. You know what is the most difficult task with the mad?"

Calvino shook his head and watched as Osborn went back to work. On the left side, stairs were being built to allow the mermaids to enter the tank.

"Keeping them occupied. One patient was given a broom and told to clean the leaves from the footpaths. After the footpaths were cleaned of any sign of a single leaf, a doctor friend of mine found the patient halfway up the tree, shaking it, sending a shower of leaves onto the footpath. The patient climbed down and quietly continued with his work. Happy that he had established some sense of productive contribution, that some way of passing the time had been found. Screenwriters are like the patients in the nut house. They are constantly climbing trees to shake them for a few leaves and this gives them work, and work makes them happy."

"Nice story," said Calvino. "Let me put it this way. My employer is a professional storyteller, you are a storyteller, professional maybe, I haven't decided. I am a working guy. I can't judge *The Visitations*. If someone asked me if it's a piece of art, I have to say, I don't know. Work of art, entertainment or something you wrote about some people behind bars. It doesn't matter. What does matter is a little piece of information I have about a certain guidebook. *Handbook to Best Bangkok Eateries.* The word on the street is that it was part fiction. A scam. And I'm real curious whether Quentin Stuart, my client, was ever informed of your participation in this project?"

"Mr. Calvino, you continue to surprise me." "I continue to surprise myself."

"Perhaps you want to know how I got in involved in *Eateries*?"

"I thought you'd never ask," said Calvino, loosening his tie, taking one of the stools off the bar counter, setting it down, and then taking the weight off his feet. He had a feeling that Osborn had the kind of story that took some time in the telling.

Osborn lit a cigarette, looking back at his tank. "Why build an aquarium?" asked Calvino. "Underwater is the primordial state. We came from the sea. Have you read Darwin?"

"How we evolved from apes." said Calvino.

"Then you know that man evolved from sea creatures. We have sea water in our veins. I am simply returning who we are to who we were. And in that transition lies a sexual excitement. Any time a creature such as us completes a cycle, it is a cause of celebration."

"Was *Eateries* another evolutionary project?" asked Calvino.

"No, it was revolutionary. A one off. A quantum leap."

TWENTY-THREE

ALAN OSBORN'S SECOND literary grift was a restaurant guidebook, a concept hatched during the height of a rainy season several years before. He had been living on short rations, his clothes were ragged and worn, and he didn't have enough money to buy razor blades so he grew a beard, only the beard was patchy, lightly gray and wiry. Osborn showed up at the door of the da Vinci Restaurant as heavy rain pelted down, a torrent of water so thick that when he arrived in the driveway the street was already flooded and several cars had stalled engines. He rode his bicycle between two large Mercedes-Benzes, the windscreen wipers going but the cars immobilized in the flood water.

Osborn stopped and dismounted from the old Chinese bike. His pant legs were held tight against his calves with metal clips and rainwater. He knelt down and put a lock around the rear tire on the theory that no matter how wretched the condition of the bike, there would be someone who would steal it and find a market to sell it in. Not unlike the market in which he had originally bought it—the light-fingered, secondhand market—for a purple, five hundred baht. He smiled in satisfaction at all the stalled cars in the street. Even though he was thoroughly drenched from the rain, he felt happy with himself. Those rich bastards were going nowhere, and he had arrived, he told himself.

His hair dripped rainwater as he came through the door and asked to see the owner. Osborn looked pale, so pale in fact that the veins in his face took on a ghoulish hue of blue as if his face had been blotted against a blueprint of a Sukhumvit thirty-story high-rise condo project. The Thai staff stayed clear of him, thinking that he might have been a ghost, or sick from one of the diseases that had laddered down from the airborne colony, or that he had gone mad with too much rainwater seeping into his brain. He appeared to be the kind of personage that his ancestor would never have painted into one of the seascapes, hoping to sell the result to a middle-class home owner looking to cover a blank space on a sitting-room wall.

The restaurant owner, a large man with a thick neck, mid-thirties, his shirtsleeves rolled up to his elbows, sported a bushy black mustache that covered his upper lip. He narrowed his blue eyes as Osborn gave his flawless pitch in upper-class English, explaining in detail how the planned guide to *Bangkok Eateries* would focus the bright beam of publicity on the restaurant and many *farang* customers would brave the Bangkok traffic to fill all of his tables. Rainwater dropped from his nose, his arms, his clothes—indeed Osborn appeared to be leaking from every orifice—straight onto the floor, creating large puddles. The owner's attention was divided between Alan's pitch and the rate of water running off Alan's body and onto the restaurant floor. Finally, after a few more minutes of intense monologue, he persuaded the owner to sign a contract and contribute a healthy amount of money.

"A full-page display in *Bangkok Eateries* is quite reasonable, I should add."

"How much?" asked the owner, snapping his fingers for a waiter to bring over a mop.

"One hundred thousand baht," said Osborn in an earnest, convincing and firm voice. "Say a deposit of ten thousand baht will hold you two pages."

The owner shrugged his shoulders, asking another member of his staff to bring a towel for Mr. Osborn who was standing in a small pond of water on his expensively tiled floor. The waiter arrived and started to clean the floor, hitting the head of the mop against Osborn's leg. He did not move.

"Ten thousand baht?"

"I meant to say seven thousand baht."

"Son, that is a lot of pasta," said the owner. He liked the fact that Osborn held his ground.

"Actually that is for our deluxe two-page display and I will put da Vinci on the cover."

"You don't look at all well," said the owner.

By this time Osborn's teeth were chattering, goose flesh covered his arms, and he looked very close to fainting.

"No real writer ever looks well. If you don't suffer for your art, then you are nothing but a vulgar man of business. Please sign the contract here," said Osborn, taking a paper from a plastic pouch and placing it on the table.

Without reading the document, the owner signed where Osborn pointed with a dripping finger. The waitress drooped a towel over his outstretched hand and retreated.

"When is the last time you had a meal?" asked the owner.

Osborn looked up at the ceiling, pursed his lips. "Exactly two and half days ago." He wiped his face and neck with the towel. "I was traveling third class on the train to Penang. My forty-ninth visa run."

"A forty-nine-run man. Very good," said the owner, sounding impressed. He poked his finger at his own chest. "Me, I'm sixty-three-run man next month."

"My advice is to avoid the third-class railcar on the Penang train. The food is nonexistent. There is chicken, mind you. But the chickens are alive and in crates and they keep you awake all night."

"Why don't you have lunch. As my guest."

"That is very kind of you. I accept." He draped the towel around his neck like a boxer.

After Osborn finished the second plate of seafood pasta, the owner came over and sat down at the table, holding the contract that he had signed. He had the look of someone who had some second thoughts.

"The other restaurants in this guide, are they respectable?" asked the owner, his bushy eyebrows shooting up to form a solid line a few inches below his hairline.

"Five-star is the minimum requirement for acceptance into the guide. We want only the best. After all, there is a high standard to be maintained as well as my personal reputation as a writer," said Osborn.

"You've done books before?" asked the owner. "Sir, I am famous in England."

"This is Thailand."

"Fame does not necessarily travel on the same plane. Or train."

"You are expecting fame to arrive any day?" asked the amused owner.

Osborn smiled. "Rome wasn't built in a day."

"But it was built."

"With your faith, how can I not build such a Rome in our adopted city?"

If the owner smelled a grift, he did not let on. He let Osborn eat his pasta. He allowed Osborn to leave with a fat check, and what more faith is necessary than the writing of numbers on a check payable to bearer?

After the tropical stormy afternoon when Osborn had pedaled his bicycle into the driveway of da Vinci's, his luck had changed. The meeting had been an omen. In the days and weeks that followed, every subsequent restaurant and hotel in the Sukhumvit Road area turned out to be an easy mark. Osborn had created the perfect formula, the moneymaking machine: he knocked over each resident managing director, who were mainly *farang*, by producing the signed contract he had acquired with the owner of the da Vinci restaurant and a photocopy of the check.

"He is a sixty-three-visa-run man. An old Bangkok hand. No one's fool," Osborn would say to remind them. Someone who knew the score had taken the plunge so the scheme couldn't be all bad. Pulling seniority of time in the country over another *farang* was a favorite way of pulling rank in the Big Weird.

Osborn soon discovered that showing the da Vinci contract was like showing a piece of paper with an official authorization to print money. The other owners and managers signed the same contract and paid up a healthy deposit. Osborn had obtained a considerable sum of money and soon discovered he had hit upon a book-writing scheme that was almost too easy. The success went to his head, and within two months Osborn, having succumbed to a bad case of The Sickness, had spent all of the deposit money he had collected from dozens and dozens of restaurants and hotels; it had all gone on women and drink. Not that the money had been badly spent; that wasn't the point—the point was there was no money to print the book. All the profits, except for seven hundred and twelve baht, had been completely exhausted. He no longer had sufficient funds to pay the Chinese printer, and the printer—having seen Osborn arrive on his bicycle—absolutely refused to extend a single satang of credit. He required cash, full payment up front.

Osborn was at the very low point of his life, not because he had blown other people's money on women and liquor, but because he was in great danger of not being able to buy women and liquor for the following week. He was broke. So broke, in fact, that one of the go-go dancers had thrown him out of her squalid slum quarter because he no longer had enough money for his own share of the rice. She threw his few articles of clothing, three cassette tapes, a suitcase containing some books and all of his contracts with restaurant owners, into the *soi*, hands on her hips as she watched him picking up his meager belongings. And then she came up with the big idea that saved the day.

"Go Soi Cowboy. Sell ads to bars. Make money or don't come back."

"What a brilliant idea," said Osborn, picking up his few clothes from the street where the *ying* had thrown them. "Only someone with a fourth-grade education could have figured that out."

"You not smart with money, you not eat."

He picked up his shirts and trousers. "At least you didn't cut them with a razor blade," he said, smiling.

"What for? They already all cut up."

He looked at a tear in the pocket of a shirt. "They could use some mending. Do you think that you might be able to sew this . . ."

Before he could finish the sentence, she threw an empty Mekhong bottle at his head. He leaned to the side, and it smashed against the pavement.

On that note, Osborn left the slum, his clothes and few belongings stuffed into his suitcase. He rode his bicycle all the way to Soi Cowboy, the broiling sun overhead. It didn't matter. He had confidence, and knew he would succeed. Osborn hadn't felt this good about himself or anything else since that rainy day when he got a free lunch and a signed contract and a check for a lot of cash. His fortune had, in other words, changed.

TWENTY-FOUR

SOI COWBOY. WHAT was there to say? It was best described as an entertainment strip running between Soi 2 and Asoke with both sides of the soi lined by dozens of go-go bars, mostly single shophouse bars, shabby, dark places which had retained the look from the old days and a few hole-in-the-wall restaurants. Soi Cowboy was like a small-time blues band with a select, local, committed fan club; the members of the band changed over the years but no one really cared, and an entire city grew up around it as if embracing it as this radical flash from the past, a relic, an eyesore from the 25th floor of a new condo where the few inhabitants who occupied the premises had sufficient money to think that such carrying on was suspect, if not downright evil, and petitioned authorities to close down the music, to put the band out of business, but the band still played on, night after night, for that specialized audience that remembered the old times before the five-star hotels on every block, before the fast-food chain every half block, and the Benz stalled in heavy traffic every hundred meters. Many of the regular customers had suffered The Sickness for so long that they were like the Grateful Dead of Bangkok, and some of the workers they bought for the night were not that much younger than members of that band.

Osborn had traveled on a straight line from a crowded slum room to Soi Cowboy—finding that most of crowd moved with him. He had locked in to the daily commute of the hundreds of working *yings*. But they were not carrying all their earthly belongings and riding a bicycle along Sukhumvit Road. He entered Soi Cowboy, got off his bicycle, and walked along the rows of empty bars, *yings* squatting out front, eating noodles, sticky rice, fish paste, drinking water and squinting in the sun as Osborn pushed his bike past them. Home territory, he thought.

He made the rounds, first stopping at the Blue Fin, because he knew that if he succeeded with the mamasan who ran that restaurant, the rest of Soi Cowboy would be easy. The mamasan who had seen and heard about every grift that had ever gone up and down Sukhumvit Road—and that was about every grift invented in the head of man or woman—sat behind the bar counter, picking her teeth with a toothpick, looking at the contract he had laid out on the bar for her to sign, and asking Osborn to translate the legal document into Thai.

She remembered Osborn because he had dropped quite a lot of money in the Blue Fin buying bar *yings* lunch, dinner, and drinks. *Farang*s like Osborn were like gold mines. But they were more like gold mines inside a volcano, which could erupt at any moment, swallowing all profits, life, happiness, and the lunch menu.

"Your *tilac* say you crazy, Khun Go," said the mamasan because Go was much easier to say than Osborn.

"That's because she loves me. She's crazy for me," said Alan. "I make her happy. I have no money, but it doesn't matter. She wants me. She will take care of me and look after me. She told me that no matter how poor I am she would always be there," he said, lying between his teeth, his suitcase on the floor between his feet.

"I don't believe that girl Daeng love you if you have no money," said the mamasan.

"You are a superb judge of character. One can't expect Daeng to indulge in free love, can one?" He sighed, looking around the restaurant.

"I will likely die single unless I can find a woman who will give me sex on credit."

"You right. You die single man. So why you come here?" she eyed him, throwing away her toothpick. She picked up a large wooden phallus with her right hand and turned it slowly into the palm of her left hand as if it might be a weapon in a tight spot if she were cornered.

"I've come to discuss a business venture."

She laughed. "Hah, what business you want with me? Monkey business?"

"The guidebook business. I want to make your establishment famous. Thousands of rich *farang*s will wish to spend large amounts of money here."

"You bullshit, Khun Go. Daeng say you talk bullshit every day." She paused, cocked her head to the side, watching the television set on the wall above Osborn. "So you understand why I don't believe you, yes?"

Daeng had definitely bad-mouthed him on Soi Cowboy. It was time to go to plan B.

"Many hotels and restaurants have great faith in me. Let me show you." He took out the da Vinci contract and put it on the bar.

"It says here that da Vinci has committed to one hundred thousand baht," said Osborn in Thai.

The mamasan tapped the wooden dildo, the size of a horse's femur, on the paper. A couple of customers in the back thought she was chopping up the ingredients for a spicy Thai salad. One *farang* got up from a table in the back near the toilets and took her picture, smiling, a gold tooth catching the flash.

"Winci. Who's that?"

"No, it's da Vinci. He's very famous. His restaurant is on Sukhumvit. He has the carriage trade."

The mamasan knew nothing and cared nothing of the carriage trade.

"Never heard of him or his restaurant." She said this as if she were the definitive expert. Since the name of da Vinci had never come to her attention, then he might as well have been living on Mars.

"My dear lady that may be the case. But he's a sixty-three-visa-run man. He's a veteran. And his restaurant is top drawer with all the *farang*s."

The light went on inside Osborn's head: the light said bottom drawer.

"Luke's Guest House and The Happy Night Coffee Shop also are in the guide."

She had heard of the guesthouse and coffee shop off Sukhumvit Road; they were establishments, which allowed her *ying*s inside. That proved to be the dealmaker.

"You do business with Luke's Guest House?" She tapped the wooden dildo against the side of the bar, as if the sound was helping her to think through something. "Not only do I do business with Luke's Guest House, I have the honor of showing one of their short-time rooms on the cover of my guide."

That did the trick and the old mamasan counted out a deposit on the bar counter, "You cheat me, Khun Go, I have you killed for four baht. No problem for me. So you not take money and think you can fuck me around."

"But mama, the thought never crossed my mind. You are doing the right thing. Believe me."

"I not believe *farang*."

"A wise racial decision. On the other hand, you are showing there are exceptions to every rule."

"You not forget. Four baht," she said, drawing the two fingers of her right hand underneath her throat, and sticking her bloated tongue out of the corner of her mouth.

"Erotic as always," said Osborn, walking backwards out of the bar.

Then, that same day, he got the Yings Feast Bar to give him a deposit, and so did Green Parrot and a half dozen other bars in the Plaza, Soi Cowboy, and Patpong. Before Daeng learned about the new source of money, Osborn rode his bicycle to Thonburi and paid the Chinese printer in small bills, twenty baht, fifty baht and hundred baht notes, simply to have the satisfaction of watching him spend a great deal of time counting and recounting the money on a small wooden table.

Osborn slightly regretted that he had pre-sold the *Bangkok Eateries* guide on the basis that only high-class, five-star establishments would appear. In the final version, there were several slight alterations; for instance, the Green Parrot bar appeared in the centerfold with bikini-clad beauties, wide-eyed and smiling, their hands wrapped around chrome posts. One of the owners was grinning into the camera as he sat on a stool. On the spine of the book, the author's name read Orson Welles and an old studio shot of Orson Welles in full white beard with a cigar hanging out of the corner of his mouth appeared on the back cover.

After the first edition of *Bangkok Eateries* sold out, Osborn had decided immediately to launch a second edition, and sent Daeng around to da Vinci's to get a new contract and more money from the owner. But she returned empty-handed, after being told that the only reason the owner had given a deposit in the first place was he had felt so sorry for his impoverished condition that day, that he had allowed his sense of compassion to overrule his business sense; and that this could only happen once in a lifetime, especially since the staff at the Green Parrot had been on the double-page spread that he had been promised. Besides, the restaurant didn't need the publicity since it was already the most famous Italian restaurant in Bangkok.

That very evening Osborn had met the bar owner and signed a contract to construct an aquarium for bar *ying*s. He still lost Daeng, who ran off with a Frenchman who had signed a contract with an American naval officer to sell one hundred tons of potatoes to the fleet every time it docked in Pattaya. Her new boyfriend's slogan was, "You fuck a *ying*, but you make love to good food and wine." He was very French.

Daeng had dumped him to go into the potato business with a *farang* from Paris. She could connect to potatoes, as a potato was part of her world of earth, water, weeding, planting, and harvesting. But writing and selling books in Bangkok, that didn't make sense to her.

"Who like reading books?" she had asked him. "Go anywhere look at people. What they do? No read book. One-hundred percent, sure."

Osborn did not have an answer for her (though they weren't eating potatoes either), and once again his clothes were in the *soi* and he was stuffing them into a suitcase as a Number 8 blue bus, spewing clouds of black exhaust, bore down on him as if he were a target in a shooting arcade. As he hurriedly scooped up the clothes, he came to the realization that a bar *ying* underwater was a new, untested, untried theme and he could not really blame Daeng because she had decided to go with the sure thing.

TWENTY-FIVE

THE LAST THING that Pauline Cheng had thought would happen was that Vincent Calvino would ask her out for dinner. If he wanted information, then he could have simply come around to her office. Making it a social occasion was an indication that he wanted something more. She was intrigued enough to say yes, though she immediately regretted the swift acceptance of the invitation, thinking that Calvino would believe she was easily available. She should have played the game better, she had thought to herself. It was simply too late to back out with any degree of grace.

"A man wants one of two kinds of women. One who isn't bright enough to notice the things that he says or does. Or one who is so bright that she notices everything for what it really is and understands it is better not to let on that she knows. This is the smart bitch category. The smart bitch keeps her insights and knowledge to herself."

She looked pleased with herself, touching her wine glass to her lips.

Calvino thought about this for a moment. "There is a third kind of woman," he said.

"Yeah, and what would that kind of woman be?"

"She is bright enough to notice what a man says and does but isn't bright enough to understand that no matter how hard she tries, she can never change what a man says or does."

"Do you think that you are an expert on women?" asked Pauline Cheng. Her smiled deepened.

It was as if she had tossed a stun grenade at his feet; the intention wasn't to kill but to scare the target away. He tried not to look scared and to think fast. Pauline was an extremely smart woman, reminding him that in the Big Weird there were lots of very clever, cunning women but a shortage of women with an educated intelligence, with a tongue that wasn't tailored to please as much as it was to find the precise words, shaping ideas like one of the ice sculptures found in five-star hotel foyers.

"I'm still trying to figure out whether this is a male city or a female city. *The Art of War* says an army should only attack female cities, what do you think, Pauline?"

"To attack is not to win the battle," she said. "I didn't know that private eyes liked reading about war."

"Only if they want to stay alive in Asia," said Calvino.

"Did you invite me to dinner to discuss a book?"

"Actually I had a fable in my mind. One my mother taught me as a boy. I learned very young not to cry wolf unless there is a wolf at the door. And, right now, you are the wolf at my door. I watched Slugo and Ice working online at the cybercafe. And I saw how WULF wiped out Ice's avatar."

"You picked a good time and place to continue your women's studies program," she said, breaking into a smile. "Tell me, did Slugo freak out?"

Calvino shook his head. "He just giggled. Ice freaked out, screaming and crying. She couldn't understand why you wanted to break her rice bowl."

"You still don't understand what it is about, do you? What Slugo is trying to do?"

"Enlighten me."

She pushed her plate aside. "Ice isn't just a bar *ying*; if that were all that's involved, who would care? But Slugo is using her as the prototype for his three-dimensional avatar. If he perfects this avatar and the environment where males can have their own interactive avatars, he will spread his technology to a hundred, a thousand other sites. The night world in this city will sprawl everywhere, and nowhere in cyberspace, coloring the attitudes, judgment, feelings men have about women. Digital sex, digital rape, digital degradation, and throw in a million pixels worth of humiliation. No one should allow that to happen to another human being.

"He thinks it's just a big computer game. Slugo has his brain hardwired like a thirteen-year-old kid. He doesn't see the bigger picture. For Slugo, Alpha Domo is a computer game. He can't see the damage that he's doing. Or he doesn't care about the implications of what he's doing. And there are other Slugos in Japan and America with their own Alpha Domo dreams, which are nightmares for all women. A vast universe filled with cyberspace brothels. If that were to happen, then all women would be doomed. Whatever gains we have made in respect and dignity will be destroyed."

"And you have appointed yourself the guardian of woman-kind?" asked Calvino. "Coming up with an effective means of censoring the Web is a project that the Chinese should be more than happy to fund."

"To protect yourself against violence is not censorship. To think otherwise means you've not understood a single thing that I've said to you." There was anger in her voice.

"Did Sam McNeal share your vision of using WULF to stop Alpha Domo?"

Now she smiled. "Business is never that far away from anything I do," she said.

"That makes us alike," said Calvino. "Well, did she?"

"In a lot of ways, Sam was supportive. But her heart wasn't in it. Computer avatars were too abstract. Slugo made her laugh. He charmed her, telling her stories about his childhood. His wealth impressed her. His Harvard degree impressed her. Sam was impressed by the wrong things in men."

"And what did Sam say?"

"She said that any man who was rich and funny could win over any woman. And, of course, Sam was right."

"Did it surprise you when Sam shot herself?"

The question didn't catch Pauline Cheng off-guard.

"Sam was unstable. And she was in an even more unstable relationship. Suicide is the alternative that people choose when they pass beyond the point of understanding, the point where there is only pain, loss, regret, and such a debt can only be cleared through death. Sam reached that end point, put a gun to her head and pulled the trigger." Her eyes narrowed as she acted out the sequence of Sam's final moment, pressing two fingers to her temple and dropping her thumb as the hammer of the revolver.

"And you think that Sam killed herself because of Nakamura?"

"I don't think anyone can answer that question. The last person to come up with an answer would be Ben Nakamura."

"Sam sent him a lot of e-mail before killing herself."

"He was a fool," she said.

Calvino saw a cloud of emotion in her eyes. "Because he wouldn't go along with the scheme

to help a Chinese electronic component company, the same company which also supplied components for the Chinese Long March -B rocket?"

Now it was Pauline's turn to laugh.

"You've been talking to Ben. The switch to Chinese components by the contractor in this project was perfectly legal, all aboveboard. Transparent. The group head made a business decision to switch components.

The components involved had nothing to do with the -B rocket. It was Ben's red herring. Sam suggested that Ben try to explain the position to his Japanese employer. There is nothing criminal in asking someone to give an explanation, is there, Mr. Calvino?"

"Depends on whether the explanation involves other things."

"Such as?"

"Maybe Ben knows about one of the Chinese strategies from *The Art of War*, a variation on the old bait-and-switch scam. Promise to deliver the dragon, but deliver the Phoenix."

She shrugged. "Ben said no, he wouldn't help. He wasn't interested."

"And that's when the e-mail campaign started," said Calvino.

"E-mail was invented for bad relationships. No, I am not surprised. American women come down with as severe a case of The Sickness as a man. Sam reached the point of no return. She lost it."

"She had a little help from her friends in WULF."

"Meaning?"

"Sam didn't write all the e-mails sent to Ben."

"Sisters help sisters. Brothers help brothers. Nothing an Italian from New York is surprised to hear."

It had been a long time since someone had called Calvino that in Bangkok. After years in the city most *farang*s stopped thinking ethnically and geographically. They became what the Thais called them: *farang*—a group that supported each other, looked after one another in an interlocking network of friendship. They had shed the debts of nationality and ethnic differ- ences and merged into a new breed who resided on the edges of Southeast Asia. They were a small colony that had taken root in a foreign soil that promised the Thais nothing.

Pauline leaned over, reached into her briefcase, and pulled out a book, which she slid across the table. Calvino read the title: *Handbook to Best Bangkok Eateries.*

"You know that Osborn wrote this book?"

"Yeah, I know," said Calvino, trying to look surprised that she had any interest in Alan's book venture.

"There's something you may not know. Osborn is going to sell advertising for Alpha Domo. You don't think that Slugo is doing all this for the love of Ice or hacker satisfaction, do you? Yes, Osborn wrote this book. And he has the contacts to turn Slugo's platform into a commercial site. Frankly, I am surprised that Quentin Stuart would allow Osborn to author his biography."

"Who said he doesn't know all about Alan's history?" asked Calvino.

Her eyes narrowed. "I don't believe that he knows about Alan's venture with Slugo."

"How did you find out? Did Slugo tell you? Or did Alan?"

"The information is out there if you know where to look."

The problem with smart people is that they understand the intelligence of others.

"So does it really matter whether Quentin knows or not? Osborn's a writer, and sometimes those kinds of people don't behave the way normal people behave, you know what I am saying?"

"And you are normal?" asked Pauline.

Calvino threw up his hands. "Of course, I am normal."

She ran her tongue across her lips, which had a shiny gloss of red lipstick. The side of her mouth curled in a half smile. "In that case, I guess I can trust you with what WULF plans to do next to stop Slugo and others like him."

"Hey, what's not to trust?"

TWENTY-SIX

CALVINO ARRIVED AT the Plaza about midnight after seeing Pauline Cheng home and having a look at the layout of her garden and house. He had arranged to have a heart-to-heart conversation with Slugo, in order to get his version once again about Alpha Domo and to see if the story about Osborn selling commercial spots checked out. Walking inside the Plaza, the place looked different because the climate of the times was different. It was crawling with uniformed cops and the customers that stayed behind were the hardcore. Those who remained in the Plaza had all the classic signs of chronic sufferers of The Sickness; there could have been bombs going off, small arms fire, and they would have stayed on, buying lady drinks, talking to the talent.

The news reports could not have given a more depressing story for this group. A police crackdown was in full swing and it had hit the entire Bangkok entertainment industry. All of Bangkok's nightlife venues, each and every bar, pub, disco, nightclub, pool parlor was given an ultimatum—obey the official order or else. Special forces from out of town swept through the Plaza, fanning out through the bars, checking IDs of each and every *ying*, turning on the lights, guarding the doors. The punters who sat in the corners had spent a year's savings so they could afford to fly economy class to Bangkok, settle in for their annual treatment. These unpackaged *farang*s did not by temperament deal well with authority invading their playground.

He found Osborn squatting in front of his yet to be completed Mermaidium, smoking a cigarette. He hadn't moved from his position earlier that day when John had appeared out of the blue and tried to kill him. What had changed were the mirrors in the back of the tank area. Osborn had watched Calvino come into the unfinished bar. There was no one else inside.

"I am learning to watch my back," said Osborn. "Lots of police around tonight," said Calvino. Osborn nodded. "Yes, a detachment arrived about fifteen minutes ago."

The police crackdown order had been given many times before and it meant two weeks and the crackdown was over. The crackdown operated on a wholly novel approach. The government had set aside 8 inactive posts for the police. The crackdown only worked if there was also a crackdown on the cops who were running the crackdown. Six inactive posts for commissioner-level rank or higher, 14 for deputy commissioners to commanders, 4 for deputy commanders to superintendents, 196 for deputy superintendents down to inspectors, and 88 for sub-inspectors. No one would suggest firing a cop that let a bar or club operate later than one or two in the morning for discotheques;

transferring them to an inactive post was a sufficient indication that the crackdown was to be taken with a great deal of seriousness.

Calvino squatted down beside Osborn and studied his face in the mirror.

"You've not returned to talk about police matters, I take it," said Osborn.

"This isn't about *Bangkok Eateries*. It's about you working with Slugo to sell advertisements on the Internet."

Osborn smiled. "Oh, Slugo's cyberspace grift promises to be a very successful scam. But *Bangkok Eateries*, the true, inside story, would make a splendid film. Don't you think?"

Slugo waltzed in with a bar *ying* on each arm. He was turning to each *ying* and speaking in Thai, "*Yom pae*—I surrender." The bar *ying*s loved to hear that expression; it gave them visions of a white flag being waved overhead by a *farang*. The objective of each *ying* was to find a *farang* who would surrender without much of a fight, succumb to The Sickness and gladly hand over lots of money. But, in reality, it was rare to find many *farang*s who knew the Thai expression, creating the irony that a *farang* who knew the expression knew too much—he knew the terms of surrender.

The dancers sat on the stools holding their colas as Slugo went up and patted Calvino on the back. "Calvino will soon have his own story for a film. He is going to be a star, an international box office hit and one day we can say that we knew him."

"This is becoming a disease," said Osborn. "Really, it is quite disturbing."

"What is this script about, Slugo?"

Slugo leaned over and kissed one of the *ying*s on the forehead.

"Sex is a midnight echo, and in those vibrations is the syntax of our DNA code. The real-time sexual act is limited by what one's genetic material permits. The story is how the digital Ice is liberated from prison walls of the biological Ice's sexually. Genetic destiny. Sex. Computers. Drugs and rock 'n roll. And there is a private eye named Calvino. All of it is set in the future. That is the script."

Osborn moved closer, "Of course, you know that he is quite mad."

TWENTY-SEVEN

LOVE AND HONOR are gone from the earth. Now the sky is black and silent and we wander the shoreline, searching in the darkness for what I have lost, what you have taken from others, what they have taken from you, and what can never be replaced. Trust. How can I ever trust another man after the way you abandoned me? It was so easy for you to go. I gave everything to you and it wasn't enough. You took and took, consumed by faith and trust, until there was no more to give. No more. Then you threw me away. One day you will be punished for what you have done, Ben. You will feel the pain that I feel.

Those words had appeared in Sam McNeal's last e-mail sent to Nakamura on the night of her death. Appearances could be deceiving, especially when someone was sending e-mail using the Internet account of a dead person thinking that she was alive. The e-mail arrived in Nakamura's mailbox on the night of her death and from the time of the message, the words had been sent after her body had been found.

Knowledge of her death had not filtered to whomever

in WULF was assigned to write, or at the very least, send Sam's letters to her ex-boyfriend. Calvino had held back some of Sam's e-mail messages until he had done more background investigation into their authenticity. He had failed to anticipate that a week later he would be inside Quentin Stuart's study, looking at the opening sequence of a screenplay in which one of Sam's e-mails—one which he had not delivered to Quentin—formed the opening lines of dialogue for an American female character named Dawn who was clearly based on Sam McNeal. Quentin said that it didn't matter that in life Sam could not have written those words; what mattered was that the language worked well in the script he was writing and that screenwriting should never be tainted by trying to force the characters and the story to mirror the actual events from which they had been drawn.

As Calvino stood in front of the desk, Quentin did not look up from his Remington manual typewriter. His fingers gracefully struck the keys at high speed; after a moment Quentin paused, his reading glasses with the thick black frames balanced on the end of his nose, and his lips moving as he silently read back a line of dialogue. As the light from the side window fell across Quentin's face, he might have passed for Hemingway in his later years. He worked slowly over the contents he had finished typing. Suddenly, he pulled the page out of the typewriter carriage, carefully put the page on a neat stack of pages, and pivoted around in his chair. Calvino couldn't quite take his eyes off the ancient typewriter.

Inside his jacket pocket Calvino had a copy of Slugo's script idea—all about the use of hardware and software one hundred years into the future, and here was a screenwriter who was using a nineteenth century machine. How Slugo's story synopsis ended up inside Calvino's jacket as he stood in front of Quentin was the direct consequence of breaching Calvino's law of fair exchange. He had pumped Slugo for information about Pauline, and rather than paying him on the spot, he had made the mistake of owing Slugo a favor. There was no free information any more than there was free sex in the Big Weird. The cost of information about the exploding Chinese -B rockets and how to connect the fallout to Pauline, he had to admit, had come from Slugo. And he called in the favor. Pitch his script idea to the man. To the greatest screenwriter of them all: Quentin Stuart. Calvino thought that would be easy but he had forgotten about the Remington typewriter. Now he looked thoroughly disillusioned about selling a hi-tech science fiction story to Mr. Stuart.

"You know, a lot of people who come into my office gasp in horror when they see me writing scripts on a Remington. I had one young guy tell me he had never seen a real Remington before, outside of a museum. Until I tell them I never worry about my Remington coming down with a virus, updating the software, buying more expensive chips to improve the speed, and I don't worry about power-cuts costing me a week's worth of work."

"I thought before we go upstairs for lunch, you could pitch your script idea," said Quentin.

"Have you ever used the Internet?" asked Calvino. "Or, do you ever wonder how cyberspace might change a lot of things, like entertainment?"

"I'm too old, too sick to start on something like that.

The Remington has been my friend for more than half a century, why abandon her now?"

"If it's all right with you, I think that some other time might be better to make the pitch. It's not quite ready."

"As you like. Sometimes it is better to wait. You only get to pitch a film idea once. People listen because they want to like it. It either flies or never gets off the ground that first time. There is no such thing as a second pitch. Unless you are talking about baseball."

Calvino glanced down at the top page of the script with Sam's words in the dialogue. He had spent enough time on Slugo's recalled favor, and it was time for him to go back to work on the case.

"If you had Sam's e-mail all the time, why didn't you tell me?" asked Calvino.

"That's what I am paying you. How do I know I have all the e-mails she sent? How do you know my files are complete? In fact what you gave me wasn't complete."

"Some of the e-mails may not have been Sam's." Quentin sighed, shaking his head. "Does it really matter who was the author?"

"It matters," said Calvino.

"If I told you I already had her mail, then you might not have given it priority, and I might have lost a chance to see how reliable you are."

"You're using Sam's words in one of your scripts," said Calvino, looking up from the page.

Quentin Stuart slowly removed his reading glasses as if he were in the presence of a slow learner. "Vincent, a writer is like a cuckoo; we lay our eggs in the nests built by others. They are our eggs but the warmth needed for incubation is borrowed from the ass-end feathers of other birds in the flock. Though in this case, Sam was paid by me to work as my research assistant. She was my employee. The final product is never the nest; it is the hatched egg. The script."

"But the film is about Sam, am I right?"

"*Temporal Target* is about young foreigners with too much money living high above the mean streets of Bangkok. They get together to form a very private members-only club. Membership is limited in the *mem-farang* Russian Roulette Club. While the men are members, the guests, the shooters, are women only. Women had the guns; men watched as they pressed the barrel to their forehead and squeezed the trigger. It's a thriller with the woman hero trying to stop a friend from crossing the line and taking the biggest risk of her life. Sisterhood, love, betrayal, and death played out against the backdrop of the most exciting, modern city in Asia. Now, that is what is called a pitch in the business," Quentin said.

"When you sell a film you have to hook the producer with an idea that has legs."

"It sounds like a remake of *The Deer Hunter*," said Calvino, reading the rest of the page.

"*Temporal Target* is not a remake. It is an original script. There's nothing about the Vietnam War in this movie. It is modern, hip, very 90s. A movie rich in texture, one with characters so real that you can't take your eyes off them."

"Let me guess, you're aiming for a young audience. Those who are bored, in between values, who toy with the idea of death as if it were another consumer product in a shopping-mall window," said Calvino, laying down the page.

"Brilliant, I should hire you to do the publicity. That's the concept exactly. Temporal means limited in time and it also means the temples of the skull. The main character of Dawn finds the only way to stop her friend is to take her friend's place, thinking that once she sits at the table, experiences fear of such mortal danger, the friend would call it off. End it, throw away the gun. The friend has satisfied whatever primeval need she had to experience danger. She finds, to use your words, death is not a toy."

"In reality, Sam killed herself. So, if there was a friend, her friend didn't stop Sam," said Calvino.

The maid had quietly slipped into the office and announced that lunch was ready upstairs.

"We'll be upstairs in a minute," said Quentin, hands folded on his desk.

"Maybe the friend wanted her dead," said Calvino. "And maybe you are right. But where was the friend? Sam went into Ben's house like the one I describe in the script, only she is alone when she puts a gun to her temple and squeezes the trigger. At least this was my first reaction when I heard about the circumstances of her death. The more I thought about her work for me, what I knew about her family, and the more I remembered about our conversation about life and death, the more I started to doubt my first impressions about how things happened that night. I knew Sam extremely well and saw her in many social circumstances. There is something that doesn't quite fit together and that is why I hired you. To find what I believe is a missing piece or missing pieces."

"Did you ever think that Dawn in Temporal Target

should die? As a homage to Sam who doesn't come out of the story alive," said Calvino.

"Life copies art, and art copies life, to paraphrase Oscar Wilde. But in the movie business, art copies what is commercial and to hell with life. Sam loved the idea of this movie and getting it made meant a great deal to her. She threw herself heart and soul into it. She literally died for it. She was so involved with the project that it spilled over into her relationships. Especially after she split up with Nakamura, doing research assignments for the film became her passion. She lost herself in her research."

"Doing research for you didn't stop her from blowing out her brains," said Calvino.

"And I have a feeling there were witnesses in Ben's house with her that night. People who might have pulled her back from the edge."

"Or someone who pushed her over the edge."

As Calvino finished talking, Quentin rose to his feet and motioned for him to go upstairs. The table was set for three people. Downstairs, kneeling in front of the huge aquarium that he created, Osborn was looking at the fish.

"Alan, please come up and take a chair."

"I was trying to imagine what a *ying* would look like inside the aquarium," said Osborn. "A small *ying* about the size of Luk Pla."

Osborn came upstairs from the living room barefoot, wearing a torn pair of gray trousers and the same old workman's shirt that he had been wearing in the bar. He sat down in the chair opposite Calvino. Quentin sat at the head of the table. Plates of fresh salad and toasted tuna fish sandwiches were laid out in the center of the table.

"Please help yourselves, gentlemen," said Quentin.

"Mr. Calvino, you always seem to be in rooms I enter these days," said Osborn.

"I was thinking the same thing about you," said Calvino.

"Well, you know what they say about great minds. Though, I am sure it doesn't apply in this particular case," said Osborn.

"Osborn and I will take a meeting after lunch," said Quentin Stuart, using two large plastic spoons to fill his plate with salad.

The maid brought in a large glass of iced coffee and set it down beside Quentin's plate.

"I thought that was why I came here today, Quentin. To discuss Mr. Osborn's other book."

Quentin Stuart started to laugh. "I thought it was to pitch me a screenplay idea. And deliver the rest of Sam's e-mail. Osborn has already told me the entire story about his *Bangkok Eateries* guide."

"It was a lovely scam," said Osborn. He turned to Quentin.

"Has your private eye revealed his film project with Slugo? Some kind of strange science fiction piece I believe is the way Slugo tried to explain it. Bangkok in the year 2046 inhabited by bio-synthetic life forms and customers in those hazardous-waste space suits"

Calvino shook his head.

"Is that the story you wanted to pitch?" asked Quentin. Calvino frowned at Osborn, who was cutting a large piece of lettuce with his knife and fork. "The story's not ready. It may never be ready. Mr. Osborn seems to know as much about it as I do. Besides, it looks like you've answered your own question—whether you can work with Mr. Osborn.

He can write your biography and be your film consultant, too," said Calvino, a puzzled expression on his face as he looked first at Quentin and then at Alan.

Slugo had a big mouth, Calvino thought. Getting favors without paying for them always came to grief. Now he was compromised as well, since Alan, at least according to Pauline, was also doing business with Slugo, hawking advertisements for Alpha Domo.

"Don't sound so petulant, Mr. Calvino," said Osborn.

"The biography can wait until after I am gone."

Quentin stared at a large green olive pinned to a slice of lettuce and onion on the end of his fork as if he had discovered that the color green was not only used on American money. "We are beyond that. Now we are discussing a screenplay based on his experience in researching, writing, and publishing his *Bangkok Eateries*."

Calvino got up from the dining-room table and walked to the door, reached down and slipped on his shoes.

"Aren't you going to finish your lunch?" asked Quentin.

"I don't think Mr. Calvino looks very hungry all of a sudden."

"I have another appointment," said Calvino. Working for Quentin Stuart was a wearying experience with the rules changing each time he met his client, one reversal followed by another, until he realized that he had been brought in less to discover the dark forces of evil than to discover the squalid compounds that could be shaped into books and movies.

"Aren't you slightly interested in how Quentin is going to turn my book into a movie?"

Calvino walked halfway to the dining room table.

"What about *Temporal Target*?" asked Calvino looking directly at Quentin.

"It's nearly finished. So I have time to work with Osborn on *Fast Food*."

"Don't tell me. Fast as in speed and fast as in fasting," said Calvino.

Osborn raised an eyebrow and exchanged a knowing look with Quentin Stuart.

"I wish to revise my earlier observation about the applicability of the great minds quotation. Perhaps I was wrong and it does have relevance," said Osborn

"One more thing before you go, Vincent, would you be free to go to the Plaza tonight with Luk Pla and me?"

"Is this another film project?" asked Calvino.

"Say, seven thirty?" asked Quentin Stuart. "This is a personal matter. The invitation has nothing to do with getting material for a film. I am asking for your help with respect to my mental and spiritual well-being."

Without waiting for a reply, Quentin sat back in his chair and devoted his full attention to eating his salad. As he was chewing, he looked over at Alan. "I have been thinking about the opening. Your character is on one of those old Chinese bicycles that looks like it's made the thousand-mile journey with Mao, and your character looks like he is trying to pedal the last one hundred yards in the rain. He's exhausted, his face is drawn, sickly, and all around him are hundreds of motorcycles, cars, buses, trucks. He is a good cyclist but he's being chased by thugs and they are gaining on him. We will get a long shot of that chase scene in the driving rain."

Osborn screwed up his face, lit a cigarette, and shook

his head.

"I had the idea of a seashore, a landscape, and emerging, here and there, are very small fishermen. And delicate, smallish windmills. Like an English play, the story should have intelligence, elegance, class, and a bold streak of wisdom," said Osborn.

"In other words, the kind of literary elements that killed the movie industry in England."

Before fade-in had been agreed upon, there was already a major disagreement.

Osborn thought about this, exhaling smoke. "A Chinese bicycle in the rain. Why are they chasing the main character?"

"They are the brothers of a respectable Thai *ying* whose heart you have broken."

Osborn beamed. "I like that. And she wants to have me killed for revenge."

Calvino supposed that Hollywood worked that way, one man chewing salad, and another man listening, agreeing. One had power and one had hope to use power. Creativity was making up things about characters and situations which had never happened to people who had no experience of them even if they had happened. Alan Osborn and Quentin Stuart writing about an unpackaged *farang* character who had broken the heart of a respectable Thai woman was like a couple of amateurs running around a blood-splattered bathroom with buckets, trying to make a murder look like a suicide. As he left the penthouse, Calvino thought about Quentin's earlier suspicion that Sam McNeal had been murdered. Perhaps that suspicion was only another one of his momentary plot points. In a strange way, it was as if he had scripted her death, or was there some piece of information that he had been keeping incommunicado, waiting for the right moment to release it, or could it be that in Quentin's world, a week was a long time, and Sam had been dead long enough for him to move onto other projects?

TWENTY-EIGHT

AT 7: 0 P.M. Calvino quietly slipped into the nearly empty bar in the far corner of the Plaza. Young women dressed in short, pleated school uniforms, white cotton blouses with bow-ties and tartan vests, sat on the back benches, smoking cigarettes and gossiping. A half-dozen slender figures danced on the stage. A couple had their tops removed but kept on their bras—a sure sign of a crackdown in progress—and watched themselves in the distant mirrors on the walls. They were on the job, like Calvino was on the job. And as Calvino watched them dancing, while Quentin searched their faces, looking for Luk Pla among them, he realized how his job was not all that different from the job the *yings* were paid to do.

Their clients were engaged in dreaming. Dreamers provided a lot of employment in the Big Weird. They made a good living reinforcing dreams; a private eye made a living—good was another issue—from assessing the damage resulting from broken dreams, repairing the dream and delivering it back patched up. The bar *yings* and private investigators were only the tip of the iceberg of those who made a living from all of these doomed dreamers.

Quentin Stuart sat second row up, along the right hand side. Luk Pla was one row down, letting a couple of her friends admire her gold bracelets, necklace, and rings. She was nursing a cola, and Quentin had obviously bought drinks for all of the other *ying*s. There were four or five dressed in school uniforms who huddled around Luk Pla as though she were the class runt, the kid who had surprised everyone and had achieved success, returning to her school like a victorious alumna. She was the only one in the group of women who was out of uniform. Clearly a graduate, thought Calvino as he passed her, climbing the steps up a level and sliding in next to Quentin.

The old man looked nervously towards the door. "You look worried," said Calvino.

Quentin Stuart's hands were shaking as he raised his gin and tonic from the table.

"I had a little run in with Luk Pla's ex-husband. He was waiting for us at the mouth of the Plaza and came running up shaking his fists and shouting at her in Thai."

"What did Luk Pla do?"

Quentin swallowed a mouthful of gin.

"She screamed at him. Called him a stupid water buffalo in English and then in Thai. If I hadn't pulled her away, they would have definitely been kick-boxing each other in the street. And I would have put money on Luk Pla kicking the shit out of him."

Calvino remembered the so-called ex-husband, and if tradition were any guide, then the altercation was with the same guy she had shared a bag of fried grasshoppers, and he was neither an "ex" nor a "husband." He was Luk Pla's boyfriend. Marital status was often blurred in the Big Weird. There were marriage ceremonies which weren't real marriages but more like blessing ceremonies, then there were real marriages but the couple never registered the marriage, and then there existed the possibility of someone registering one marriage in one province, and marrying someone else, then registering that marriage in another province, and there was the traditional system of *mia luang*—major wives—and *mia noi*—minor wives; in sum, who was married and who was unmarried was a grab bag of different options.

Married or not, the boyfriend, was a little like Willy Sutton the American bank robber; he knew where the money was kept and had told her to go back to Quentin Stuart, as if he were a bank, and to bring back the dough. The boyfriend had a problem that bank robbers like Willy Sutton never faced. In the battle between ego to possess the woman and the greed to exploit her for his personal benefit, the pendulum swung back, ringing the ego bell with a thunderous, great force.

"Mr. Stuart, I am a private investigator, not a body-guard," said Calvino.

"You remember that period when I couldn't find her? Well, for those dark days of my life, Luk Pla came back to work at this bar. She swore to me that she never went out with another customer. That all she could do was sit in the corner, cry, and think about how much she missed me. How much she loved me. Wanted me. And whether I would take her back. She knows all the right things to say. I think I believe her."

"But you want to know if she's telling the truth?" asked Calvino.

"I thought you might be able to ask a few questions. Just to clarify the situation. I don't have that much time left, Vincent. Six months, a year, maybe more if I'm lucky. So I don't want to start over with another *ying*. But I don't want to waste time on a *ying* who is fucking around on me and then lying about it."

Calvino caught the eye of the bar owner, who was on the opposite side of the stage, holding a soda water. The owner, Harry, was one of those rare bar owners who didn't drink and who did not sleep with the help. He was a tall, slightly bald man of about fifty.

"I thought that was you, Vincent," he said as he sat down on the bench.

Calvino introduced Quentin Stuart. "I am a big fan of your films, Mr. Stuart."

"That makes us even because I'm a big fan of your bar, Harry."

"We have very nice *ying*s working here. They are like a family. We treat them right, with respect, and we have no trouble keeping them on the payroll. No thieves, drug addicts, and no mean ones. I can honestly say that we have never had a fight among our *ying*s."

Quentin called down for the Baby Fish, and Luk Pla, hearing her name in English, turned around and blew him a kiss.

Harry recognized her as she nestled into the crook of Quentin's arm.

"She's a nice girl," he said.

This made Quentin smile and hug Luk Pla. "I am feeling better already," he said.

Calvino had seen her type before working in the bars: the kind of *ying* with the eyesight of a rat moving fast as hell through a dark hotel room. She knew how to get the cheese without the trap coming down and breaking her beautiful neck. Calvino discreetly asked Harry, "She was working a few days last week. Was she bought out?"

The owner thought about this question for a second. He had hundreds of *ying*s and keeping their names straight in his mind was not an easy task. "I'm trying to think. I recall seeing her every morning at two, three. Some of our *ying*s are like that. They dance, draw their salary, the money from their lady drinks, but they don't go out with customers."

Calvino leaned across Harry and related the substance of their conversation to the old man who was growing younger and happier by the moment. Quentin's eyes glistened, wet with tears, as he hugged the Baby Fish.

"You were telling the truth," he said. "You do love me."

She smiled and kissed him on the lips.

"Love you," she said. "Love you too much."

Quentin paid for the round of drinks and wasted no time, quickly leaving the bar with Luk Pla on his arm.

"You want me to walk you out of the Plaza?" asked Calvino.

Quentin Stuart looked up from the main floor. "I recall you saying that you don't work as a bodyguard, Vincent."

He regretted having put his back up. "Forget about what I said. I don't work in the movie business either but I wanted to pitch you an idea. I think that I overreacted. If you want me to see you out, all you've gotta do is say, Vincent, see me and my lady out of the Plaza."

Quentin smiled. "I appreciate it. But I can handle myself."

"I am certain you can handle it, but sometimes having a friend along doesn't hurt matters," said Calvino.

"Vincent, it's under control," he said, patting Calvino on the shoulder and sliding out from his seat.

"He's one of the great ones," said Harry, as they watched Quentin and Luk Pla walking towards the door.

After the old man left the bar, Calvino asked Harry if he minded checking The Book. It was a capital letters kind of book, one that every bar kept that recorded each and every buy-out and lady's drink. Each *ying* had a page in the sacred book. The Book recorded the number of times that the *ying* had been called upon to treat The Sickness of an infected *farang*. The Book was guarded like a confidential, secret document; its very existence might have shattered all illusions of the nature of bar *ying* and *farang* relationships. The Sickness was fed because men believed that they were paying the bar fine for a romantic interlude with a *ying* who was attracted to him rather than like every other commercial transaction; the customer was never more than a customer. Every time a *ying* was bought out of the bar, the transaction was registered in black and white.

The business of sex was laid out like a monthly financial report, showing whose inventory had moved, who were the hot, new products, and the small group who didn't go out with customers. They existed, and because a few along the margins refused customers' invitations, the vast majority could create the illusion that they were among the refusers. Even in the case of a *farang* with a mild case of The Sickness, the sufferer wanted a Refuser;

she became his own prized possession, not shared with others, so rather than pay for play, it was love for play.

Showing The Book to an outsider was an unspoken taboo along the lines of a lawyer not revealing the confidences of a client, or a priest not repeating the stories from the confessional box. Bar owners, like the operators of Disney World, had the duty to preserve the cartoon of romance, and there was big money in cartoons, especially if they were consumed as the surefire cure for a dose of The Sickness.

Calvino followed Harry to his office in the back of the bar. They sat on chairs in front of a long wooden table pushed against one wall in the narrow room. Harry unlocked a small safe and removed The Book, which he opened and laid on the desk. He flipped to the page with Luk Pla's name and number written in black ink at the top. In the three days that she had gone missing from Quentin Stuart's life, Luk Pla had been reeled out of the bar five times. Harry looked up from the page, "Sorry, but I was mistaken about Luk Pla. She's a very good earner, that one. And I don't know how I didn't see her potential before."

"Thanks for setting the record straight. Don't worry, Harry. I won't mention that I saw The Book. The information came from a friend."

"I appreciate that very much, Vincent. I would have a small riot on my hands if the *ying*s ever knew I showed The Book to a customer."

Calvino put up his hand and drew two fingers across his lips. "My lips are sealed."

He left Harry in his office and returned to where he had been sitting with Quentin. Not long afterwards,

Slugo, his face beaming, climbed the steps two at a time, finally reaching the back, where Calvino sat alone on a bench, finishing his drink.

"Hey, I saw Quentin and Luk Pla outside. Man, does he look happy. He said he owed it all to you. I'd say you are on a roll," said Slugo, placing a manila envelope in front of Calvino. "You are his man. He likes you. He will help us get our movie made."

He looked at the envelope, then looked up at Slugo. "You ever tried using the post office, Slugo?"

Slugo giggled. "Be serious. I think you will like it. I revised the original draft that I gave to you, and in the new draft you are the hero," Slugo said, as a waitress brought him a large glass of orange juice with one of those tiny Japanese umbrellas sticking through a red cherry. "Did you talk to him about it yet?"

"Not yet," said Calvino.

"Thank God for that. The new version is so much better and it would've blown it had you told him about the original story."

"You only get one chance to make a pitch," said Calvino.

"That's absolutely right," said Slugo.

"But I don't think I am any good at pitching story ideas."

"You probably aren't. But it doesn't matter. It adds to your charm. Anyone who pitches well is thought of as, well, sleazy," said Slugo.

Calvino opened the envelope and pulled out the papers, but it was too dark to read so Slugo took out a gold lighter and held the flame close to the page.

"What do you want me to do with this version?" asked Calvino.

"Give it to Quentin. You are his fair-haired boy. I think he can get this made," said Slugo. "Even though I wrote it myself I think it's very good."

"Why would I want to give this to Quentin?"

Slugo giggled. "Remember you owe me a favor and the film is about you and Bangkok in the next century. How can you resist a film about yourself?"

He remembered the favor, the chit had been called in all right; Slugo had brought up the favor about a dozen times since he had delivered him the original treatment.

"He works on a Remington typewriter," said Calvino.

"Quentin hates computers. He has no use for the Internet."

"That's because he hasn't had it explained to him properly."

Calvino folded the envelope and put it inside his jacket.

"Why did you have to tell Osborn that we were working on a film together? Because it's your film. I am not working on any project, but on the case I was hired for by Quentin."

"Vincent, baby, this could be your big break," said Slugo. "It could change your life."

"I am happy with my life the way it is."

"Come on, Calvino. Don't you want more out of life?"

Calvino watched the dancers filing on stage.

"I'll pass your idea along to Quentin. Then we are even. The favor is paid for." He extended his hand.

"Deal?" asked Calvino.

"You don't want part of the action? You can't be serious. This film will make both of us wildly rich. You can buy your own private playground," said Slugo.

"I have parts of more action than I know what to do with. Somehow the maintenance of keeping a private playground doesn't appeal to me."

"You will change your mind. I would bet on it."

The next morning, Quentin Stuart phoned Calvino. "You know, Vincent, I had breakfast with a friend this morning who hadn't seen me in two weeks. He said that I looked totally different and that it must have been the Baby Fish. I can't tell you what a relief it was to find out that she hadn't been lying to me. That she really does love me. I haven't thought about my illness, the pain, or death since. I have you to thank, my friend."

"Yeah, sure, as long as she makes you happy," said Calvino. "By the way, you know when I told you I had this idea for a film but it wasn't quite ready?"

"I remember."

"It's ready," Calvino said. "I don't know if you're gonna like it. I know you have this thing about Remington typewriters and modern technology, but I think it is interesting."

"Why don't you come around and tell me about it?" asked Quentin.

"You mean you want to hear it? I mean with all the stuff you are doing?"

"If you think it works. Has some valid truth, then sure I want to hear it."

The old man did not want the truth; he had convinced himself that his life in the Big Weird was strangely connected to the fiction that he liked to create: bar *ying*s with honor and integrity and respectable ones with broken hearts who unleashed their brothers to kill *farang* lovers.

"I will come over," said Calvino, thinking that his hand was shaking. He had killed people and his hand didn't shake. It was this strange thing about show business. He was wondering if that was a Sickness itself and he started to think maybe he was coming down with it.

TWENTY-NINE

COL. PRATT LOOKED up from the last page of Slugo's Cyber-Eye Bureau with a curious expression on his face and found Calvino was nervously sitting forward in his chair, waiting for his reaction. Pratt had one thought in his mind: had his friend from New York City, after all these years living and working in Bangkok, gone deep inside the Hollywood dream time? Nothing or no one had ever come close to buying Vincent Calvino. Now he was sitting like a patient in a doctor's office, all the x-rays of bones and organs fastened to the lighted glass, waiting for a verdict. Was he going to live, or was he going to die? Calvino flipped through some pages, then he looked at Pratt.

"What do you think about the story?"

"You are the one who gets shot, what do you think?"

"I phoned Slugo this morning after sleeping on the story and said that you should be in the film. The tough but fair Thai cop who loves Shakespeare."

"Do I get shot, too?" asked Pratt. "The cyberspace private eye in Slugo's film who just so happens to be called V. Calvino is shot."

Calvino, repressing a grin, raised his hands and shrugged his shoulders.

"While you are reading *Hamlet*. I am joking. I am the one who is shot. You get to be a hero. And I don't see why you can't play yourself. Like the Rocky films. Stallone held out until they let him star in his own film, now look where he is. Italians hold out for something they want. I think as my friend you should be in this film."

"Your friend, Quentin, he thinks Hollywood will turn Slugo's story idea into a film?"

"I haven't asked him. I wanted your opinion first," said Calvino, sipping Mekhong and Coke from a large glass filled with ice.

"I thought you were working for Quentin on the McNeal case."

"I am working on that job. That's right. But this came up. I saw an earlier version of the script and didn't think much of it. But this draft is, well, it's good."

"You mean, Slugo thinks you have influence over Quentin."

"He knows Quentin better than me," said Calvino. "You know, they see each other at parties. They have the same friends. He's known Quentin much longer than me."

"But Quentin doesn't rely on him for anything. Doesn't owe him anything. The relationship is purely social. Fluff. With you and Quentin it's just the opposite. But Slugo already owes Quentin. He can't approach him. But Quentin has relied on you. And you've helped him.

He is obligated to you. You investigated the Englishman. He wasn't expecting that you'd come through. In the end you gave him the real story. He may have had parts of it but couldn't fully understand how it fit together. Vincent, you didn't let him down. Quentin's in a business where letting people down is a way of life. Everyday someone has their hand out asking him for something. So you stand out. You didn't take all the cash he offered you. The main thing, you deliver what you promised. Slugo saw that. And the English writer . . ."

"Osborn."

"That's the one. Even he knows you have influence with Quentin."

"So you like the movie idea or not?"

"I am thinking."

"You're being Thai. You don't want to commit yourself. Just in case the project goes nowhere. Or you are upset because this draft doesn't have your part written in. Hey, that's easy, I can get Slugo to fix that."

"You seem to have a lot vested in Slugo's film, Vincent. Is it because you are the central character?"

"Me? I just thought it was interesting. Being in a movie. Getting shot. Coming back to life. All that science fiction spin. Two hours of stuffing popcorn in your mouth, you could be watching something a lot worse. But who cares? I can just walk away from it. Investment in Slugo's idea? Who cares?"

"I guess you are going to ask Quentin's opinion."

"I don't know. Maybe he will hate it. Maybe he will think, hey this guy brings back my *ying*, finds out about the English guy . . ."

"Osborn."

"And I even clear up the circumstances surrounding Sam McNeal's death, but I blow it because I show him some dumb idea that's not even my idea. Since it is about me I am in his face like an Amway salesman trying to convince him how great it is. And he thinks, how can this guy go out and do all this stuff that I can't do, don't know how even to start to do, and then he shows up with something like this, thinking it is gonna win an Oscar or something."

"You're afraid of rejection."

"I don't wanna get involved in something that doesn't look right."

"Most of the clients who come to you have done something that doesn't look right and ask you to help them. Besides, since when have you stopped taking risks, Vincent?"

"But this is different. I don't know what it is. These guys who write movies, famous guys like Quentin, what do they really do? I've seen him. He sits around in his silk dressing gown thinking up stories, making millions of dollars, and other guys sit around doing the same thing and nothing happens except they are broke. They are schmucks. I don't know why the one guy gets the picture deal and the next guy gets swept out of the door like he's carpet lint climbed up on someone's lapel. It's gotta be something to do with the way the story works."

"I don't think anyone knows. Or if there is one person who does, he wouldn't tell anyone else. He would be the most powerful, wealthy man on earth."

"So should I ask Quentin? I mean the guy hates computers and all that high-tech stuff. And you read what Slugo wrote; it's all about the next century where computers become people, and sex is something guys in white coats put together in a lab."

"It's up to you," said Pratt.

Calvino smiled. "I knew you'd say that. Meaning I should ask him, right? I will see him tonight. I'll see how I feel. I might ask him what he thinks. I'll keep it at the general concept level. I won't get into the details. Just test the water. See what his reaction is. If he looks bored or distracted, then I'll know."

"Know what?" asked Pratt. Calvino finished his drink. "My timing was wrong."

Alan Osborn smoothed his uncombed hair with the splayed fingers of his right hand, then he adjusted his glasses; one optical lens in the broken eyeglass frames was spliced to the frame with black electrician's tape.

He was nervous as he looked through the growing crowd, wondering if he had forgotten anything. The aquarium was larger than any object containing water he had ever constructed. Getting the chlorine level right had taken some trial and error: one girl's skin had turned an orange color after she had spent only five minutes underwater. The air hoses had to be adjusted. The filter system and pumps had broken and had to be replaced, and finally the lighting had to be synchronized with the music. When everything came together, it was a work of art, he thought. The invited crowd had come for the official opening of the Mermaidium. It was like opening night for a movie, the bar was soon packed, standing room only.

The official police crackdown had unofficially ended and it was business as usual in the Plaza. A few of the hardcore *ying*s celebrated by running around the Plaza without their tops on and mooning customers on the staircases. A *farang* in his early seventies, judging from his weathered, wrinkled face and hunched over body, wore a pale green jump suit, white socks, and white shoes; he waved at them as they walked along outside the bars, wearing a black bra around his bald head like a headband. The upturned 8" C cups above his temples, gave him the look of an aged Mickey Mouse character who had been paid to greet customers as they arrived to go on the rides.

From the upstairs balconies, the **ying**s shouted at the old man, then turned their attention to a group of *farang*s who had gathered near a Middle-Eastern vendor's cart and ate shawarmas outside the Lollipop Bar. The dancers screamed at the *farang*s to bring their shawarmas upstairs for some tender loving care. Party time had again returned to the Plaza and the local punters were in their best show-me-something-different mood. Something they hadn't seen before. The hardcore chewed their shawarma sandwiches, talking about the idea of watching a naked *ying* underwater sucking on a plastic oxygen tube.

Calvino spotted Reed Mitchell with several of his friends in suits and ties, Ben Nakamura arrived alone, and Slugo came into the bar with Ice, who looked like her black spandex bodysuit had been spray-painted onto her body. Ice wore three-inch red high heels and her hair was piled in layers on the top of her head, giving her the appearance that she had grown half a foot taller since last time Calvino had seen her.

"You have my two thousand baht?" Ice asked as she peeled away from Slugo's arm.

He slipped her two greyish blue notes and she turned and ran back to Slugo, who was trying to avoid Pauline Cheng.

Pauline and several other women entered the bar, stopped, and surveyed the crowd like a commando unit preparing a surprise attack, before they moved in behind where Quentin Stuart sat at the bar. They leaned back against the mirrored wall. Quentin wore a dinner jacket and black tie, looking as if he had arrived at the Academy Awards.

Backstage, Calvino found Osborn with a plumber's wrench, working on a water pipe.

"Hello, Calvino. All the usual suspects are out there tonight," said Osborn.

"I heard that Luk Pla is to be the first *ying* to go inside the tank," said Calvino. "Aqua-Girl One."

"You heard correctly. She had a powerful argument for the job."

"Which was?"

"She will tell Quentin how much she adores my screenplay. One of the *ying*s I used for a trial run is still a lovely shade of orange and I am certain it will wear off eventually."

"Tough call whether Quentin will believe Luk Pla. About the screenplay."

"Not at all. Men nearly always believe whatever a woman tells them. Especially a woman who has a man wrapped around her little finger. Quentin would do the Bangkok Yellow Pages as a film if he thought this would make the Baby Fish happy. That's how Hollywood works. Otherwise, how else can you explain most of the films they make?"

Osborn was right; career warp, career destruction was part of The Sickness, the need to be unconditionally loved, wanted, accepted by a twenty-year-old bar *ying* who would be hard pressed to distinguish between a meatball and a tennis ball. It was called innocence, and the belief in innocence doomed a man to believe that impulse was superior to reflection, and once that line was crossed, a life of incomparable mental distortion and wobble infected the decision-making process. In the final stages of The Sickness, common sense was forfeited, experience suspended, and afterwards came the lingering, paranoid fear of a cruel punishment— exile to a land where men were automatically herded into social groups of women their own age.

"And Quentin gets the satisfaction of knowing he goes home with the Baby Fish," said Calvino. "A pioneer in underwater sexual entertainment. When you are his age, what more could you possibly want? You are Adam and you have hooked Eve."

Was the bar big enough to accommodate Aqua-Girl, Alpha Domo, and WULF members? Hundreds of people were scattered around the bar, watching each other. Everyone was claiming the same turf, and looking for a way to put their rival, alternative Gardens of Eden out of business. The fact that Osborn had created an underwater Eve, substituting old-fashioned plumbing and glazing for digital paradise made on computer terminals and launched into cyberspace, had not made him any less threatening. The Mermaidium was the real thing, no virtual reality mermaids were swimming in the bar tonight. The women were the real thing, and with the exception of Luk Pla, like produce at the fish market, they could be pulled out of the tank, dried off, paid for, and taken home.

THIRTY

ALAN OSBORN THOUGHT that Luk Pla (unlike her friend Ice) lacked the future thinking lobes of the brain, so that it never would occur to her that she had the potential to capitalize and market herself as the first Aqua-Girl to have appeared inside the Mermaidium. Still, Osborn might have been selling her short. What was to be a quantum leap in the Plaza's latest re-invention of the entertainment business was a small step for Luk Pla, who had already landed a major housekeeping deal.

Almost every fetish imagined by minds soaked in alcohol for long periods in Bangkok had been converted into a theme built into a Plaza, Cowboy or Patpong bar. Osborn believed underwater nudity was an entirely novel concept. And since it had never been tried, it was completely lost on the likes of Luk Pla, whose thought process was more along the lines of a self-contained world consisting of a few basic elements in this rough hierarchy: fun, cash, gold, fun, mother, shopping, girlfriends, discos, fun, friends, grasshoppers, sleeping after too much fun, Thai boyfriend, and *farang*s.

Working on the script of *Fast Food* with Quentin Stuart, Osborn had spent sufficient time at the penthouse not to be surprised when the old man casually asked him if Luk Pla might have the honor of being the first *ying* to appear in the huge tank. She was not an ordinary starlet. Luk Pla flat out refused. She was afraid of the water. She was afraid of putting her head underwater. She had never heard of anyone—let alone seen anyone—who had gone naked underwater before a bar full of strangers. Anything new, untested, outside the formula was not of great interest to Luk Pla until, of course, someone else was given the chance that she had passed up. So when Ice said she would do it, go in the tank first, Luk Pla pleaded, cried and nagged until Quentin Stuart had to ask Osborn if he would be gracious enough to let his lady have the honor.

Ice wasn't that angry or upset; in fact, she set up Luk Pla because she had bigger and larger plans for the Baby Fish than even Osborn could imagine. She knew Luk Pla's limitations better than most of her other friends who were even more limited than Luk Pla. Ice had tried on several occasions to teach Luk Pla how to use the Internet; but she was hopeless as a student, she daydreamed, dozed, filed her nails, and stared at the computer screen, asking, "When does the movie start?" Ice had decided that Luk Pla was not only stupid, but she was forever doomed in the old ways of making easy money. Ice felt sorry for all of her contemporaries who worked the playground circuits and who were living in the Stone Age. Down the road, Ice told herself, just maybe it would be a good thing if, like Slugo, she too could create a media star, someone whom she could manage, put out on the Net, and, of course, totally exploit for her own selfish personal advantage.

In her way of thinking, the Mermaidium gig, if played in the right way, would pay handsome dividends. Ice told her that the first *ying* to swim in that tank would be a living legend. Since for Luk Pla the concept of being a living legend had little meaning, until, of course, Ice had explained the facts of life, which one day her benefactor—Quentin Stuart—would be cremated and all she would have to her name would be the gold she wore and his one-thousand-baht urn containing his ashes.

In the mind of Ice, she had already worked out how she would get Slugo to create the Baby Fish Web page where all the *farang*s, with a bad case of The Sickness, would be invited to spend a weekend for two in Koh Sumui with the living legend of the Plaza, the widow of the Oscar-winning screenwriter, Quentin Stuart. When none of those arguments worked, Ice said, "Never mind, I don't want you to do it. I want to do it myself. I will make so much gold I will pay you five baht to walk behind me and carry my gold inside suitcases."

It was then that Luk Pla's eyes got real big and she ran into Quentin's bedroom crying, bawling her eyes out, until Quentin intervened, found out what was wrong, and got Osborn to offer the chance to Luk Pla one more time. "You have to put your head underwater," said Alan.

She cried even harder, sticking her head deep into the pillow and pulling it back to gulp more air.

"I love to go underwater," said Ice, standing at the foot of the bed. "I think I am very sexy underwater."

Quentin sat on the bed holding her, and Osborn stood in the doorway smoking a cigarette.

"Okay, okay, I do for Quentin because I love him. Not for me," Luk Pla sobbed.

Osborn and Ice exchanged a knowing glance.

"Now for some rules, ladies. I want a tasteful show," said Osborn. "Nothing sick like underwater darts or opening of soda bottles. Just acrobatic nude swimming. You see, I know that there is an untapped market for naked *yings* swimming together underwater."

Luk Pla emerged from the dressing room wrapped in a blue towel with Nana Hotel in tall letters stitched onto one edge, a piece of incriminating evidence from those few days she had gone back to work in the Plaza and likely had spent more time inside the hotel than the night receptionist. She wore plastic sandals and seven baht of gold—thick enough to look vaguely like an anchor chain. Without her make-up and her hair under a clear plastic shower cap she looked about fourteen years old. Skinny legs and arms, slightly protruding belly, gave Luk Pla an undernourished semi-African appearance. Osborn looked at her with disapproval; this was not his idea of an Aqua-Goddess. He had never compromised in his life except this one time and he felt that he was being punished for doing so. It was, however, far too late to pull the plug. When Luk Pla walked between Calvino and Osborn through the curtain, looking at the audience, Quentin Stuart leaned over and whispered loud enough for almost everyone to hear, "If she were any more beautiful God would have kept her for himself."

She returned backstage and a moment later appeared on a stone ledge. She suddenly froze at the top, as she stared down at the stone steps leading to the water. Luk Pla stared at the stones, pearls of tears in the corners of her eyes. If she backed out now, then she would lose so much face she would have to drown herself. So why not climb down the steps and into the stone-walled underwater city? She might not drown, then again she might drown in front of all those people, and think of the loss of face. She glanced at Quentin who blew her another kiss. She swallowed hard and started her descent. Halfway down she found Ice in the audience. They waved at each other.

The audience was growing restless, and someone shouted, "Is this a show?"

"When does she take off the towel?" someone else called out.

"You don't have to go in," Pauline said in a loud voice. "They can't make you."

"Why don't you go in, Pauline," said Earl Luce, who was taking photographs of Luk Pla and some very unsavory looking characters at the bar. "Show some flesh and sisterhood solidarity at the same time."

Pauline cupped her hands over her mouth, and shouted the WULF slogan, "*Mai yom pae*—Never surrender."

"Your Thai is terrible," said Slugo, who was sitting a couple of bar stools away, in a loud voice.

"Go to hell, Slugo."

"But I am in heaven already," he squealed with laughter.

This only enraged Pauline who shouted support to Luk Pla a couple of more times before falling into a sulky silence.

Earl caught a photograph of Pauline looking like an aging cheerleader for the politically correct Dallas Cowboys. He clicked off shot after shot, as her hands came down from her mouth, he captured that certain look rarely caught on film: an expression of pure disgust, revulsion, and hatred mixed in equal parts and the firestorm of rage in the eyes and in the angry shape of the lips.

Luk Pla finally reached the bottom step that was at water level. She hooked her toes over the edge of the stone and looked down at the water, swallowing hard, she rotated around towards the audience, allowing her Nana Hotel towel to fall to her feet. Instinctively, she covered her breasts and searched to find Quentin on the bar stool who was still blowing her kisses. She took a couple of deep breaths, closed her eyes and fell forward into the water. Water splashed against the glass housing her magic kingdom, spraying the front row of customers. So far, she had forgotten everything that Osborn had taught her in an afternoon rehearsal, except one thing: she reached over and grabbed the thin plastic air hose, slid it into the side of her mouth and began her voyage to the bottom of the tank. She pulled off the shower cap and her long black hair fanned out like a huge sea creature above her head.

Luk Pla sat in the lotus position on the bottom of the stone grotto next to the pirate's treasure chest, staring out at the audience with a dull, pissed-off look, which seemed to say, how did I ever get myself into so much cold water? Then the lights on the floor of the Mermaidium came on, throwing hues of blue, red, and yellow through the water, washing over her body, turning the fragile woman inside the twenty tons of water into an Aqua-Goddess with a seven-baht chain of gold around her throat. At the far end of the Mermaidium, the four-meter-high waterfall was illuminated in the golden glow of light.

"I wish that Sam were alive to see this," Quentin Stuart said, as Calvino took the stool next to him.

"Sam liked large fish tanks?" asked Calvino.

"She loved Luk Pla's body."

Calvino had known about Ben Nakamura, Sam, and the threesome they had together with Ice. He had taken that as part of the typical experimentation that happened in the Big Weird. But he was revising his conclusions about Sam's sexual preference, knowing that experiments can be addictive and move from being an experiment to a way of life. That, in the Big Weird, *mem-farangs* sometimes came down with The Sickness.

There was no question about Luk Pla changing underwater. After a couple of minutes her entire face changed. The fear and loathing had vanished. She had been reborn as a natural water baby. After ten minutes, Osborn rapped his knuckles on the glass window of the tank. Her eyes wide open, she smiled at Alan. She looked like she would like to stay underwater all night long, as if she had found some silent, peaceful world she had always longed for and thought existed only inside air-conditioned shopping malls.

Osborn gave her the thumbs-up signal, moving his head up at the same time. After her head broke the surface of the water, Quentin was on his feet, clapping his hands. A few others clapped as well. Given the hardcore *farangs* in the bar, no one would have bothered to clap for Luk Pla, except out of respect to Quentin.

He ran up to the top of the tank and threw the towel over her shoulders. Then he kissed her on the cheek.

"You are all disgusting pigs," shouted Pauline Cheng and she and her two friends marched out of the bar, a trail of catcalls following them.

"Oink, oink," Slugo snorted, his face twisting into the shape of a clenched fist as he could not restrain his laughter and joy. A few other customers joined in the chorus, making their own pig-like noises.

A few minutes after their departure, another *ying* was in the Mermaidium, half an hour later, eight more dancers had stripped off and had slipped inside the water, making Ice think her idea about Luk Pla becoming a Plaza legend would need some serious cyberspace bullshit if she was going to make it pay off.

As they were on their way out of the bar, Osborn collared Calvino just outside the door.

"Everyone said they loved it," said Osborn.

"I wish that I could go to bed just once knowing that I had gone the whole day without someone telling me a lie."

"What you should wish for, Alan, is that you can go to bed once without telling someone a lie."

"Now that indeed would be difficult," said Osborn, grinning.

Calvino started to follow him out of the door but there were so many people around Quentin that he decided it wasn't a good idea to ask him about Slugo's screenplay. There would be a better time and place.

THIRTY-ONE

QUENTIN STUART PROUDLY left the bar with Luk Pla holding onto his right arm. Her hands were wrinkled from being underwater for so long but she glowed as if she had been reborn. She had a bounce in her step as they walked through the crowd. The bar had been filled with hordes of *farang* customers and a thick layer of cigarette smoke floated at nose level above the bar surface, driving Quentin out into the night air. There was hardly any difference in the air quality.

Luk Pla stopped at the food stall a few meters outside the bar, reached down and picked up the vendor's six-month-old baby. Quentin beamed as Luk Pla kissed the baby's fat cheeks. Calvino stood alone just outside the entrance, holding a glass of Mekhong and Coke; bar *yings* drifted in and out, paying him no notice. Their Bardar readout, the rough equivalent of radar to detect the presence of a customer, computed that Calvino was neither going to buy them a drink or buy them out.

He was on the job. There was no point of even thinking about good bar karma with a *farang* whose mind was solely on doing the job.

"Come on, darling, it's late, we have to go. Somnuek is waiting with the car."

"You go to the car. I come. One minute. Promise." Quentin hesitated, looking suddenly deflated that he had given her a polite order. Her response was with a direct order of her own, one quite to the contrary of what he really desired. He caught Calvino's eyes and shrugged his shoulders. Why not indulge her whim? He stood below the red neon sign reading Lollipop. Quentin Stuart was the kind of man who made no attempt to hide his emotions. It was as if moods scripted his body, a good mood, watching Luk Pla swimming in the tank had created a mature, lively character in his fifties; then, moments later outside the bar, with Luk Pla's sudden withdrawal of attention, his mood turned to defeat, hatching a disturbingly old character in the Plaza.

He looked like an old man with a slack jaw, eye-sockets deep and black in the night, hunched-over shoulders, with the shuffle of the elderly using a walker. Calvino continued to observe Luk Pla as she fussed over the baby; she had lost any interest in the old man—he simply had stopped existing in her world. She was at home in the playground; it was the one place where she belonged. Feeling ignored and helpless, Quentin slowly moved down the driveway, turning into Soi Nana. For a few seconds, Calvino thought about going after Quentin, asking him about the film Slugo wanted him to help with. But he couldn't bring himself to follow the old man, who looked so diminished and beaten-up. It wasn't right talking business in the middle of someone else's personal anguish.

Several dancers came up to Luk Pla and the baby. They passed the baby around, joked, laughed, and examined each other's gold ornaments. A couple of minutes later Somnuek, Quentin's driver, appeared at the food stall and went directly up to Luk Pla. He saw Calvino a few feet behind her. From the direction of Sukhumvit Road, the night sky turned an incandescent whitish blue as if someone had shot off a number of blue flares. Some of the bar *ying*s hanging around gathered in front of the entrance of the Plaza to get a closer look.

The old *farang* with the black bra around his head stared up at the sky, his mouth wide open.

"Boss says time to go home," said Somnuek. He spoke English for Calvino's benefit.

"Tell him I take taxi home. I want to go disco first." A loud explosion echoed from Sukhumvit, sounding as if terrorists had set off a car bomb. The blast knocked out the electricity and all the lights went out. And the violent boom sent a shock wave through Luk Pla, who handed the baby back to its mother. She looked frightened as suddenly the Plaza was shrouded in darkness. Mamasans and *dek serves* (who did the heavy lifting, delivering customer drinks, collecting the bill) and bar *ying*s began lighting dozens of candles. There was chaos as patrons ran out of the bars. Each bar soon had the flicker of candles throwing dark shadows over the customers and the *ying*s.

Somnuek, who looked tired, disturbed by the blast, and angry, closed in on Luk Pla, stopping a few inches from her face. His face turned red as he spoke, moving his hands as if he were slicing an invisible loaf of bread in the air. There was something in the power of his voice, his words, his movements that overwhelmed Luk Pla with a sense of real fear. Her smile had been erased and she looked worn down, defeated. Whatever Somnuek had said to her, it had worked, and together they walked away from the bars, turning by the foreign exchange booth. People swarmed past on all sides.

Calvino saw Somnuek and Luk Pla swallowed up by the crowd. He had never seen a *farang* send his Thai driver to collect his live-in girlfriend from the Plaza before. Many odd events happened in the Big Weird, and as far as Calvino was concerned, this was well within the range of weirdness.

Some gut instinct told him to follow it through. He had been to a lot of Thai funerals for dead *farang*s. Many dead men he had known had died because their desire for excitement and adventure had overtaken the slow horse cart of fear, and instead of slowing down around the curve, they sped up, hitting death head-on. They forgot that there was no playground any more than there was a free lunch. Caution and carefulness were casualties in the Big Weird; and once they were gone, it was only a matter of time before there would be a back alleyway ambush. Calvino followed a few feet back, as he was curious to see if Somnuek had managed to win the argument with Luk Pla.

It gave him no pleasure to discover that he picked it right. Two shots rang out. The sound of small caliber shots froze the crowd of people who had gathered at the mouth of the entrance to discover the source of the explosion. Bomb-like blasts followed by gunshots. It was a busy night in front of the Plaza. The motorcyclists at the corner of Soi Nana and Sukhumvit raced to the scene of the gunshots. Calvino pulled out his . 8 Police Special and made his way through the crowd. Luk Pla lay in the street, her hands pressed against her stomach as a pool of blood leaked through her fingers and onto the pavement. A .22 caliber pistol was no more than a foot away from her. Somnuek and Luk Pla's Thai boyfriend—Somchai, the name came back to Calvino— were circling each other in the darkness with the cat-like rhythm of two edgy kick-boxers. Calvino holstered his .8 and knelt down on one knee beside Luk Pla, raising her head up from the pavement. With the blackout, it was difficult to see her face.

"Where are you shot?"

She was sobbing, rolling from side to side and clutching one hand.

"I don't want to die. I am too young. Please, help me. Please don't let me die."

"You're not going to die," said Calvino, calming her.

"Pain me so much. I know I die."

She was convincing enough for Calvino to think that she might not make it. He had heard two shots, but in the darkness of the street, it was impossible to tell whether both rounds had hit her and where the bullets had done their damage.

"Why Somchai shoot me, Vinny?" Calvino didn't have an answer.

As he looked up, Somnuek had landed a foot with the full forward thrust of his body on Somchai's jaw. The gunman folded, fell down in the street, knocked out cold, as several brown uniformed police ran up, guns drawn, shouting at the crowd to clear away. The police did what Calvino had expected. They handcuffed Somnuek and Luk Pla's boyfriend, Somchai. And not too soon, as Somchai's motorcycle buddies moved in close, ready to tear Somnuek apart. As Calvino let the police go about their business, he lifted Luk Pla off the pavement and, holding her in his arms, as blood dripped from her mid-section, took several steps forward through a crowd of people who were trying to look at Luk Pla. She had taken a direct hit, Calvino thought. For the first time, he thought she might not make it and he saw the old man across the street.

"Oh my God," Quentin Stuart moaned. He looked down at Luk Pla, who opened her eyes long enough to see him.

"Darling, why?" He was shivering as if he had the chills. He had written movies where many people had been killed in gunfights. But this wasn't a movie; it was the real thing—actual blood, real pain, and the distinct possibility of death.

"Get into the car," said Calvino. "We've got to get her to the hospital."

Quentin's new Mercedes was parked in the Nana Hotel lot. He put Luk Pla in the back with Quentin and closed the door. There was blood smeared on the side of the car, leaking inside the seats and covering Quentin's trousers. One of the police ran up to Calvino as he had gone around to the other side of the car, and demanded to know what he was doing. Calvino stood with one arm swung over the opened door on the driver's side.

"We take her to the hospital. She's been shot."

No ambulance would be dispatched to collect a bar *ying* with gunshot wounds. No insurance, no credit cards, no likelihood of payment translated into a no- show. Quentin was her insurance card, and that would have been a difference. But the explosion on Sukhumvit had everyone running around in a panic. Nothing was working. It was possible the hospitals might have a power problem. The best Luk Pla could hope for was that a couple of friends would put her in the back of a tuk- tuk and take her to the police hospital. And if she didn't bleed to death on the way, she might just make it.

But one hospital would accept her as a patient, and Calvino knew that hospital as did the cops. And besides, it was the best hospital for someone in her condition: a patient with multiple gunshot wounds. Doctors at the police hospital knew the difference between the exit wound of a .22 and a 9 mm. They had practice in identifying different rounds by looking at the damage left behind.

"Take her to the police hospital," said the officer, taking in the make and model of the car. Calvino's jacket was unbuttoned, and, beyond the blood-soaked shirt, the cop's eyes picked out the brown leather holster and Calvino's . 8 Police Special nestled underneath his left armpit.

"Okay, no problem. We got to move or we are going to lose her," said Calvino.

The cop, his right hand resting on the butt of his .45, gave another hard stare at Calvino's holstered handgun.

"We go now," Calvino said. "You see who shot her?"

"Her boyfriend. The young guy named Somchai. The other man is Mr. Stuart's driver," said Calvino.

"Love affair. No good. It makes Thai husband crazy," said the officer. "You stay at hospital. Now give me your gun."

Calvino pulled his arms away and let the officer remove his . 8 Police Special. The officer touched the end of the barrel to his nose and sniffed. "I have a license to carry," said Calvino. "It's in my wallet."

"Impossible for *farang*," said the officer.

"Yeah, impossible. But possible, too," said Calvino, smiling. His use of the contradiction impressed the officer that this *farang* understood a certain way of thinking and being in Thailand. "Col. Prachai made it possible."

The officer looked at the . 8 Police Special and handed it back to Calvino.

"See you at the hospital," said the officer. He turned and walked away.

In the rear seat, Calvino saw the old man rocking back and forth with Luk Pla. Quentin carefully lifted and then cradled her head, brushing back her hair with his fingers. Calvino pushed the driver's seat back and started the engine. He looked in the rearview mirror.

"Papa, am I gonna die?" asked Luk Pla. "Why did he shoot you, darling?"

"Somchai think I am fucking Somnuek," she said, half crying, half laughing. "He not believe that Somnuek is your driver. He think Somnuek and me take money and not give him. Somchai very much love money." Before she could finish, Luk Pla had passed out, and Calvino had turned left at the lights onto Sukhumvit Road and, honking the horn, threaded his way through the traffic, which had backed up to the expressway entrance. The lights were not working, and the intersection was a tangle of cars and buses. He looked up and saw what had caused the explosion: an overloaded transformer had blown up, knocking out the local power grid. He did what any local driver would have done—he pulled over into the oncoming lane, forcing the traffic to the side.

"How bad is she?" Quentin asked in a thin, feeble voice.

Calvino knew that with gunshot wounds, bad or good was measured in units of time, and units of blood. "She was hit in the hand and took one more in the gut."

Quentin was looking at his hand as they crossed the railroad tracks, and by then they had entered a new power grid, and he was able to hold out his hand and see the blood from the nearby streetlights. He touched Luk Pla's blood on his fingers. His carefully manicured fingernails were stained a dark red.

"She's losing a lot of blood." Then he started weeping, his head tilted down, the tears falling onto Luk Pla's long black hair. "I should have insisted that she come with me. It's my fault, Vincent. Don't you see, I was weak. All my life I have been weak with women when I should have been strong. I should have demanded that she take my hand and go out of the Plaza with me. Now this. This beautiful child. And she might die because of me."

That was the hallmark of real-life violence: it didn't give a rat's ass for beauty, children, fairness. Violence cared nothing about second chances or heaven and hell.

At the Police Hospital, the surgeons operated on Luk Pla's stomach, where one of the bullets had found its mark. The Police Hospital doctors had a great deal of experience with gunshot wounds. The bullet, which punctured Luk Pla's gut, had missed her vital organs, and after removing about half a foot of intestine, they sewed up the ten-inch wound that began just below her navel and came to a dead end at the bottom of her rib cage. There were tubes in her nose and overhead an IV was connected to her arm.

Seven hours earlier the Baby Fish had had an oxygen tube stuck in her mouth, and now she had one stuck up her nose and was fighting to climb back from the land of the near dead. Somchai's first bullet had gone straight through her hand and her hand was now wrapped in thick bandages. It was .00 a.m. when one of the doctors came in and said that Luk Pla had a good chance of making it. The doctor was Chinese, early thirties, wearing gold-rimmed glasses. Several long strands of hair were curling out of a mole on the right side of his face.

The doctor casually examined Luk Pla, pulling back the sheet and looking at the wound in her stomach. He whispered to a nurse who nodded. Quentin, who had been dozing on a cot, pulled near her bed, broke into tears and hugged Calvino.

"She's going to live, Vincent."

Calvino stood up and went over to the doctor and spoke to him in Thai.

"How good are her chances?" asked Calvino.

The doctor without any change of expression said, "Fifty-fifty. If she makes it, then she'll never have children. That's bad for a Thai girl. Sometimes it is better not to live."

"Mr. Stuart is covering all of her bills. He would be grateful if she didn't die."

A few minutes after the doctor left, a nurse came in and hooked up a new IV line to the other arm.

"After losing Sam, I seriously don't know if I could take the death of another woman in my life. I don't have the strength for it." He lay his head back on the cot and stared up at the ceiling. Calvino thought he would go to sleep and was about to leave, when the old man leaned up on one elbow.

"My American wife nearly killed me. That's why I left Hollywood. Not long afterwards my marriage to Rebecca ended. That was more than ten years ago."

"Are you saying your wife tried to kill you?" asked Calvino.

"The next best thing. She tried to get me to kill myself. And I have never told anyone this story before. An original story, a true story and it doesn't happen very often in Hollywood or anywhere else that someone has such a story." His eyes were black, swollen, and he looked like he had less of a chance of pulling through the night than Luk Pla on the bed above him. Calvino took his hand away from the door and sat back down on the chair.

"Does this original story have something to do with Sam McNeal?"

A grin crossed his lips at warp speed. "Why else would I bother to tell you?"

There were other reasons, of course. Incoming women and outgoing women were like mortar rounds for the screenwriter, thought Calvino. This time there was nothing fake about Quentin's expression, nothing to indicate that he was about to attach some commercial spin, a practice pitch to see if the characters and plot worked their magic on the listener. The old man had something else on his mind. He was planning to make a long overdue confession, a testament as to how he had come down with The Sickness.

THIRTY-TWO

QUENTIN STUART'S DRIVER, Somnuek, crept into the hospital room and approached the old man. He walked in the half-stooped-over position of a peasant approaching the lord of the manor. As he came closer, Calvino could make out his features more clearly. His mouth was a thin line; he had bloodshot eyes, the whites gone yellowish, and in the half-light, his pock-marked complexion and thick mustache obscured his upper lip and gave him the look, not so much of a peasant, but of a Southeast Asian drug lord on the run from the DEA.

"Can I go home, boss?" Somnuek asked.

"Somnuek, Khun Vincent says that you saved Luk Pla's life," said Quentin.

The driver stared at the series of tubes running into Luk Pla before he glanced at Quentin. He moved forward a step. Luk Pla's head was turned to the side on the pillow, her eye sunken and black like she had been beaten up.

"You did good," said Calvino in Thai. "*Khun tham dee.*"

"Police say Somchai go to prison for long time. If Luk Pla die, a very long time."

Quentin shuddered. "You go home. Come back to the hospital tomorrow at eleven-thirty."

"Yes, boss," said Somnuek, standing there blinking. "Oh, Somnuek here is one hundred baht for your dinner." He held out one red note and Somnuek stepped forward, waied him, and took the note.

Then Somnuek turned away from the bed, his head slightly bowed, and walked out the door like someone who was confused as to whether he had won or lost.

Quentin stretched out on his cot, rubbing his stubble of a beard with the fingers of one hand as if he were lost in the depths of thought. "Her name was Rebecca. Tall, blonde, with those kind of long legs you see once or twice in a lifetime and most of the time, if you find legs like those, they are attached to a body out of a horror film. She was working for the Los Angeles Times and had been sent to do a feature about me. I had a housekeeping deal with one of the studios at the time, so I had my own office and parking space. Parking and the location of the space are very important on the studio lot. It's a little bit like gold chains for a bar *ying*.

"The first thing I remember when she came into my office was that when she sat down, she crossed those legs, and smiled, her full lips pulled back to show a set of perfect teeth. Shrewd eyes, blue, an aqua blue that you see in late afternoon off the coast of Greece. She started by asking me the usual stuff. Where do I get my material? Do I write about real people or are the characters drawn from inside my head? What had it been like to work with the greats like Marilyn Monroe, John Wayne, Cagney, Sly,

Eastwood and on and on. The kind of loopy questions I had been asked for years and years. In Hollywood, writing is an industry, and writers are industrial workers. The only difference is that writers get invited to better parties. Of course, if you are a writer you are going to make your life romantic simply because women want to sleep with men who can inspire romance. Nothing was more guaranteed to cause a sexual frenzy among women working in LA than a man with a screen credit to his name.

"Most of the time, when I was interviewed, as soon as I heard the standard questions, I turned on my internal tape recorder where I had stored all these answers over the years, and hearing myself talking, a disembodied voice; I knew that I had succeeded in detaching my mind from the interview and went on to think about more useful, pleasant subjects like whether I had a chance of sleeping with the woman doing the interview. In the case of Rebecca, I was thinking if I took her out to lunch where would I take her? I figured she was mid-twenties, and the way she crossed and uncrossed her legs, the tongue touching those full lips, that maybe it was going to be my lucky day.

"I had just been divorced from my fourth wife and had turned forty-six years old. About your age, Vincent. In those days a forty-six-year-old writer in Hollywood was in his prime, and a woman in her mid-twenties would not dismiss him as some old fart who was the same age as her father. Today, at that age, I would have been a target for a sexual harassment suit. In Hollywood today, the lawsuit would be the best way for her name to appear in the newspapers and her career would be launched.

"Thirty years ago in Hollywood, it was a different place. At the time I met Rebecca, Hollywood was still in the golden era. I took her to one of the top Hollywood restaurants where everyone called me Mr. Stuart and gave us the best table. We drank a bottle of wine at lunch and she began calling me Quentin. I didn't object, in fact, I encouraged her. I casually reached across the table and touched her hand. Nothing approaching a grope, mind you. It was more like one of those subtle brushes over the top of the knuckles. Then she told me about her boyfriend who was a graduate student at UCLA and how they had been living together for nearly two years. "She asked me how I thought about writing, and I told her that every writer's life is the search for creative singularities—that tiny atom from which an entire imaginary universe is inflated. Without finding that singularity there is no act of creation. No universe. Once the writer found it, then the process of creation began. The first draft took the inflation to the halfway mark. The second draft finished the size of the universe. With the third draft came the formation of galaxies and solar systems, while the fourth draft was spent on the details of relationships, dreams, sorrows, and desires. Writers are universe manufacturers. Finding a singularity and building a universe is an act of God. The problem with Hollywood was there were too many wannabe Gods and too much bad physics, and the universe was a sterile place full of special effects but devoid of the human dimension.

"After I paid the check, I asked if she would like to see my house. It could be background material for her story, I said. That made it easier to say yes. Then I told her it was on the beach, and I could see that this fact had an impact, created the right impression, but I needed something more to close the deal. That's when I told her I wanted to make a confession. Off the record, because I didn't want it in the article she was writing. I said that I hated Hollywood because it made writers into whores humping typewriters for money. Destroyed their creativity, mortgaged their souls, and sold their destiny all for a few bags of silver, when what they should have been doing was writing stories which took audiences to the edges beyond infinity.

"Years later she asked herself aloud at a screening of one of my films when she caught a certain line of dialogue, how she had been so inane, so brain damaged, to be taken in by such a stupid, meaningless, bullshit metaphor as 'edges beyond infinity.' It was the same line that I had used to get her to the beach house that first day we met.

"At the beach house we sat outside on a wide verandah drinking our second bottle of wine. And Rebecca asked me if I didn't want to write screenplays in Hollywood, then what kind of writing did I want to do? Like most screenwriters, I was prepared for that question with a half-completed novel. I went inside and brought out the manuscript. I even remember the title: *The Marble Piano*."

"The story was about a young boy who had been given a marble piano by his crippled uncle. The uncle had been wounded in the third wave landing at Normandy Beach. The marble piano was a gift. An to uncle received it from a nurse he had met in London. It was an exact replica of a grand piano, and the nurse told him that it came with a legend attached: that whomever could make music with this piano would run like the wind, have the strength of the young, and the wisdom of the ages. The nurse was killed a week later in a bombing raid in London. And all that he had to remember her by was the piano. The nephew got the piano from his uncle, who had grown resigned to the reality of his handicap and, while amused by the legend, had no faith, no belief.

"One day, the boy's father heard music coming from his son's room. It was midday and when he opened the door the music stopped, but he found his son seated in front of the tiny marble grand piano. When the father asked where the music had come from, the boy pointed to the piano. The father laughed, shook his head, and challenged the boy to play, slapping a five-dollar bill on the marble piano. The boy struck the marble keys and nothing happened. The father scooped up the five dollar bill and walked out of the room. Later, the father told his older brother who had given the boy the piano the story, but contrary to what he had expected, the older brother didn't laugh. He looked off into the distance and lit his pipe. The nurse had told him that playing the piano was an act of faith. That was the hurdle most men who had been broken—and most men were broken in one way or another—could never jump.

"I stopped reading and looked up at Rebecca. She had a single tear, which had cut loose from the lower rim of her right eye, and it hung there for a instant, then splashed on her cheek. 'I didn't want to make you cry,' I said to her. 'But a moving drama about faith, about belief and innocence is what you should be writing,' she said.

"I agreed with her and told her that after my housekeeping deal was finished, I would have saved enough money to buy the one year I needed to finish

The Marble Piano. That was my dream, I told her.

"We watched the sun set over the ocean. It was a very quiet and peaceful moment. She relaxed, leaned her head onto my shoulder, her long legs stretched out on the verandah. I asked if she would like to move in and live with me, be part of my life. I felt her head shift on my shoulder, and as I turned, she was looking directly into my eyes. 'Roger said he would kill himself if I ever left him,' she said. 'Who is Roger?' I asked her. Of course, he was the graduate student boyfriend. We made love that evening and the next morning she left the house. It crossed my mind that I might never see her again. That "never" proved to be a Hollywood never, meaning that afternoon she phoned to say that she had packed her things and wanted me to meet her at the house. I was there in fifteen minutes and had the house open and waiting for her. I asked her what had happened to Roger. She showed me the letter that she had written him.

"It was short and sweet. *Dear Roger, don't make a complete mess of it. If you are going to do it, then do it right. I recommend the enclosed.* She signed it simply: *Rebecca.* I looked at the clipping enclosed with the letter. It was an advertisement from one of those handgun magazines for a nickel-plated . 57 magnum pistol. Here was the woman who had been softly crying on the verandah as I read about the little boy's faith in making music from a marble piano, and the same woman was coldly, with premeditation, about to send her boyfriend an efficient way to dispatch himself. Women are practical; indeed they are born professionals in their practicality. Their temporary descent into romantic adventure is always provisional, marginal, and controlled.

"Rebecca taught me a great deal about women. Women are much tougher than men. Their diminutive size is deceptive because in terms of tolerance for pain and patience for revenge, no man can ever equal these qualities women possess in abundance.

"For the next twenty years, Rebecca and I were like a hand and glove. Inseparable. The fact that I never managed to get around to finishing *The Marble Piano* became the kind of standing, inside joke married couples share.

"When I finished a new film, and we would go out for dinner to celebrate, Rebecca would raise her glass, and say two words, 'Marble Piano.'

"And I would take a wad of hundreds out of my wallet, fan them in the air and say, 'Sound of music.'

"She travelled first-class to Europe with me, and to Latin America, and to Asia. I was hot then, and I got writing assignments in many different countries. It never occurred to me not to take Rebecca along. We had the best of everything. The best hotels, limos, and three- star restaurants. We were as close as two people ever become, finishing each other's thoughts and covering for each other's lies in a community that wouldn't know truth if it took a healthy shit on its face.

"Twenty years is a long time, Vincent. Long enough to make you think that you had beat the law of physics. You know, the law, which says that all mass is subject to the law of gravity and that no matter how hard you try, the momentum of an object will decrease its speed over time and space. The same is true of a relationship. The initial boost of those emotional engines gives you such a great amount of thrust you feel that the acceleration will continue forever. But there is no perpetual motion machine. And there is no relationship with enough sexual fuel to resist the forces of gravity. The forces of repetition and routine start to pull you back to earth. Before you know it, before you can stop yourself, you are tumbling helplessly into bed with another woman.

"What I am trying to say is that I had an affair at year twenty into my marriage with Rebecca. Of course, there had been some indiscretions along the way. Curled up in the back of a limo in the streets of New York. In the toilet of the Concorde twenty minutes after lifting off at Heathrow Airport. The usual blow-jobs at the studio; those were more like perks of the job rather than anything else. In truth, there had been only one affair, and that was with a black woman named Joanne. I was sixty something and Joanne was twenty something. In other words, about the same age as Rebecca when I first met her.

"Joanne lived in a rat-trap apartment which she shared with a couple of junkies who played in a local band. This band had gigs in the kind of clubs that you needed bodyguards to get out of alive. She had two-story legs, large, full breasts and a head of hair that would have touched both sides of the Holland Tunnel if she walked down the center lane.

"Rebecca hired a private investigator because she had her suspicions I had been steering off course for some time and she wasn't aboard. I was sloppy, forgetting about a picture of Joanne, which I had used as a bookmark in some damn script the studio sent over. Her investigator tailed me and took his own pictures. He must have had the hotel room next to the one Joanne and I were using. I came home from the studio one night. Rebecca had the table set with our best china, candles were lit, and a bottle of champagne was in the silver ice bucket.

"That afternoon, I had phoned to say that I had just signed a new housekeeping deal, and my agent had negotiated a percentage of the gross on a three-picture deal. It was a great deal of money. She said that she had a little surprise of her own. There was, I noticed, a slight chill in her voice at the time and it went straight up my spine. I told myself after I put down the phone that I was imagining things. That is the classic mistake, to override your own instinct for disaster.

"Rebecca and I never got to the first course, or to opening the bottle of champagne. The photographs of Joanne were laid out like a deck of cards around my dinner plate. In the photos, black and white, were Joanne and me looking like pages out of the Kama Sutra; we were in sexual positions I didn't even know I was capable of until I saw the prints. When you are caught like that, there isn't a lot you can say. She asked me if I loved the girl, and I told her the relationship had been strictly sexual which wasn't one hundred percent true, but truth wasn't something that seemed appropriate at that moment.

"Rebecca asked me how long I had been seeing the girl, and I told her about three months. Taking the liberty to divide the actual time by two. She asked if I wanted a divorce, and I told her that I would never see Joanne again. She sat there in candlelight and asked me how I could have been so cold-blooded. I reminded her of the gun ad she had sent to Roger, the boyfriend she had been living with when I met her, and she said that was different. It was a joke. This was not a joke. This was dead serious.

"Most men say their life flashes before their eyes at such a moment. For Quentin Stuart, it was his assets that flashed through his mind. Christ, the house, the boat, the cars, the stocks, and I had told her exactly how much I was getting on the new housekeeping deal. I was like a little boy. I couldn't wait to tell her, and now it would be impossible to lie and say the studio had canceled my contract and thrown my ass off the lot. I was fucked. She knew I was fucked. From the way she smiled, it was written all over her face. Then she did a remarkable thing, she reached across the table, gathering up all the photographs, touched them to one of the candles and let them burn to ashes in her plate. I was so grateful I got down on my knees and wrapped my arms around her and wept.

"A couple of years passed. I kept my word and didn't see Joanne again. During this period, Rebecca developedaninterestinthe paranormal,the supernatural, and the mystical. She said the interest had always been there and the reason she fell for me was that I was working on a novel about the supernatural. I had heard music coming from a marble piano. And, before long, she had pulled me into an orbit of people who started showing up at the house, people who called themselves a variety of things: channels, guides, seers, fortune tellers, and healers.

"We had bought every New Age book, the crystals, the tarot cards, runes; we paid a grand each to have our charts done, another grand each to have them interpreted. The charts and the cards indicated that we were living in the wrong house. Rebecca, with one of the wind and fire consultants, a small-boned Chinese man, found another house two miles farther along the beach, one of the houses with four split levels, red wood balconies, a 180-degree view of the sea, a dock, a huge swimming pool and a two and a half million dollar price tag. We bought the house. Rebecca took up painting strange, cosmic images—or at least that was what she called them. They could have been anything. But we had them hanging in every room of the house. You couldn't get away from these nightmarish visions. It was like she was testing me in an odd way.

"One night when I came home she was painting, and as I poured myself a Black Label on ice, she told me about this extraordinary psychic who lived in the Valley. She was an old Polish woman who spoke broken English with a heavy accent, and this woman had named herself Gabelle.

" 'Why Gabelle?' I asked her. Her story was that in the seventeenth century she had been a French tax collector. And 'Gabelle' was a kind of ancient Gallic tax paid in salt. The fact the old witch was a Pole rather than French was an apparent inconsistency. But one that only appeared on the surface. She claimed that she had been French in a previous life. Once you start on that road of mysticism everything has an explanation from past lives. There is no cause or effect that can't be explained by something you did a hundred and fifty years ago in another life. And Gabelle had been reborn into this life to collect taxes again. This time she had been reborn to read the spiritual tax forms of rich people in Los Angeles. Rebecca had taken over a couple dozen photographs of herself, me, various relatives and friends.

"She taped the session and that evening she played

the tape as we sat on the balcony overlooking the ocean. Gabelle would look at Rebecca's nephew and say, 'He's a very old soul. He's had between twelve and eighteen prior lives. In one life he was your father. In another life he was a monk and you made confessions to him. You will always be close to him. In this life there is an unbreakable bond between the two of you, as if you can read each other's minds.'

"Then she showed the old woman a photograph of me, and she studied it for a long time, 'He is a sensitive man, someone who has lived many, many lives and has returned this time to work out unfinished business. And that is to find someone to share his soul with. You are his soul mate, and nothing can ever change that. For as long as the two of you live, there will be a bond that no one can break. But until the two of you recognize that you must give the other the freedom to explore an independent life, you will be condemned in the next life to repeating the mistakes you have made this time around.'

"Rebecca made an appointment for me to meet with Gabelle. I thought this was going to be a waste of time. Some old Polish witch with sagging jowls and cataracts trying to make out faces from old photos. To please Rebecca, I went along, taking an envelope of photographs. The old woman, and I say old though she was about my age, took me into a modern kitchen with all the modern appliances, including a TV set turned on to a movie channel. As it turned out, one of my old movies was on, and I took this as an omen. I sat at the table and Gabelle poured me one of those small European cups full of black tea. Then she took my photographs out of the envelope and proceeded to read the relationships, the personality, the connections, the past life occupations of each person.

"She came to one photograph that I hadn't remembered putting in the envelope. I was in the photo along with a woman named Beth Cumberland. I had known Beth for more than ten years. She had been a guest at our house many times, and even bought one of Rebecca's strange paintings.

"Gabelle fingered the photograph, turning it one direction, then another, saying with those watery Eastern European eyes, 'This woman is your soul mate. You were born to be with this woman. Each person is born to find that one, single other human being that he or she belongs to, is born for in this life. This is your soul mate. If you are not with this woman for the rest of your life, then your karma will be stained with blood for the next cycle of ten lives. The blood of others will wash over those lives in a waterfall of anguish and despair. She loves the water, doesn't she?'

"And I had to say, that, 'No, Beth actually hated boats. And I had never seen her go into the water.'

"Then she said, 'But she likes looking at the water.'

"And I said, 'Yes, she loves looking at the sea.'

"And the old woman said, 'That's what I meant by her loving the water.'

"Now, if I hadn't wanted to believe all of this, I would have seen the old woman was fishing, leading me on. But this was such powerful stuff, and I was thinking about the next ten lifetimes. That's when I took my eye off the ball, when I should have been asking myself what the fuck was happening in this life? I made the classic mistake of ignoring any evidence that suggested she was off the track. Like most people, I wanted to believe that there is some larger purpose than working, eating, fucking, and taking a final ride in the back of a hearse.

"That night over dinner Rebecca asked me how the session with Gabelle had gone, and I told her everything except the part about Beth being my soul mate. I practiced deception, in other words. She was delighted with the reading and asked me to play the tape from the session. I said that I had lost it. What I had done was courier a copy of the tape to Beth Cumberland, and asked her to meet me that weekend at one of those out of the way spots in the Valley that no one in our set would ever be caught dead inside of. She admitted that she had had strong feelings about me from the first time we met but had kept them to herself. The prior life business made perfect sense to her. We started to see one another after that. First we kept our meetings to once a week, then they crept up to twice a week.

"When I asked Rebecca for a divorce, she had no objection so long as she kept the house, the cars, bank account and a healthy cash settlement. I had no objection to her keeping the art. Beth made a similar deal with her husband, who happened to be my agent, Sam McNeal's father. Not a year after the two divorces, Beth went to see Gabelle, and it was long enough for the old woman to have forgotten about me. So that when she read Beth's photos, her life partner, her soul mate was Harry McNeal.

"As it turned out Rebecca had set me up with the old witch. She had envied Beth and thought she was attracted to me, and she had never forgiven me for the humiliation she had suffered over the affair I had had with Joanne. She had been betrayed and she waited until she had planned every last detail before she pulled the rug out from under me on her terms, and on her timing. And when she did, I landed on the hard ground. There was nothing to break the fall. Beth left me. I lost my agent. Everything I had worked for all those years in Hollywood was gone as well. For whatever reason, it was Sam McNeal, of all people, who felt sorry for me. And I was the one who had broken up her parents' marriage.

"The only thing the old witch said that came true was the bit about my karma being stained by the blood of others. Innocent others. Rebecca is telling everyone in Hollywood that I was personally responsible for Sam's death. That Sam would never have gone to Bangkok unless it had been to follow me. She has been telling people in the community that I may even have driven Sam to put that goddamn gun to her head and blow out her brains. I know that girl, what she had been through, what she was capable of doing and not doing. If there is a killer, Vincent, it would go a long way to rehabilitating what little is left of my reputation in Hollywood."

Quentin fell asleep as he finished, his mouth open, his hands folded under his head, knees curled up to his chest. He snored lightly. The room was otherwise quiet. Luk Pla slept on her bed. The old man slept on his. The very old and the very young are united in the way they sleep, going into the fetal position, the original moments after birth, after leaving the womb. That is how Quentin slept; it was the position in which Luk Pla slept as well.

Calvino sat in the darkness, thinking about the old man's story, thinking about the story that Slugo had written. He also thought about Sam, and for the first time understood what had drawn her to Quentin. There was more than appeared at first glance; in Bangkok there was always more below the water line than above the surface. Alan's Mermaidium had been a metaphor for life. Luk Pla had been submerged underwater, and looked free for the first time that Calvino had ever seen her. Truly happy. Then she had been shot and had been unconscious, fighting for her life, under a different kind of water, a different kind of freedom.

THIRTY-THREE

"YOU USED TO cite Shakespeare more often," said Calvino, as he peeled the shell off a large prawn. He sat at a table in the kitchen of Pratt's house. It was the middle of the night, and everyone else in the house was sleeping.

He had told Pratt the entire story that Quentin had told him; and then he had told him about the shooting on Soi Nana.

" 'But it is doubtful yet whether Caesar will come forth to-day or no; for he is superstitious grown of late, quite from the main opinion he held once of fantasy, of dreams, and ceremonies, it may be, these apparent prodigies, the unaccustomed terror of this night, and the persuasion of his augurs, may hold him from the Capitol to-day,' " said Pratt quoting Act II, Scene I, Cassius's speech.

"I like the part about the dreams and ceremonies. It makes me understand why a Thai can love Shakespeare," said Calvino, wiping his fingers on a cloth napkin. "In the city men get lost in their dreams and ceremonies. Women, too. Like Caesar, dreams and fortune-tellers hold us up, keep us away from the business of life."

"I talked with the officer who was on the scene at Soi Nana last night," said Pratt.

"And?"

"He said you pulled a handgun on him."

Calvino raised an eyebrow. "You believe him?"

"But you did draw your gun?" asked Pratt.

Calvino nodded. "When I heard the shots."

"How long did you have your gun out of the holster?" asked Pratt.

Calvino peeled a shrimp, dipped it into a small plate of red sauce, and popped it into his mouth. "Less than a minute, then it was back in the holster. There wasn't a cop around when that happened. Is this going to cause a problem?"

Pratt smiled and shrugged his shoulders. "It's too early to know. But I don't think so. You have to be careful about taking out your gun. It's better not to show it in public."

This dressing down had happened before; it had become a ritual, of sorts. Pratt would advise Calvino to carry a gun but not ever show a gun, and Calvino would argue that there was no point in carrying a gun if some maniac with a gun was shooting unarmed people and he couldn't respond.

"Next time, I will only take out my gun in private." Pratt nodded, watching his friend eat shrimp.

"A stomach wound is usually a bad one," said

Calvino. "It tears things up inside." "You think the girl won't make it?"

"It's hard to say. The doctors don't know. When I left the hospital, Quentin was looking very bad. Stuck together in the ICU. She was no more than a kid, and he was older than the ancient mariner. Two dying people find they have more in common than with anyone else. I guess age doesn't matter at that point."

"Did you talk to him about your film idea?" asked Pratt.

Calvino shook his head. "But he told me a story. A long story about his fifth marriage in California."

"Five marriages?"

"And five divorces. The last one was an incredible story. The divorce was messy."

"It follows. Hollywood people invented messy divorces," said Pratt.

"And in his story there is a connection to Sam McNeal's family," said Calvino.

"I had the idea his interest in the case was not exactly what he told me at first."

"Nothing is ever as it appears at first," said Pratt.

"Another Shakespeare quote."

Pratt pushed away his coffee and stretched. "Another Pratt quote."

"Too many special effects," said Calvino.

He had left out some of the internal thinking behind the conclusion and that left Pratt confused. "What do you mean? With Luk Pla tonight?" asked Pratt.

"I mean Slugo's script. It's all special effects. I was thinking that it would be costly to produce. The part about Einstein as a talking head of lettuce, for instance."

"That could be educational," said Pratt.

"I am thinking about giving the story back to Slugo."
"But I thought you owed him a favor."

Calvino sighed. "That's the problem. Favors come at a much higher price than straight transactions."

"Favors are the price you pay for having friends," said Pratt. "Especially ones who pull their handgun in public."

"I deserved that," said Calvino. Pratt did not disagree.

THIRTY-FOUR

ALAN OSBORN, HIS hands folded around a cup on the table, sat beside a Thai woman named Somporn. Reed Mitchell stretched his legs out, taking up the full bench on the opposite side. The three of them occupied a back booth in the Thermae, a coffee shop on Sukhumvit Road that offered much more than coffee. Osborn had been listening to Somporn talk nonstop about her new life in Montana. Her hair was cut in a punk style, with two beaded braids of hair resting halfway down her right temple. She was early thirties, large lips, wide mouth, a square, Mongol face and, as she talked, Somporn gestured with hands covered with gold and silver rings. Each ear had been pierced nearly a dozen times and tiny stars, crosses, monkeys, and dogs were assembled up and down her earlobes.

Reed yawned and glanced over his shoulder. Neither man seemed particularly surprised to see Calvino arrive in a fresh suit and shirt, clean-shaven, smelling of cologne, at five-thirty in the morning.

"It's Calvino," said Osborn.

Reed slouched all the way down so that he couldn't be seen from the bar.

"That guy is starting to get on my nerves," said Reed. "Every time I look around, he's in the room."

"I rather like him," said Osborn.

"What's he lurking around Thermae for this time of the morning? I don't get it."

"Why don't you ask him yourself?" asked Osborn as he waved at Calvino.

"Now why did you do that? He might not have seen us."

"Don't be stupid. Of course, he would see us. The place is nearly empty."

Calvino took his time at the bar, ordering a drink, looking around the room. The number of working *yings* had dwindled to a few hardcore regulars, the oldest, most broken-down women who, like the apples that never get picked out of the market basket, stayed on not so much out of hope but out of habit and no place else to go. A couple of women were half asleep behind the tables and inside the booths, and occasionally, a head would pop around the booth, looking for a *farang* with The Early Morning Sickness. Someone who was in need of an early morning fix. There wasn't so much competition at that time of morning and even the very old women stood a chance of being selected by a soul haunted by desire; no time for idle chatter or to be too choosy, only time to negotiate a short short-time deal before the traffic jammed every lane of Sukhumvit back to Soi 6 .

Calvino had gone home and changed, then had taken a taxi to the Thermae. He had a call on his answering machine that Earl Luce had some prime information connected with the Sam McNeal case. Earl had been taking photographs of some car-crash victims near the Thermae at the time he phoned, and he said that he would stop in the Thermae for breakfast. That was good enough for Calvino. Was Earl heading home or was he stopping in for a quick ringer check? But Earl was an old hand and knew as well as anyone that ringers were hard to come by at five in the morning.

The jukebox played a Thai love song about broken hearts. The interior of the Thermae looked like a badly organized wake and just about anyone on the stools around the bar could have played the role of the deceased. No one was drawing straws for the part; at the same time, no one was moving either. Five-thirty was dawn in the Big Weird; the goddess of the dawn was Eos, but no one ever claimed, at that final of all stops, at the Thermae, to have bumped into Eos or any other goddess. That time of the morning all the Thermae goddesses had long ago gone to sleep.

Calvino slid into the booth next to Reed.

"I see you before," said Somporn, as she suddenly came to life.

He looked at her and tried to remember Somporn's face. She wore one of those tight-fitting bodysuits that women wore in health clubs, and a pair of jeans. He couldn't place her. He drew a complete blank.

"Six years ago, I come here to find man. I not like. Okay for young girl, but they not think of about future. You not stay young for long. Then new girl come along, and then what happen? You got no future. No girl like a man who say bad thing about her. Treat her like a dog. Not see she have eyes, nose, mouth, and heart just like the man. She want a good life. She not want to fuck strange man. But what can she do? She have no choice to get money. Very big headache.

"I never go with different man every night. I go with man two weeks, one month. Like that. Then I find a man I like and I stay with him for five years. He a German man. I want baby. I tell German man, give me baby. After first year, he buy me monkey. I call her Jackie. Monkey very stupid, very spoiled. I put dress on Jackie. I even buy her Pampers. But Jackie is monkey, and monkey is not baby. Then after two years, I say, where is my baby. I want. And German he come back with second monkey. He call this one Greta. I think Greta better than Jackie. Not so spoiled. Nice monkey but I getting old, and still no baby. We together five year, and he give me monkey named Eddy. That monkey very smart. Smarter than the German I think.

"Three monkeys and five years I think German never give me baby, just waste my time. I tired looking after monkeys so I throw him out with the monkeys. I marry with American. Straight away he give me baby. Then one year later, second baby. I come back for holiday, I feel lucky. Have husband, have two babies. No Germans. No monkeys. This is my rule." She fingered her golden earrings.

"You see this one? That's for Jackie, and this one for Greta, and on this ear, you see that earring? It's for Eddy. Now only monkeys I have are gold monkey I keep in my ear, and every time I look in the mirror, I see three monkeys, and I say, you smart girl, get rid of German, keep gold, get babies with American husband, and have future."

"I think I'm going to go insane," said Reed Mitchell. "The sun is up, I have to go to work in three hours, and what am I doing? Listening to Somporn's talk about babies and monkeys."

"You can blame me. I was explaining to Somporn about revenge, and how it can work as a perfectly valid defense in Thailand," said Osborn. He had a small spoon, which he used to mindlessly stir his coffee.

"Hey, whatever you do, don't step on this man's shadow," said Mitchell.

"In the insane asylum over on the Thonburi side of the river, there was a mental patient who attacked another patient who was working in the kitchen. The attacker used a knife and opened a considerable wound in the other man's shoulder.

"When asked why he had attacked the patient, he replied, 'He stepped on my shadow. I saw him step on my shadow.'

"And as far as I know the authorities accepted that as a valid defense. Keep your foot out of another man's darker side or he might take revenge. This Somchai character will likely come up with something equally improbable, and he will be back on the streets sooner rather than later," said Osborn.

"I feel sorry for Luk Pla," said Mitchell. "Bad luck."

"Is that the girl who get shot?" asked Somporn, and then answering her own question.

"Alan he tell me and I feel very sad for her. Young girl. What future she have? Shot in heart."

"Shot in the stomach and hand. She had a bad night," said Calvino.

"Yes, I forget, you have big-time police connections," said Reed Mitchell.

"So the pond scum who shot her may actually get what he deserves. That poor girl. Is she dead?"

Calvino shook his head. "No, I think she's gonna make it."

"Wow, that had to be something. Shooting someone on Soi Nana in front of a hundred witnesses. What a nitwit," said Reed Mitchell.

"The owners were extremely happy with the Mermaidium," said Alan.

"Customers hung on until after three in the morning. Everyone thought the evening was an unqualified success. A new star was born. A new star was shot. The gap between fame and assassination is now less than three hours. Since I have a script-meeting tomorrow, I must go home and rest my mind."

"Try washing it out with a good book," said Reed Mitchell.

"You are jealous because I am doing a script with the great man. And you are left to soil your greedy hands toiling in the factories of commerce," said Osborn as he eased himself out of the booth. He stretched his arms, yawning. "I never know whether to say good night or good morning when I leave the Thermae," he said.

"You might try mixing in the occasional 'great' or throw out a 'bad' just to keep your friends off balance," said Reed Mitchell.

"My friends are off balance to begin with," said Osborn. "Or they wouldn't be my friends."

"I go with you," said Somporn, and she lifted a black bag onto the table and opened it, tilting the bag so that

Osborn could see inside.

"What's she got in there? A stuffed monkey?" asked Reed Mitchell.

"A pair of handcuffs and sheets of latex. What Americans, I gather, must use in the bedroom these days."

Mitchell pulled the bag over and peered inside, and he looked over at Calvino.

"He's not joking."

"I married lady now. I don't fuck man. But I make him happy," said Somporn, smiling.

"Tell you what, Alan. I'll give her a thousand baht if she handcuffs and wraps you in rubber. Think of it as performing art. And, who knows, you might like it. Bringing back memories of boarding school."

"Somporn, you are a jewel in the Thermae crown, but I must go home and sleep. And I am afraid we English haven't quite worked latex into our mating rituals," said Alan.

"I not go back to America for two weeks. Maybe tomorrow or next day," said Somporn.

She slid out and walked with Osborn towards the back entrance.

Calvino sat with his back against the booth, staring directly at Reed Mitchell. It didn't look like Earl Luce was going to show after all. But it wasn't a wasted trip; it gave him the opportunity to try out another theory as to the circumstances surrounding Sam McNeal's death on Reed Mitchell.

"I think Somporn and Alan make a great couple. What do you think?" asked Reed Mitchell.

"Did you and Sam make a great couple?"

"You are looking sadder than usual, Calvino. But then you're entitled. You must have had a very rough night."

Calvino waited as the waiter set down a cup of black coffee and moved away from the table.

"You put the bullet in the gun Sam used," he said.

"Pull in the reins on that horse, it's gone real lame. I put the bullet in Sam's gun? Why would I do something stupid like that?"

"Because you wanted *Moving Target*," said Calvino.

"*Temporal Target*," said Reed Mitchell.

Calvino smiled, "Yeah, that's the script I mean. She was going to help you get involved with the old man on the script. But Quentin Stuart had a different idea about Reed Mitchell. You weren't part of the picture. Quentin wanted to make up something to Sam, something that had happened a long time ago. He felt responsible for her mother and father splitting up. He owed Sam a big one. He was trying to pay down that debt when you came along. And you found out that the project belonged to Quentin and Sam and you decided on some creative revenge."

"Calvino, you are starting to make me nervous."

"You should be nervous. You killed her."

"She killed herself. Everyone knows that."

"Why do I keep telling myself, Sam must have had some help?" asked Calvino. "And one more thing, I have this feeling she didn't die alone at Nakamura's house."

"If any of this were true you would be on to your Thai colonel buddy to throw me to the crocodiles. You know what joy that provides the locals when a *farang* is swallowed up in local scandal."

"What I can't figure out just yet is how you got the bullet in the gun without anyone seeing you. Without any evidence that it was you and not her that put it there."

"I hate guns," said Mitchell, avoiding direct eye contact with Calvino.

"Have you asked Quentin about Temporal Target?"

"You mean whether I can get involved?"

"Something like that. Play a role. Share a credit."

"He has a lot of other things on his mind. Like his girlfriend getting shot. And his health going downhill like a dropped rock. Besides, it would be too painful for him now."

"But later on, when the pain of Sam's death goes?"

"Hey, the man's got the big 'C.' He's going to be trading one pain for another."

"Except Sam probably told you that he writes to keep his pain in check."

"I thought that's why he kept Baby Fish around."

It was time to get down to reality. Calvino waited as the waiter set down a cup of coffee and plate of bacon and eggs. He made no effort to touch the food. Instead he stared hard at Reed Mitchell.

"Quentin told me that one of the studios hires a flatbed truck to go around once a week to pick up all the scripts people send in," said Calvino. "The workmen fill that ten-wheel truck to the sky with all of those 120-page scripts. All those stories written by people with dreams, with hopes, with one aching desire."

"Which is?"

"To see their name on a film. Have people talking about them. The usual perks. Getting the best tables, getting the best women. Breaking out of the cycle. A

Thermae girl breaks out of the endless cycle of monkeys from the German by marrying an American. We break out by going into the movie business. You know what else Quentin said?"

Mitchell shook his head.

"There are no Oliver Stones, Kevin Costners, Tom Hanks, or Mike Tysons in places like Bosnia. Killers, yes. Bad guys, yes. Meaner, tougher, more ruthless and violent. Probably. But it don't matter because they are faceless, nameless. It's like they don't exist. The same in Tibet, Turkey, Laos, Albania, Iran. Most of the people in those countries know who Mike Tyson is. They know Tom Cruise. They even know the famous dead like Elvis, Wayne, Monroe. They know Donald Duck, Mickey Mouse and the Lion King. What doesn't occur to most Americans is that most countries of the world only have local celebrities. A hundred miles away they are nobodies.

"America is in the celebrity export business. They have a lock on it. When you think about it, most countries don't have a single living human being in the entire country who is recognizable once he or she steps outside of the country. Huge populations in China run around like ants. They crawl along a tiny path, and disappear without a trace. No one in the world mourns their passing because they never knew that person existed. Disney cartoon characters like Goofy have a longer shelf life than three billion human beings. You've got to laugh at a world organized that way.

"You have to cry a little for the people who think turning themselves into a cartoon is going to give them immortality. But whether I like it or not doesn't much matter, Reed. That's the way of the world. It's the way people think, live, and it's a reason for dying, it's a reason for helping someone to die.

"The only way off the back of that flatbed truck into the studio executive's office is through the good offices of someone like Quentin Stuart. All those thousands of dreams going up in smoke each week. I can see a guy like Reed Mitchell thinking to himself, I'm not going to be one of those schmucks. I am no flat bedder. I got the world by the tail because I have access. I'm off the truck, man. I'm in the driver's seat. Except Sam just found something about that picture she didn't agree with. She saw you in the driver's seat and her with ten thousand faceless women riding in the back"

Reed Mitchell was smart enough to know the score of how the police worked in the Big Weird. He was right that if Calvino had the evidence, then he would not have bothered tracking him down at the Thermae at half past five in the morning for a face-to-face chat. Mitchell would have been in police custody, eating red rice off a tin plate. Calvino believed that Reed Mitchell had wanted the chance to be a Hollywood writer, and he wanted to grab that brass ring bad enough to set up Sam McNeal just like Rebecca Stuart had done in order to destroy her husband and Sam's parents' marriage.

It wasn't a photo session with a sham fortuneteller named Gabelle either. Reed Mitchell would have been too clever to run that one again. What better alibi than a room of witnesses who saw the deceased shoot herself? A room of friends expecting a party, willing to believe that everyone was bonded the way expats sometimes became emotionally connected.

In Bangkok no one wanted to be an orphan; everyone sought attachment, affiliation, support—a network that would be there in case the weirdness descended on their head. The conventional wisdom on the expat circuit was that orphaned *farang*s were created by their own hand and not made by others. People spent a lifetime circling around their destiny trying to find the strength to flick open a switch blade and stick it deep into the face of anyone who would rob them of what belonged to them.

Earl Luce appeared at the back of the Thermae wearing his crash helmet. One of the *ying*s screamed, thinking her nightmare hadn't stopped when she opened her eyes. As Earl came over to the booth, Reed slid out.

"See you around, Reed," said Calvino.

Reed said nothing as he walked passed Luce, and threaded his way among the empty tables and out the back entrance. "He's usually so funny," said Earl.

"No one's funny at this time of the day," said Calvino, watching Reed leave.

Earl pulled off his helmet and set it on the table. He pushed back the coffee that Reed had left behind, a plate with a half eaten hamburger on it and some shriveled up, cold French fries.

"You know, I think I may have the person who can tell you a few things about what happened the night Sam McNeal killed herself," said Earl.

"You have my full attention," said Calvino, looking at the plate of cold eggs and bacon. He picked at them with his knife and fork, gave up and drank his coffee.

"I owe you one for the jam you got me out of last year. Let's say this makes us square."

Seven months earlier, Earl Luce had got himself busted in a police sweep of motorcycle drag racing on Ratchadaphisek Road. He had been hanging out with the bikers when the police arrived and Earl made a point of photographing the police beating one of the bikers. With Col. Pratt's intervention, Earl Luce was released but his camera with the film was missing. It was a compromise, and after one night in a Thai jail, it was a small compromise, the charges were dropped and Earl walked away a free man. He understood the risks an unpackaged *farang* without affiliation ran in pursuing the shadows that fell over the Big Weird every night.

THIRTY-FIVE

AFTER A COUPLE of hours' sleep, the cold nose of Joy nudged his arm. Calvino climbed out of bed, took a cold shower, dressed, and listened to the pile drivers as he shaved. He fed Joy two cans of tuna mixed in cold white rice. Outside his apartment, he saw a pack of soi dogs tear into the bamboo garbage baskets, which were lined up along the driveway. They were hungry. The entire city had this nonstop hunger. He walked past the dogs, which many years ago had stopped noticing him. He was part of the neighborhood. Then he took a taxi back to the Police Hospital opposite Erawan Shrine. Earl Luce was waiting, his Leica hanging around his neck. He carried a bag over one shoulder.

"Hey, it's Vincent Calvino, looking like a robber's dog." Earl was hamming it up. They had only seen each other a few hours ago and Earl was acting as if they hadn't seen each other in years.

Calvino smiled. "I still haven't seen the photos of your Bangkok dog autopsies."

"Wait for the book," said Earl.

They had worked together a couple of times for insurance companies, including the time the *farang* was pulled out of the Chao Phraya River after being submerged for five days. And it was Calvino who had been at the police station with Earl's motorcycle helmet under his arm as he was led out of jail.

"How's it going, Earl?"

Then Luce arched one eyebrow as he looked at the woman who stood next to him, "Khun Vinny is my mate," he said.

"You know mate is the Aussie word for *puen*." The Thai word for friend registered and the woman nodded, grinned.

"I hear you are working for Quentin Stuart. In the movie business. Moving ahead, are we? Not just another dropkick Yank, but you've moved up the scale to become a Hollywood hanger-on."

Earl's friend moved alongside Calvino. From the flaming red backless cocktail dress, the Adam's apple, and breasts that were too good to be real, the extra large high-heels, it was as close as one could get to a dead certainty that the friend was a *katoey*. A doctor's scalpel had reequipped the creature into a woman.

"This is Porntip," said Earl. "We've come to see the boyfriend."

Porntip fluttered her long, fake eyelashes.

"Earl told me that we have a common friend."

"Who might that be?" asked Calvino. "Her nickname is Ice."

Why doesn't that surprise me, thought Calvino. Ice seemed to have her nails into just about every counter-culture group in the Big Weird.

"Quentin's friend, Luk Pla, took two bullets last night in front of the Plaza," said Calvino.

Earl lit a cigarette and sucked in long and hard as if he was going to inhale the entire cigarette on the first hit. His eyes were ringed with black like someone who never slept, or like a raccoon, someone who only went out at night. In Earl's case, both were true.

"Porntip's *farang* boyfriend had an unfortunate accident in prison. First the drongo gets his ass busted for heroin. Turns out that he was a diabetic. He needed his kit to inject himself. The guards thought he was just another junkie wanting a fix so they wouldn't give it to him.

"He said, 'Hey, man, I'm sick. I am gonna die without my insulin.'

" 'Fuck that. Die you bastard,' they said. After a few days, true to his word, he went into shock and corked it. Porntip wants some pictures so she can make a case against the cops. Maybe she can get the family to hire you. The guy's family has some money."

Porntip's garlic breath was close to Calvino's face as she whispered, "His family is very rich."

"How well do you know Ice?" Calvino asked her. He had heard most of Earl's version earlier in the Thermae, but he had left out the part of how Porntip had a plan of her own to try and get money out of the police. That was a nice twist, thought Calvino.

"Why you want to talk about her?" asked Porthip.

"Because women around Ice seem to be getting themselves shot. Those close to her are getting shot. Not that I am saying you are a close friend of Ice."

This wiped the smile from the katoey's face.

"Many guns in Thailand. Can be dangerous sometimes."

"Maybe she talked about her friends getting shot." He looked over at Earl, who winked.

"She told me how this *mem* shot herself."

"*Farang*s have a helluva time staying outta jail and staying alive," said Earl.

"Earl, your observations are most useful."

"I reckon you're right. Why don't you come along. I'll do my job, and you can do yours," said Earl.

They walked down the hallway, the katoey wedged between Earl and Calvino. She was the center of attention, smiling, holding her head high, chin pointed up. They walked straight into the morgue. Earl lit a hand-rolled cigarette, rolled another one and handed it to an attendant who was eating a bowl of noodles.

"You got a *farang* in here?" Earl asked, he half-turned and winked at Calvino.

The attendant nodded, spooning in a mouthful of noodles.

"Great, we'd like to have a look if that's okay. Don't want to disturb your lunch or anything."

Earl lit the attendant's cigarette and then they followed him through a set of doors into a room with heavy metal fridge doors on the walls. He pulled out one of the drawers and loaded the corpse onto a stainless steel table and wheeled the table to the center of the room. There was the color of the Big Weird sky all over the body. The aftermath of an autopsy had left a long, crude gash in the main cavity and thick, rough stitches zigzagged along the edges of the skin. From the perforated body, fluids, with the viscosity of thin maple syrup, leaked onto the table and dripped onto the floor. No one said anything as Earl opened his bag and changed the lens on his camera. Calvino watched as the attendant held up a hand.

"Wait," the attendant said in Thai.

"Wait for what?" asked Earl lowering the camera. "Jesus, I want to get this job over with."

Porntip had gone pale, tears smeared her make-up, making her look more like a man by the minute.

The attendant walked over to a set of stainless steel drawers and removed a long length of plastic hose. He walked back to the table, dropped his cigarette on the floor drain, then he stuck one end of the hose into the body of the dead man and began sucking on the other end as if he were siphoning petrol. At the last moment, he pulled the hose out of his mouth, the yellowish liquid spilled down the drain.

"Fucking gross," said Earl. "You see that Calvino?"

Porthip was vomiting her guts out down the same drain, holding her head between her legs. She gasped for air. No question about it, Porntip was a mess. Earl snapped several shots of her bent over retching down the same drain that the hose was carrying the run-off from her dead boyfriend. The attendant pulled the hose out of the body, lit another cigarette, and sat down on a folding chair to one side. Porntip was wobbly as she rose to her feet. Earl had his shots of the emotionally worked-up katoey and, after that, he took no notice of her as he circled the table, the flash showering the room with a brilliant, incandescent light. Calvino helped Porntip move away from the table and the body.

"These shots ought to look good in the family album," said Earl, changing lenses. "Here's a picture of our son on holiday in Bangkok. Looking a bit drained." Like many photojournalists, he talked to himself as he worked a job. He never stopped talking; he could have talked under wet cement. It was a way of keeping himself assured that he was still alive, something he did as he waited out long stretches during the night, standing a lone vigil for the next act of Big Weird violence to leave a subject for him to photograph.

"What did Ice tell you about the night that the *mem* killed herself?" Calvino asked.

At first Porntip either did not hear or she did not understand what Calvino had said.

"Ice?"

"Your best friend."

"Oh, Ice."

"She told you the story about the *mem*?"

"She saw mem kill herself," Porntip said, covering her mouth with both hands, showing her long, red nails.

"I promise not to tell anyone. Please don't tell her that I tell you. Pleassse." The shock of the body and all that vomiting had softened up Porthip.

"Ice saw the mem pop herself?" asked Calvino.

Once again Porntip nodded. She had the look of someone telling the truth, but, then, she had the look of a woman when she had been born a man.

"Was there anyone else in the room that night?"

"Lots of people," said Porntip.

Earl had stopped shooting and was packing away his equipment. He rolled himself another cigarette and watched the attendant finishing his bowl of noodles.

"The guy didn't even gargle before he tucked back into his noodles. It makes you wonder what would put him off his lunch," said Earl.

"Did Ice mention any names of the people who were there the night Sam died?"

"Hey, Calvino, the next thing you'll be sticking a hose down my client's throat for information."

Calvino ignored him. "Well, did she?"

Porntip gave a sly smile, fluttered her eyelids, "You want me break my promise?"

Calvino removed a blue thousand baht note from his wallet and held it out.

"Corruption is a contagious disease, Calvino," said Earl, his eyes buried in dark, sunken eyeholes flashing as the money came out.

Porntip took the money and handed it to Earl.

"Your fee," she said.

"Earl, you surprise me, I thought you had been vaccinated for all communicable diseases."

Earl handed her three rolls of films.

"I'm keeping the blue as evidence so when you come to trial, they can nail your ass," he said.

After they were back on the street, Earl disappeared on his motorcycle leaving behind a haze of blue smoke. Calvino took Porntip into the hospital canteen and ordered coffee. What he got in return was two more names at the scene of Samantha McNeal's death. The names of two people close at hand: Quentin Stuart and Luk Pla.

THIRTY-SIX

OY WAS A *dek serve* working the floor at Lollipop Bar. That meant that her job was taking drink orders, delivering drinks, emptying ashtrays, and collecting chit slips from the square plastic boxes placed in front of each customer. Most of all, it meant that Oy worked fully clothed. She might have been mistaken for any other waitress in any other restaurant or bar except she had the face of a goddess. The *dek serve* often got more action than the dancers. Think about it. The naked dancers were making a certain kind of statement by what they were not wearing; the dek serve, by wearing clothes, appeared normal, and for a lot of *farang*s, they fell straight through the clothing trap, and when they hit bottom they were impaled on a long spike just as sharp as any laid by the bar *ying*s who displayed the endgame spotlighted in their birthday suits.

They fell into two categories: *dek serve* shy-form: young, shy lass not yet ready to display their bodies and *dek serve* flawed-form: older and divorced, they bore stretch marks from childbirth, motorcycle accident and major surgery scars, the wreckage on the body skillfully hidden under their clothes. The rule of thumb did not always hold. A cunning *ying* with pretty face but otherwise loaded vile deformities might get away with pretending to be a shy dek serve. With visible body flaws, customers wouldn't bar fine them. They would never dance on stage; they would undress only in dark rooms. Oy was a *dek serve* flawed-form.

Oy sat on a chair, which was pushed next to Luk Pla's bed. When Calvino came into the room, Oy was leaning over the bed and hugging Luk Pla gently, like a mother hugs and rocks a baby; only Luk Pla wasn't a baby but a bar *ying* with some significant medical problems. Oy held the Baby Fish carefully so as not to dislodge the tube inserted in her nose or the other tubes, held by tape and attached to needles, inserted into the veins of her arms.

The Baby Fish had a puffy face, bruised and discolored; it was difficult to tell from where Calvino stood inside the door, whether her eyes were open or shut, whether she was sleeping or listening, or listening in her sleep. Oy released her grip on Luk Pla, letting her down easily on the bed, adjusting her head so that it rested in the center of the pillow. Form was important, so the way Luk Pla's head was positioned on the pillow mattered in the way flowers arranged in a vase mattered. There was a right way, and wrong way. After fluffing up the pillow, Oy collapsed back in her chair, exhausted and distraught. Out of the corner of her eye, she caught Calvino standing near the door. She was putting on some lipstick, looking at herself in the mirror, when she became aware of Calvino. Oy might have been a mere dek serve, but she had picked up a few of the bar *ying* tricks such as using the mirror to scout the room.

"My name is Vincent. Vincent Calvino," he said, walking forward, pulling up a chair and sitting down.

"I see you before. And I see you the night Somchai shoot Luk Pla."

Oy had a good memory for faces, for names, for nationality, for those who left large tips, for those who were Cheap Charlies. That memory would have been at work, capturing those who were at the scene of a shooting. She had never once danced on stage. If nothing else, Oy wore more clothes than the other *dek serve* in the bar, giving her a romantic eighteenth-century milk maiden look that drove the English patrons crazy as she hovered over them and delivered their drinks. Calvino remembered her face, the eyes, the mouth, the perfect nose and chin. He was neither particularly surprised to find her sitting at Luk Pla's bedside nor surprised to discover that Quentin Stuart had gone home.

"Did you see Khun Quentin?" asked Calvino.

"He go home. Old man stay up too late. He look bad. I think he die soon," said Oy. She had the ability to show irony by making one of those half-smiles; one side of her face smiled while the other stayed non-smiling.

"How long have you been here?"

Oy had no idea about the passage of time. She might have been in Luk Pla's room ten minutes, or for half a day. "Khun Quentin phone Ice and he say for Ice to phone me. He want me to talk with Luk Pla. Tell her not worry too much. Not useful. Think too much is bad. Give you a headache. He old man and maybe she not beautiful to him anymore."

"You have Ice's mobile number?"

"Have. She give me, I get her customer, she give me commission," she said, reaching into her handbag and taking out her little black book. She found the number and gave it to Calvino. With the arrival of the packaged *farang*s, more and more of the *ying*s had the money to buy mobile phones. The trendy ones found that they could use their customers as a mirror to reflect what was cool, what was in, what was desirable, hip, and American.

Ice scouted cyberspace on a rented computer and still kept close tabs on her regulars in the city who dressed in suits and worked out of the office buildings up and down Silom and Sathorn Roads—the parallel rails of the financial institutions and big business enterprises of the Big Weird. Her mobile phone memory was loaded with office numbers of her regular customers, and she loved speed dialing down the directory until she found someone at the other end whose voice chords seized up, growing thick simply hearing her voice, The Sickness slamming into them like a freight train hitting a ten-wheeler straddling the tracks on Rama IV Road.

Oy, however, was not as successful or as lucky in matters of getting *farang* cash cows for that mid-afternoon short-time in a curtained motel. She was not plugged into the high-tech future. No mobile phone. No computer. She might as well have been working in the Stone Age. She was a milk maiden with few cows to milk but she put up a brave face and scraped by as a *dek serve* who had a respectable record in the amount of tips she could slip unnoticed by the rest of the staff into her bra.

Oy had been bouncing around various bars in the Plaza for more than a couple of years and had been born in the same Isan village as Luk Pla and somehow, so Calvino was able to gather, they were distant cousins. The connection was strong enough to convince anyone around them that they were genuine sisters. But their pathway to the door of opportunity inside the Plaza had not been the same. Oy had worked in the kitchen of a restaurant on the way to the airport. One of those local places that foreigners would never find, and if found, they would never go into. A hole-in-the-wall restaurant where local customers sat at small wooden tables, and alternated between hacking up gobs of fungi colony waste, slurping their soup, and spitting chicken bones on the floor. At the end of the night, the floor looked like a chicken massacre.

One night while she was working near the stove, a pot of boiling water was accidentally dropped down her front by a guy who had smoked two joints and drunk half a bottle of Mekhong. She was sixteen years old at the time and untouched by the hand of a man. Oy had the face of an angel, the kind of face no customer could take their eyes off, inviting, soft, warm, caring, with a hint of sensual pleasures. But her body had been damaged beyond repair. She had the body of a melted angel; one God had held too close to the sun. Her skin puckered into ripples and waves, hundreds of them rolling from just below her neck and extending below her stomach. She had been sculptured into a *dek serve* flawed-form.

The main consequence of the accident was that Oy lost her nipples in the accident. What remained was a pair of beautiful nippleless breasts covered with psychedelic whorls where the boiling oil had reconstituted her flesh into images not of this world. It was the kind of work of art that would have commanded a great sum of money in a SoHo gallery in downtown Manhattan, but was neither art nor commerce in the Big Weird. The hot oil had also destroyed her pubic hair. When Luk Pla had first introduced Oy to the old man as her best friend and told him the full story, Luk Pla insisted that Oy take off all her clothes to show the extent of the damage.

Quentin studied the breasts and the pubic area, and that afternoon, he arranged for several merkins to be made in New York and shipped by FedEx to Bangkok. Five days later, the first time Luk Pla helped her put on a merkin, Oy stood in front of the full-length mirror for hours with tears in her eyes. Luk Pla also had tears in her eyes. So had Quentin. They all cried together as Oy stared in the mirror at her merkin. She had been repaired, just a little. Enough to give her back something of the woman she wished to be.

Her body had in some real way died and been reborn as a piece of art. Boiled to racing stripes of wavy tissue that was rubbery to the touch. That was a death of beauty worth weeping over; that was a death that even those with an acute case of The Sickness found themselves crying over until they could cry no more.

Oy was the perfect tonic for Luk Pla on the day that the doctors told her that she wasn't going to die after all. But her body had one very ragged, hooked, ugly scar that made the Baby Fish look like she had been caught, gutted, sewn up, and thrown back in the sea. She needed reassurance and Quentin made all the necessary arrangements through Ice for her to have some feel-good company.

When Ice delivered Oy to Baby Fish's room, she *waied* Quentin, and he *waied* her back. Oy threw herself on the Baby Fish's bed, pulled back her bed clothes and stared at the wound. Then she started sobbing, and saying things like, "No man wanna fuck you like this." This wasn't the kind of emotional support that Quentin had in mind. It was too late, the dye had been cast, and the mostly unconscious Baby Fish was slobbered over by Oy who totally lost all composure. By the time Calvino had arrived, Oy had been alone with Baby Fish long enough to recover her need for food. She had eaten a bowl of noodles, an apple, half a plate of rice and chicken, and a banana as she watched the saline bottle gurgle beside Luk Pla's bed.

Calvino left the room, found a pay phone and tried to call Ice's mobile. Pay telephones on the streets were hotwired to deny access to long distance calls and could not distinguish a phone call to London from a mobile phone on Silom Road. He loitered in the hallway until he remembered that Quentin had bought a mobile for Luk Pla. As he went back into the room, Oy had partially pulled down her own top and Luk Pla sat up in bed half-naked. Her hospital gown crumpled as if she were undergoing a medical examination.

Oy was doing most of the examining, her face a couple of inches away from Luk Pla's stomach, having peeled away the bandages, she touched the puffy red ridges with her finger. Luk Pla looked straight ahead like a zombie still under construction, but this did not stop Oy from touching Luk Pla's hole left by the bullet, and her own scars, measuring one against another.

Calvino stood silently inside the room watching the two women. In the Plaza there was constant comparison of legs, breasts, thighs, and fingernails. It was like an inventory of the goods for sale. There was a saying that the Plaza had taken the "*bah*" out of banana, leaving Nana, but couldn't take the *bah* (the Thai word for crazy) out of the *yings* who worked in the bars. Given the amount of damage they had incurred before taking the job, not to mention the damage on the job, it was a miracle any of them were sane.

From the look of the room and the dancers, Oy had alternated between bawling her eyes out and eating her way through a large amount of food. A line of snot dripped off the plastic tube stuck inside Luk Pla's nose. Calvino took another step and cleared his throat. Oy looked around, terror in her eyes, her mouth full of banana. Luk Pla lay impassively with the sheet pulled to her chin.

"I need to use your mobile phone," Calvino said to Luk Pla.

She said nothing, her expression remained unchanged as one hand with the IV line attached snaked out of the sheet and pointed at a large black handbag on the cot where Quentin had been sleeping the night before. Calvino reached inside and as he took out the mobile unit, it started to ring. He punched the receive button and took the call.

"Baby Fish?" asked the caller's voice, recognizing a read out of Luk Pla's number on her own mobile phone.

"Ice?"

Calvino had guessed it right. "I was going to phone you."

"You know how many times I hear that bullshit line? About a million times."

"Ice, sweetheart, it's Vinny you are talking to." "You stole Baby Fish's mobile." For some reason that Calvino never understood, Ice used Luk Pla's English translated name rather than her Thai name.

"I am talking to you."

"Where are you?"

"At the hospital with Luk Pla and Oy. Where are you?"

"In the fucking traffic on Rama IV. Let me talk to Oy."

Oy adjusted her top so she was fully covered and took the mobile phone from Calvino. She sat on the edge of the bed and, switching between Thai and Isan, explained in graphic detail Luk Pla's scar. The conversation, at least at Oy's end, veered over body damage, the price of rice and chicken, the Mermaidium opening, fucking, guns, *farang*s, a sick sister, scars, making merit, and the stability of the prevailing price structure for a short-time.

Ice had clearly moved up on the social scale of the bar scene; she no longer took motorcycle taxis but sat in the back of air-conditioned taxis doing the Bangkok crawl, alternating between telephoning her clients to confirm appointments and telephoning her friends to seek sympathy for how hard she was working and wondering if she should be putting up her short-time rates to three thousand baht. Everyone needed a goal and Ice's was three blues for an hour of special off-line treatment. Slugo had taken Ice out of the Plaza but he hadn't managed to take the Plaza out of Ice; nor did he even try.

THIRTY-SEVEN

THIRTY MINUTES LATER, Oy was still talking on Luk Pla's mobile phone, when Ice came into the room. They continued to talk for another thirty seconds, waving at each other and giggling. Then Ice ran over to the side of the bed and pulled up Luk Pla's hospital gown and screamed.

"Baby Fish. The bastards! What have they done?" Luk Pla, all freshly drugged up, opened her eyes and forgot where she was. Forgot she had examined scars with Oy. She had a blurred image of Ice in her standard racing-around-the-Big-Weird gear: Microsoft baseball cap worn backwards, black leather pants and matching top unbuttoned to show a nice, large cleavage, and hanging from both her earlobes were large gold earrings in the shape of a lotus in bloom. Around her throat she displayed six baht of gold chains. Ice was looking more and more like her cyberspace avatar each time Calvino saw her. Virtual reality and reality had blurred with Ice.

"Baby Fish, your body all cut up," she said. Oy started to cry. "My body's much worse."

"Your old man, see this? A scar like this, he's never gonna keep you."

Luk Pla made a movement, which looked like a nod, tears began spraying out of her eyes. Words started to form then aborted. Her lips moved but no sound came out. She tried again, saying in a hoarse voice, "He still think I beautiful."

"Sweet mouth bullshit," said Ice, mixing her Thai and English in bar *ying* fashion.

"He not ever leave me," said Luk Pla, who was blubbering.

"They all leave," said Ice. "Get new girl, young girl, or go back home. Is that right, Khun Vinny?"

"All is one of the three-lettered English words you should unlearn. Let's talk about a party you went to not long ago, Ice."

"I'm a party girl. I don't want to talk parties. Can't you see how much Baby Fish has pain?"

"The night Sam killed herself. You were at Ben Nakamura's house and there was a party."

"Who told you that bullshit?" Ice shifted around on the bed, hooked her ankles together, her hands on her hips in a defiant fashion.

"You told someone you were there when Sam blew out her brains."

"What a blew out mean?" Sometimes a *ying* like Ice pretended she had some big gaps in English when she knew perfectly well what was being said.

"Let's not change the subject. She said you were at Nakamura's house that night. And so was Luk Pla. And

I want to know who else was in the room."

"Porntip, that bitch, I'll kill her. I make a phone call now and in two hours she'll be dead in a *klong*," said Ice. "I see her downstairs trying to pick up an old man with broken leg. Can never trust *katoey*. I am a stupid girl sometimes."

Calvino sighed and started to walk toward the door.

"Where you going?" asked Ice. She sounded anxious and the old confidence in her voice was gone.

"You won't talk to me, but maybe you will talk to the police. I am going to file a report. I figure as an accessory to the murder, you'll be out of action for a couple of years. During your prime working years. Eating prison red rice rather than penthouse caviar. I have to admire that you would put principle over profit," said Calvino.

"Catch you later, Ice. Because you are only going to be free in virtual reality."

Ice leaped off the bed and grabbed Calvino's arm. "How I know the *mem* going to shoot herself in the head?"

"I think you might have gone paranoid, thinking she was a WULF hitman."

"You think a woman not shoot straight like a man?"

"That's the point. You are a straight shooter. Maybe you did her. Even Slugo said your leather outfit was hand-tailored out of Kevlar."

"So what?"

He decided to go straight for the only question that mattered.

"Did you kill Sam?"

"Me? Ice killer? I think you bah."

"Who else was at Ben's house that night?"

Whether she had become the city's first digital bar *ying*, no one could verify, but she was definitely the most famous online avatar. With Ice, no one could be certain if her avatar had been stalked by a cyberspace killer. The volunteers drawn from the ranks of international vigilantes serving as members on their vigilance committees; their mission was to whack every Third World sexual avatar including Ice. Pauline, as the mastermind behind WULF, had revealed herself early on, as if she had nothing to hide.

WULF was not really much of a clandestine operation. Her Bangkok BBS was the number one suspect in a short list of censorship borgs implicated in giving Ice's avatar a virus three times before the afternoon Calvino had been present at the cybercafe when he saw the avatar zapped with his own eyes, and heard Ice screaming as if she had taken a bullet. Four times Ice had been snuffed out in cyberspace and each time Slugo had rebuilt her virtual reality self, giving the revised and improved avatar a vaccination against the latest series of WULF viruses. All this cyberspace assassination was costing Ice big-time in terms of the bartered short-times she had given Slugo for his avatar building, and she thought there was a fifty-fifty chance that Slugo had sabotaged her avatar himself once or twice so he could barter for another batch of free short-times from Ice as payment to rebuild cyberspace Ice. Virtual reality programming for sex wasn't money in the bank, but it was the next best thing.

Alpha Domo was Slugo's baby, and he had worked to create an avatar that was WULF hacker-proof, or so he claimed. Ice thought the sabotage theory was closer to fifty-fifty because Slugo was doing okay on his stockpile of free Ice short-times simply by whacking her competing avatars which had started to muscle in on Ice's turf, taking away some of her business. Slugo prided himself on the high body count of dead avatars which had strayed into Ice's domain. More violence was happening in cyberspace than in all the bars of the Plaza combined; there was a lot at stake: face, cash flow, turf. Ice wanted all three and so long as she had Slugo wrapped around her little finger with the three-inch red fingernail, she was reasonably confident of winning.

Going around the BigWeird nightspots dressed exactly like her avatar was Ice's statement that she wasn't afraid of any fucking virtual reality WULF rough types who had been launched into cyberspace or the bitches who had moved in on her home turf. Now she looked tense, unsure, and had drawn in her claws, having moved from attack mode to defense mode, to the mode of ulti-mate confusion—something that happened when Ice was being squeezed to tell something as radical as the truth.

"Okay, but no police, promise? No bullshit promise. But a real promise."

She pulled a face at Calvino, pointing her mobile phone at him as if it were a pistol.

"Who was there?"

"Baby Fish."

A tiny scream came out of Luk Pla's mouth.

"Baby Fish said she is very sad. But she not kill Khun Sam. The bad thing happen. Now a bad thing happen to her. Karma. And her old man was there, too. Khun Ben. Sexy man. Khun Reed. He joking, joking all the time.

Khun Pauline. She not like Thai girl. Mean Chinese eyes. And, and—let me think. Khun Sam, of course."

"You sure there wasn't someone else? Maybe you are protecting someone. Like Slugo."

"I tell you lie, I cut myself here," she said pointing at one wrist and then the other one, making a slashing gesture across each one with her long, red fingernails.

"Slugo said Khun Sam not want to live any more. She tired. He say, she have death dish."

"Death wish?"

"Whatever," said Ice. "So her wish come true. Slugo very romantic like all *farang*s. Very smart and very stupid at the same time."

"A real Lord Byron."

"Khun Brian? How you know about him? You tap my phone or what?"

"Forget it," said Calvino. "Who does Slugo think helped Sam put a bullet in her brain?"

"Slugo is, how you say? Alpha Geek. Unless he's online, surfing, he stay sad. Bitch about this, about that. That I don't know shit. He get everything from cyberspace except air, food, and pussy. Slugo, he tell me that mem-*farang*s make Khun Sam into a marty."

"A Marty? You mean martyr."

She shrugged.

"Marty, martyr. Death dish, death wish. Same fucking thing."

"I hear that you slept with Sam, too," said Calvino. Ice didn't so much as flinch. She switched into her cold stare; the look which matched her street name.

"It's my job. Why not? Sleep with her, sleep with Slugo, sleep with you, what's the difference?"

She had a point. Calvino studied her face, which had shifted into the innocent, simple, smiling Isan. She could still call up that childlike face as if all she had to do was boot a piece of old software. It was amazing how much Slugo had taught her in such a short period of time, and it was just as amazing that she could transform herself from peasant rice farmer to cyberspace superstar by the mere physical act of changing her expression. Her mobile phone rang and she unhooked it from her silver belt. She spoke a few words.

"Show time," Ice said.

Calvino wasn't going to let her slide out the door so fast and without one more try to get some solid information about the night Sam died.

"Did you see the gun?"

Ice rolled her eyes. "Yes, I see the gun."

"You saw her put it to her head?"

"Yip, see that, too. Like a movie."

"Anyone else play Russian roulette with her?"

"Joking, joking Reed play."

"You see her shoot herself?"

"Scared the shit out of me. Brains all over the fucking room. I see her ghost in my nightmare. Ghost say, 'Ice, you make me happy. More happy than man.' "

"Quentin was there."

She nodded.

"And Ben, Pauline and Luk Pla." Each time she nodded.

"Anything else?"

"Where did she get the gun?"

"Don't know. Not from me, Khun Vinny. How can I know? I not ask her. After she kill herself, can I ask her,

'Hey you with bullet in the head, where you get the fucking gun?' " She had switched into her smart-assed bar *ying* routine.

It didn't phase Calvino. He just let it pass. "You see anyone put the bullet in?"

She paused a moment. "No, Ice not see a fucking thing."

She had started referring to herself in the third person. A virtual reality star had been hatched in the Big Weird. She ran over and hugged Oy, leaned over and kissed Luk Pla on the forehead.

"If Quentin leave me, you help me kill him?" Luk Pla asked.

Ice had slipped on her Italian designer sunglasses. "No problem, Baby Fish. But he's old man, very sick. I think he die soon. Not useful to kill him. He not have any time to find beautiful *ying*. So I think he keep you. You not forget one thing. Don't go back into Mermaidium in this life. And before you make love, turn out lights then you can take off your towel. You like Oy. Not so bad. You have beautiful face."

The advice and support lifted Luk Pla's spirits and she stopped crying as Ice skipped out the door, wearing headphones, her mobile phone hooked to the front of her belt, and a Sony Walkman hooked on the back of her belt. Ice was singing to herself, her large painted lips moving to the words. The lyrics were from a Thai love song, the same one that had been playing at five-thirty in the morning at the Thermae. The lyrics were all about betrayal, death, and heartache in the heartland of Isan.

THIRTY-EIGHT

THE FOLLOWING MORNING around five-thirty Calvino sat on a bar stool close to the Mermaidium. On either side were Col. Pratt and Osborn, and behind them were over a dozen police officers milling around the empty bar. Outside of the bar, another half-dozen cops huddled in pairs, waiting for further instructions. The Plaza was empty. But the area in front of the Mermaidium was filled with uniforms. All of the uniforms had arrived because the brass had discovered that a *farang*, someone with important family connections, had died, suddenly, violently, and horribly. Nathan Gold was the name on the American passport.

Beneath the water line of the Mermaidium, Slugo's naked body floated at the end of a thick metal chain. His skin had gone the yellow-grayish color of the Big Weird sky, reminding Calvino of the *farang* body which had been dragged out of the Chao Phraya River. His scrotum had shrunk, pulling his balls inside his body; and his penis had nearly disappeared into the pubic hair, giving Slugo's inert body a unisex configuration. His feet and hands wrinkled like those of a baby or a very old man.

The police, having discovered the body some hours earlier after a tip had been phoned in, were under orders not to remove it. None of the cops understood why the body had been ordered by their boss to be kept untouched inside the tank; and none of them, naturally, would have questioned such an order. They left Slugo as they had found him at 4.00 a.m., his hands tied behind his back and his ankles chained to a block of cement. His eyes and mouth were wide open, his teeth looking yellow and sharp; his final expression was one of complete terror. One half-expected a giggle to come from Slugo's mouth. But not even a bubble emerged.

Calvino was thinking that Slugo hadn't been given the chance to make that last phone call before someone had hauled him inside in the Mermaidium. He had looked at Slugo's fingernails to see if there were any signs of a violent struggle but none of the nails were broken, and there was, at least from the outside looking into the Mermaidium, no apparent evidence of skin or flesh underneath his fingernails.

Osborn sat on a bar stool smoking a cigarette and staring at Slugo's body as if he were looking off into deep space. One of the police officers accidentally hit the switch starting the waterfall and a torrent of water splashed into the water behind the body. The still waters were churned by the waterfall, making Slugo's head bob up and down, as if he were agreeing to what someone had said.

"I guess one can rule out suicide," said Osborn. Calvino sat on a stool next to Osborn. He glanced over at Col. Pratt, who was talking to another police officer in one of those hushed, private conversations. When he finished the conversation, Pratt walked over to Calvino.

"Nathan Gold was a friend of yours, Vincent," said Pratt. "Maybe you should talk with the American Embassy, be there when they contact his parents."

"And tell them their son had a swimming accident," said Osborn.

"I don't believe anyone was addressing you, Mr. Osborn," said Col. Pratt.

"Sorry, sorry. It's just Slugo was a friend of mine. And it's not easy looking at what they did to him."

Though you could never read his sorrow from the way he stared at the body.

"Any idea who they might be?" asked Col. Pratt. Osborn inhaled on his cigarette and shrugged his shoulders. "I haven't the faintest idea. Someone who was jealous of him."

"The two of you were business partners," said Col. Pratt.

"We had no conflicts, if that's what you are trying to suggest. I had no reason to cause him harm. He was my friend. We were going to have a wonderful business in cyberspace selling virtual reality playgrounds. Now it has come to this. I am sad, of course."

Pratt stared at him for almost a minute and beads of sweat appeared on Alan's forehead as he continued to meet the colonel's eyes. It was as if Col. Pratt was trying to sweat out some true answer that Osborn was keeping to himself. Osborn was always sweating and unless he was always guilty, it didn't matter very much. The murderers had gained entrance through the roof, climbed down through the toilet area. Someone standing above must have lowered the unconscious body of Slugo to an accomplice who waited below.

They had dragged Slugo into the bar, pulled him to the top of the Mermaidium, fixed the chains and dropped him inside the water. This would have required planning, knowledge of where to break into the bar, strength, timing, and an intention to send a clear message. In other words, it had to be the work of a professional crew assigned a specific, detailed hit.

Pratt, as Calvino watched, had taken Osborn through the sequence of events: from the cutting of the hole in the roof to the final moment when Slugo had been lowered into the Mermaidium. Had Osborn hired someone to help him kill the American? It didn't seem likely, but murder was a most unlikely event in most circumstances. Col. Pratt questioned Osborn for over an hour before they came back to sit in front of the body. He hoped that staring at the victim might cause Osborn to say something unexpected. But that was not to happen. In police work, there was often no long- tailed boat that crossed the wide span of open-water guilt to dock at a full confession.

One of the police officers went over and whispered something in Col. Pratt's ear.

"In the back, there is a door which is locked. My officer would like the key, Mr. Osborn."

"I don't have a key," said Osborn.

"Break it down," said Col. Pratt in Thai to the officer. "Hold on. I don't have the key, but I didn't say I couldn't open it." He was off his stool, holding two thin pieces of wire, which he had taken out of his pocket so fast that no one had noticed.

Pratt looked over at Calvino who shrugged his shoulder as if to say, "It beats me what he's doing."

"If the police break down the door, I will have to pay for it. What the killers did to the ceiling is bad enough. I will get stuck with that bill, too. I am working on a thin profit margin," said Osborn.

The door was behind a curtain in the back, and as Osborn worked the wires in the lock, Calvino stood back with Pratt. What Col. Pratt's officer had noticed was blood seeping out from under the door. A small pool of blood had formed on the floor. Osborn glanced over his shoulder, smiled, straddling the blood. He opened the door carefully as if there was a great weight pushing towards him. The smile was wiped off when the corpse of the night guard fell forward and landed in the pool of blood. He was a Thai man, late twenties, dressed in a dark blue guard's uniform. His throat had been slit from ear to ear.

"Do you know this man?" asked Col. Pratt.

Osborn nodded, his face very pale.

"He's the guard. Or I should say, he was the guard."

"Okay, you can leave for now," said Col. Pratt. "But do not leave Thailand."

A couple of the officers looked surprised at his decision. The had found a second body on the premises and their commanding officer had not arrested the *farang*, who had just jimmied a lock with a little too much skill. Osborn was allowed to walk away without any further questioning by Pratt.

Osborn turned around, "I could never leave Thailand." Then he was gone.

Calvino knelt down and had a closer look at the dead guard. He looked up from the dead man to the door.

Osborn had opened the lock as if he had a key, and he had done it with a couple of pieces of wire. That was impressive.

"What do you think, Vincent?"

"He's been dead a couple of hours is my guess," said Calvino. "He must have surprised whoever killed Slugo. They killed him, used his key to stuff the body into the storage room."

"Any idea who might have done this?" asked Pratt, moving away from the body.

He shrugged his shoulders and rose to his feet as a police officer took pictures of the dead guard. "I don't know. But I would start looking real hard at people who sub-contracted some parts for -B Chinese rockets and for some other people connected with Pauline's WULF. Slugo passed me information about her involvement. I had dinner with Pauline Cheng a couple of nights ago, and I, can you believe this, told her I had a private source who linked her to the Chinese sub-contractor. She let me believe that Ben Nakamura had marked her. I let her throw me off. She must have known that night that the information came from Slugo."

"A woman couldn't have done this," said Pratt, looking back at Slugo's submerged body. "Or done the guard. Did you see the bruises on the guard's face?"

"If you think Osborn did it . . ."

"No, I don't. But he had access to the bar and, it is his tank. He built it. The two of them had some kind of Internet business project. We have to look at all the possibilities. He is one of them, though I don't personally think he's dirty."

"Slugo wrote the script and asked me to help him pitch it to Quentin Stuart. So that makes me one of the possibilities," said Calvino. "My motive? I get rid of him so that I can steal his story."

"His bar girl, Ice, had a better motive and opportunity," said Pratt. "With Mr. Gold out of the way, she takes over his Internet business. She stands to make a small fortune. At least, that is the view of Mr. Osborn before you arrived on the scene. By eliminating the middleman, she stood to convert their joint venture into a sole proprietorship."

"Except for one thing," said Calvino. "What's that?" asked Pratt.

Calvino said, "She's out of business."

Calvino stared at Slugo's body. The waterfall had been turned off. Air bubbles formed around the hair on his chest and stomach. One of the cops in the back room had hit a button and a million bubbles flooded the tank, shifting the body. As the head turned, for the first time, Calvino could see where it had been bashed in and was leaking gray matter into the water.

"There is another possibility," said Calvino. "Pauline Cheng. All Pauline had to do was make a phone call, Pratt. She's riding with some influential people in the Chinese community. She phones someone in Hong Kong, who phones someone in Manila or Singapore, or Hong Kong, and they fly in, do the hit, fly back out. Untraceable. No local hitman to be dragged in who immediately confesses and reenacts the crime before the media cameras, spilling his guts that the Chinese had hired him to knock Slugo on the head and leave his body inside the Mermaidium."

"So I take her in and question her. What is she going to say?" asked Pratt.

"Me? Little me, involved in the murder of Nathan Gold? Slugo, the greatest computer mind in the city, someone that I disagreed with, to be sure, but admired. Sure, arrest me. But I will have your badge and your balls. My friends, one thousand strong, will write letters to everyone in the police, the Ministry of Interior, the Parliament, the *New York Times, Newsweek, Time magazine, CNN.* And they will go on the Net and post on every board that they can find in cyberspace that the Thai police force are harassing and abusing women. I am trying to help women get out of prostitution, and the police, who have their hands in the trade, seek to persecute me."

Pratt sighed. "Yeah, that's about how I see her playing it out as well."

"I feel responsible for what's happened," said Calvino. "You said Pauline hated his Alpha Domo project."

"No question about that. She wanted that project killed off. And now the creator of the project will no longer be sending Ice's avatar into cyberspace. The virtual reality Ice is as dead as Slugo."

"The department is going to take a lot of heat over this murder. Mr. Gold comes from a very wealthy family in America. One that has political connections. Vincent, this is a major headache."

"I know. Slugo's family is rich enough to hire their own private investigators, charter a 747 and fly them in, and put them up at the Oriental Hotel for as long as it takes to get some answers," said Calvino. "All that digging by outsiders makes for a messy time."

" 'The evil that men do lives after them, the good

is oft interred within their bones,' " said Pratt, quoting Scene II, Act III, *Julius Caesar.*

"You take in Ice and charge her, you probably can even get a confession from her, the heat is off you, the department, and who would miss another bar girl who has gone to prison for murdering a *farang*? But Ice is the last person in the world to have killed Slugo. Like I said before, without him she is out of business. She's doomed in cyberspace. The next time WULF knocked off her avatar, she's out of the virtual reality business. And she's back in the bar."

"I'll still have to talk to her, Vincent. These *yings* can do irrational things. Even if it costs them, they can kill in a moment of rage."

Pratt stared at Slugo in the Mermaidium. "Does this look like a moment-of-rage murder?" asked Calvino, and answering his own question, added. "It looks like a professional hit."

"You can't blame me for wishing Ice was behind this," said Pratt, sighing. "It would make everyone's life so much easier. My superiors' life for example."

"That's exactly what Pauline would have hoped for. She gets two for the price of one. The only problem with that option is you, Pratt. You have integrity, and in Bangkok, integrity can bring you dishonor before it delivers honor."

"I'll take the risk," said Pratt, studying Slugo's body.

"No bar girl could have arranged a hit like this."

Calvino smiled, leaned over, and put his arm around Pratt's shoulder. "I have this strange feeling that Mr. Nathan Gold and Ms. Samantha McNeal ran into the same problem with Chinese component parts."

"What component is that?"

"Remember in Slugo's script, he used the expression 'T-486' as a story component. I am willing to bet that is the same part that caused the Long March -B to explode. If we did a little digging, I would double that bet."

"What's the bet?" asked Pratt.

"Pauline had applied pressure to get the T-486 accepted by Ben's people in Tokyo, and she leaned on Sam. All Sam had to do was convince Ben to recommend the T-486 component for the telecom project," said Calvino. "But Ben wouldn't agree."

He slipped the tattered copy of *The Art of War* out of his pocket and opened it.

"Listen to this, Pratt. 'Before action starts, appear as shy as a maiden and the enemy will relax his vigilance and leave his door open; once the fighting begins, move as swiftly as a scurrying rabbit and the enemy will find it is too late to put up a resistance.' "

"Someone lured Mr. Gold to his death," said Pratt.

"The question is who and why. You might think that you have the answer, but proving it is another thing."

"I am thinking about that." Calvino lifted himself off the stool.

"If you are right, it might be a good idea to keep some distance. I don't want to fish your body out of a tank."

Calvino glanced back at the body. "I'll be seeing you around."

THIRTY-NINE

QUENTIN HOVERED ABOVE the aquarium; dressed in a blue silk dressing gown and Chinese slippers, he took a child's delight in feeding his prize fish. When Calvino walked down the stairs and into the living area, he heard the old man talking to the fish.

"Eat, my darlings. Next life you will come back bigger and stronger. Next life we will meet again."

Then his voice blurred, filtered out as if his thought processes had interrupted the sound track. In a low voice, the old man was talking to himself in Death talk as the fish circled, tails flashing, to the top of the tank, their jaws snapping pellets of food. Quentin's skinny ankles had turned a purplish color. Deep inside the body's organs was a messy reorganization of cells into chaotic spheres, attacking and defeating the normal cells, as if what was normal no longer had the will, or the ability to resist. The final effect was nothing like a good-put-out-your-lights heart attack. A smash straight to fade-out ending.

As Calvino watched him feeding his beloved fish, he thought how cancer was more like one of those slow-motion tackles from behind on a down-field runner. A diving tackle by a flyweight, third-string player making that luck-out-of-nowhere contact, but without sufficient strength to knock down the runner. Instead, the tackler latched onto the lower body, slowed him down, inch-by-inch. Just enough force to add extra weight, opening the opportunity for others to catch up and finish him off, take him down to his knees, and finally flatten him out, belly down, face in the turf. Quentin looked like he had a few more yards left in him before he went down hard, went down for good and for the count.

"Vincent, I have been waiting for you. I thought you would never come." There was a hint of dissatisfaction in his voice. He had spent a lifetime of having others waiting on him and now, at the end, there was a certain humiliation in waiting for others. It was almost worse than death itself.

"Slugo's dead. He was killed sometime early in the morning, and his body stuffed in the Mermaidium."

Quentin turned, his mouth opened. "My God!"

"He was found stripped naked and anchored under-water," said Calvino.

"But who would have done something like that to Slugo?"

"The world is full of unanswered questions. Like why did Sam kill herself, and whether you will dump Luk Pla for another Baby Fish because she has a long, ugly scar on her stomach," said Calvino.

Quentin stopped the feeding, and looked around

at Calvino who stood at the foot of the staircase, arms folded behind his back.

"I know how to please a woman. But I never discovered how to live with one. A scar doesn't enter into the equation," he said. "I will never leave Luk Pla. But I don't know how much more I can take."

He looked rattled, thought Calvino, as he crossed the open floor area, past the fish tank, moving in behind the bar, opening the fridge, and pulling out a can of cola. Calvino flipped open the tab and took a long drink. Beads of sweat had formed on his forehead. He put the can down on the bar.

"You know, Mr. Stuart, I haven't quite figured out why you hired me. Why you tried to pay me all this money to find out information about Sam McNeal's death when, in truth, you knew all of the time that she had shot herself. You were present in the sitting room, watching, waiting. You saw her pull the trigger. You saw the consequences of her suicide right up close, I mean, you didn't have to read about it in the newspaper or look at the photographs of her laid out in the morgue.

"She shot herself right in front of your face. You couldn't have been more than four, five feet away. You probably walked out the door with part of her brains splattered on your silk shirt. So I am thinking to myself, why does a Hollywood legend hire a private eye in Bangkok to find the so-called killer of Sam when he was at the scene of her death? And I ask myself, why didn't he tell me that he was at Nakamura's that night? Instead he invites me to his penthouse and lets me interview Nakamura without saying so much as a word.

"On that first day I came to your apartment, you could've said, 'I was in Ben's house. I saw it with my own eyes. I still don't believe it. But it happened. She died and I watched her die.'

"But you didn't say that. And I have been asking myself, 'Why did he play it that way? Is it because he's a screenwriter and people in Hollywood play life like a movie? They don't see life the same as guys like me? Hey, who am I, just another guy from Brooklyn who knows nothing from nothing.'

"So, as you can see, I am a little hot from the weather outside, that I am used to, but I get really hot when I have a client who wastes my time running around the city when all the information the client needs, he already has."

Quentin waited a full minute after Calvino stopped talking, watching him take another drink from the can of cola before he even blinked. Calvino emptied the can and set it down on the counter.

"Are you finished, Vincent?"

"You know what, Mr. Stuart? I am finished. With the case. With you, your deathwatch, your friends, everything in the field of vision. A friend of mine was killed this morning. Not a great friend, but a friend. Someone I liked. Someone who did me favors. Someone with dreams. But no hard feelings. I will be happy to give you a refund."

He pulled a wad of hundred dollar bills out of his jacket pocket and put them on the counter of the bar.

"Keep the money. And you are not finished with the case. Not by a long shot."

"Give me one reason why I should help you." Quentin left the room and returned a few minutes later with a large coffeetable book on handguns of the world. He opened the book on the bar, and there was a photograph of a Smith & Wesson . 8 caliber hammerless safety pistol. It was a five-shot handgun which had been tested by the U.S. Army in 1889.

"Because some sick mother fucker put a bullet into an empty gun. I collected guns and this Smith & Wesson was one I could not bring myself to part with even after I had sold all the rest of my guns.

"Whoever put the round into the Smith & Wesson is likely the same person who killed Slugo. Vincent I owned that gun. It was my fucking gun. Do you read me? My gun, the one she pressed to her head and used as the instrument to kill herself with. I have a crazy ex-wife in LA."

Calvino looked up from the picture in the book. "Rebecca," he said. "You told me the story in the hospital."

"Yes, I told you the story about Rebecca. But what I didn't tell you is something you should know before you decide to dump me. Rebecca hired one of your competitors, a private eye on Silom Road."

"An agency you tried to hire before you came to me," said Calvino.

"Vincent, the lesson of life in Hollywood is always go with the brand name."

"Unless you are forced to go with a nobody," said Calvino.

"Don't take it personally. But I was lucky I didn't hire them. Fortunately, they were incompetent. Rebecca had first found out about the gun that Sam had used not from her private dick but from Sam's father. She knew that this Smith & Wesson, because it was an antique, could be easily traced to me. Rebecca decided not to tell the Thai police authorities that it was my handgun that they found in Sam's hand. And, in return, true to form, Rebecca has demanded one very large amount of cash.

"Her theory is that I am responsible for Sam's death. Perhaps I am, in her view, criminally responsible. The Thai authorities might wish to question me. They might wish to imprison me. And assuming I survived more than a week in a Thai jail, they might wish to try me for murder. My motive, in Rebecca's mind, you might well ask. Quentin Stuart, screenwriter, had vowed to carry on the cycle of revenge established years ago. And how else would you expect someone like Rebecca to think? She thinks I set up Sam's death as another way to punish Beth, Sam's mother, for leaving her soul mate. Rebecca's thinking is sick. There are many sick people who would happily share her thoughts. And you must admit, if she went public to the talk shows, to the newspapers and magazines, there is just enough evidence for Rebecca's purpose. She would make a small fortune in selling the story of how Quentin Stuart, an old man dying in Bangkok, had given his ex-wife's daughter the handgun to kill herself."

"What does Rebecca want from you?" asked Calvino.

"If I don't agree to her financial terms, to destroy me. Meaning a clean, neat five hundred grand transferred to her account in LA. That amount of money will wipe me out. I would be left with nothing. Even these wonderful fish would have to go. Baby Fish would swim downstream looking for someone else to catch her. I am no fool."

"How did Rebecca find out about the gun?" asked Calvino. "I mean a local murder in Bangkok is not going to be news in LA."

"Sam's father flew in to make the arrangements to have Sam's body flown back to LA. The Thai police showed him the handgun that Sam had used. He signed a receipt and they gave him the gun. He took it back to LA. Somehow Rebecca had dinner with him and he showed it to her. She remembered the Smith & Wesson. She had used it to shoot at sea gulls from the second-floor balcony of that new house I told you about. There is a wheel of grief, a wheel of pain that no one ever seems to break free of in this life."

"But was it your gun that Sam used?" asked Calvino, holding onto the bar with both hands.

"Of course, it was my goddamn gun. But I kept that firearm unloaded. I checked it myself. It was clean. I personally slipped it into Sam's handbag at Ben's house that night."

"Quentin, why would you be putting a handgun in a lady's bag?"

"It's a long story," he said.

"Long or short, it doesn't matter. What matters is that it is true. And not another one of your Hollywood outlines for a movie."

A faint smile crossed the old man's cracked and dry lips. He looked tired, chronically exhausted, thin, pale, his hair uncombed, and his face covered with a white stubble. If life was a marathon, then from his appearance, the old man was closing in on the tape strung across the finish line.

"I have been too hard on you, Vincent. But everyone in the room that night swore a pact that we would not disclose that any of us had been present. Can you imagine what the Thai authorities would have done had they discovered we were in the room? All of us would have been eating a diet of red rice, sleeping on straw mats, and smacking mosquitoes with our bare hands. I am a very ill man, Vincent. I need daily medication, and constant medical treatment. I have a small fleet of doctors who give me injections, radiation treatment, study my sonar scans and blood tests. Going to prison for a day would have finished me. No one else was anxious to step forward either. Ben, Reed, Pauline. And can you blame them? Poor little Luk Pla, she almost jumped out of her skin, and Ice wasn't all that thrilled by what she had witnessed. The point is, going forward would have changed a suicide into a possible murder investigation and it was my fucking gun that Sam used."

They went into Quentin's office, and the old man rummaged in his desk drawers, opening one, shutting it, then opening another, looking for something.

"Writers are like dictators, and we live in a region of the world where the dictators have larger audiences than writers," said Quentin as he searched in a drawer. "Just like a dictator, we exercise power in an utterly and totally ruthless fashion, killing off any character we think will give us an advantage, our audience a thrill. For reasons or for no reason. Sometimes to evoke strong emotions in our audience; other times because murder, more than any other act, is a high-speed engine to drive any kind of narrative; and some brave soul challenges our authority, then what? You don't have to look very far to find the answer.

"The dictator carries out his purges in the streets, back alleys, and detention cells. And writers, what do they do?

They hire a private eye to investigate their enemies. So what does this mean, Vincent? Simply this: once you divorce power from authority all you are left with is imaginative power. You don't need an army to maintain imaginative power, but you do need an audience, one that believes in your power. An act of faith is required for such a belief, and a lot of people in Hollywood believe they discovered the magic formula for making such an audience throughout the world. And that's why the Osborns, the Mitchells, the McNeals, the Slugos, come to me, because they think I have that magic, and I can pass it on to them. I can anoint them with stardust."

Finally he placed a polished cherry wood presentation box on the desk.

"Open it."

Calvino was thinking there was a gun inside. But he was wrong. As Quentin lifted the lid, he pulled out a small marble piano. There was a small bronze plaque above the keyboard, and it read: "One day you may learn the magic of the music, Rebecca." When Calvino looked up, he saw that there were tears in the old man's eyes. Quentin sat back in his large, leather chair, his pale blue eyes fixed on the ceiling, and Calvino heard the story of what happened the night of Sam McNeal's death from the mouth of a professional storyteller.

"Imaginative power," repeated Quentin, as Calvino removed the small piano.

The way Quentin started the story was to cover the last couple of weeks of Sam's life, which had been a frantic sprint from the shadows that had been tracking her.

371

According to the old man, Sam had taught him breathing exercises that she had learnt after years of intensive ballet training, skills she later honed and refined by years of meditation practice. Controlling her breath had become a zen-like ritual for her, and she believed that if Quentin could master these techniques. He would acquire the watchfulness required to experience each breath; he would observe the actor—the persona of Quentin Stuart—in the act of inhaling and exhaling, watching this self breathe, feeling his breath, finding the void between each breath, and by doing so, he would come to know the very force of life in the rise and fall of such a simple act made non-automatic. That was the theory Sam had advanced. At the end, however, her theory did not hold and she killed herself.

She had confided her most intimate thoughts to Quentin, especially during the time of her break-up with Ben Nakamura. During the middle of the crisis in her personal life, they had been working together on the script for *Temporal Target*. When she wasn't with Quentin, Sam was spending a great deal of her time with Reed Mitchell, and as they grew closer, she began bouncing ideas in the script off Reed, ideas concerning the characters, plot, and the structure of the story. Reed encouraged her, he promised her that he would be her sounding board for any aspect of the project. Reed had sent her pages and pages of notes as the script for *Temporal Target* evolved, and after a couple of weeks, he had started to talk about *Temporal Target* as "their" project.

Quentin had warned her that the first rule of writing was never to discuss a project with anyone. There was no exception to the rule. Friend, family, lover, or seat passenger on a flight to LA. All writing-in-progress was always confidential and top secret. Real writers never talked about what they were doing. Never.

Don't give them anything. Not even a small hint as to the subject matter, title, characterization, plot, location.

The second rule of writing was to cultivate paranoia. Like a dictator assuming everyone around him is trying to assassinate him. A knife stuck in the back, poison poured in the wine, a bomb set under the table. Instead of trying to take his life, they wanted to kidnap his project, hijack his concept. He told her stories of how some writer would be talking about a project over lunch in the back of a restaurant, and the next week there would be an article in Variety about how such and such a studio had optioned a project, which bore a striking resemblance to the one overheard in the restaurant. How mail boys and secretaries had photocopied scripts and passed them on to others in the business for a fee.

FORTY

SAM McNEAL FELT vulnerable after Ben had decided that a bed full of bar *ying*s was more inviting than she was. And she blamed herself for pushing Ben too hard on the Chinese component parts deal. It had seemed simple at the time. She had wanted to help Pauline out. It seemed like such a small favor at the time. Business deal had a way of going sideways; one person promising ivory chopsticks but delivered wooden ones. Everything had gotten fucked up. Ben left her. Pauline had blamed her for not making good on a small favor. At least Reed Mitchell made her laugh; he was fun, and seemed genuinely broken up over events. Quentin smiled and then began his story about one of his last meetings with Sam.

"No one was asking Ben to commit a crime," Sam had confided in Quentin.

"What was the big fucking deal?" Quentin had asked her.

"Ben said why should the Japanese help the Chinese?"

"And I got in the middle of World War II before I even knew what had happened," Sam said. "Ben thought I had gone over to the Chinese side, and all that I said was that Pauline was just as much an American as he was and what was all this bullshit about him being Japanese and her being Chinese. After all we were all living in Thailand."

"I never trusted Nakamura anyway," said Quentin. That only made her feel defensive. "It was my fault," she said.

"You just gave him an excuse," Quentin had said. "He wanted to play alone on the playground."

She had sighed and shook her head. "You don't know how Ben thinks."

"I don't want to know the little bastard either," Quentin had said.

Not long afterwards she had taken up with Reed Mitchell and it didn't take much time before she found herself involved with another kamikaze pilot who had been assigned by a massive international company to fly corporate missions for them in the Big Weird. By then, it was too late to bail out.

She was in no emotional condition to admit that she had made a second mistake and to throw over Reed Mitchell, who was a young, good-looking guy and who was showing a real, passionate interest in her at a time when her own self-esteem was at an all-time low. He appeared to be that rare kind of *farang*: one who had not come down with The Sickness. Her relationship with Reed, however, did not come without costs; the schedule of costs was like a balloon-payment mortgage. Easy payments at first, effortless, and then a massive payment notice is served. In Reed's case, he didn't waste a great deal of time before serving notice for the first heavy payment. It started with his making demands over the script; he had begun to change the script she gave to him. He had the work on his hard disk and at night, after they made love, Reed was at the computer, changing dialogue, changing story, changing just about anything he decided needed to be improved. Afterwards, he printed out the revised draft and gave it to her, telling her to take it back to Quentin, saying she had worked on it overnight, and had added a few minor changes.

"What is this, Sam?" asked Quentin, looking up from Reed's printout.

"Changes," she said softly. "A few changes."

Sam started to cry, and told Quentin the whole story. His advice was to blow Reed Mitchell off. Sam said that Pauline Cheng had given her the same advice, and Quentin said that perhaps Pauline Cheng had a brain after all and that she should listen to Pauline.

"Sure, easy for you to say. I listened to Pauline about Ben and look where that got me," sobbed Sam. "I was the one who was blown off. Besides, Pauline thinks all *farang* men who live in Bangkok are fucked up emotionally," said Sam.

"Generalizations like that happen when the thought processes go haywire," said Quentin. "I take back what I said about her having a brain."

"She's been a very supportive friend, Quentin." He decided not to point out the contradiction inherent in her view of Pauline's role in her love life.

The next night she lay in bed next to Reed Mitchell, feeling wanted, feeling desired. The next installment payment for his performance was a demand for him to be present the next time that she worked on the script with Quentin. Sam approached the old man with the request.

"If he could just sit in on one meeting," she had pleaded.

"It doesn't work that way, Sam. If he sits in on one meeting, he will want to come to the next meeting, and the next. There will be no end to it," Quentin said. "Let me tell you something, darling. In all my years in Hollywood, I never collaborated on a script with anyone. Some asshole at the studio might have brought in another writer but that was different. That's how the business works. A script might go through a dozen writers before a studio signs off on it. The screen credit might end up looking like a roll call for the dead pulled out from some monster car crash on the Santa Monica freeway, but I never worked with another writer. But I broke that rule for you."

"You only broke it because you feel guilty about what happened between you and my mother," she had said. "And you think by helping me that you are repairing what was broken and beyond repair."

"Yes, and because I think you had a good idea. Guilt coupled with a commercial idea was good enough reason to break a lifelong rule and to share a credit. But please, Sam, tell this Reed character that no fucking way am I going to have him at our working sessions."

Matters were not to end either that cleanly or that simply. Having miscalculated Quentin's reaction, she felt like a fool. Reed Mitchell had anticipated resistance from Quentin and had prepared himself with a game plan to fight back. One evening, as Reed finished revising the four pages of script that Sam had brought back after her working session with Quentin, he read each page out and Sam sat across from him and listened. Then he handed her the pages and had her read each line of dialogue.

"Don't you see how much better this version is? I mean, the old guy isn't doing his best work here. He's not at the top of his form. You can't be blamed, you haven't done this before."

"Neither have you," said Sam.

"But I have seen hundreds and hundreds of movies. I have studied them. Memorized them; every shot, every cut. And I am telling you what you just read is much, much better."

"Quentin won't change his mind. I know him. He will just dig in deeper. So let's forget it."

"Hey, now that is your problem. You don't have a creative mind."

"According to Quentin, I do." She twisted her head toward the mirror and looked at herself and Reed.

"What does he know? He helped you write that shit you brought home in a doggy bag."

"If you are so down on him, why do you want to bother working with him?"

They were a couple, she thought.

"Because he is the tunnel to Hollywood," said Reed, wrapping his arms around her, unhooking her bra, his fingers finding her breasts and squeezing them. "Fast track. Speed of light into the belly of the beast, and the old monsters are eating the story before they even know it has gone into their system. Quentin can do that. He can open any fucking door in Hollywood. But once you go in, then you have to have more than your dick in your hand. What you've been writing with Quentin doesn't even qualify as a dick."

"What more do you want me to do, Reed?" She pulled away and turned her back to him.

"We stage the Russian roulette scene. What do you say?"

"Which one?" She half-turned so that he could see her face but not her breasts.

Reed Mitchell had already decided how to answer that question. "The scene we worked on tonight. Why don't we have a little dress rehearsal. Like the pun? And let's invite Quentin and a few friends along to watch. Let's make it a must-be-there, insider social occasion. He likes showing Baby Fish around town. We give him the opportunity to display his Baby Fish, and he gets a chance to watch us make this scene come alive."

"Where are we going to get the gun?"

"I have read two books about Quentin's obsession with guns. He has collected enough guns to arm the Cambodian army. Let him supply us with the hardware that we need. Since he's your best friend, you shouldn't have any trouble asking him for a gun."

"In Bangkok? Quentin has a gun?"

"Of course, he has one. You told me that you saw it one day in his desk drawer. An ancient Smith & Wesson. A collectible that he couldn't part with. Remember, dummy?"

She regretted having ever told him that. Playing dumb, only made her look dumb and she hated herself for giving away too much too soon.

"What do you want me to do?"

"Borrow his old . 8 Smith & Wesson," said Reed.

"I am not going to steal Quentin's gun," she said. "Who said anything about stealing it, dumbo. We need it as a prop. Afterwards, you give it back to him. I mean, did you really think we wanted to keep it?"

"This is crazy, Reed."

"But you can do it. He adores you. I adore you. Borrow Quentin's gun."

She caved in, hating herself, knowing how much Pauline Cheng would abuse her for not standing up to Reed. It was a repeat of her relationship with Ben. But she couldn't help herself, and what harm would there be in borrowing Quentin's gun? He had once told her that if there was anything that she ever needed, then all she had to do was ask. Quentin would be there for her. It was an unwritten rule that they never talked about the relationship Quentin had had with her mother. Somehow her presence was always in the room with them; Sam looked like her mother, same chin, mouth, eyes. No question that Quentin would have done anything for her, so she talked herself into borrowing the gun.

The concept of *Temporal Target* was, despite Quentin's protest, a modern version of *The Deer Hunter*. A 90s free fall into the hell of a Southeast Asian tiger. The premise was that Bangkok had a class of rich and bored expats. These excitement junkies were on the prowl for new kicks; men and women looking for a new edge to hang their toes over. The old guy bar scenes were boring, déclassé, choked with unpackaged *farang*s in the final stages of The Sickness. These new cool, packaged *farang*s mostly avoided the bars unless they were going slumming. The clubs were their niche; a hangout where they could throw around lots of money, believing that they were in the presence of exclusive women.

Then one night, a small group of expats decided to slam against the back wall of their own imagination; they had nowhere else to go, nothing else to see or do, and that left them flirting with the whore of death. One member of the group comes up with a new twist on the old linkage between blood, death, sex, and musical chairs. Two beautiful hookers would be chosen for the evening of entertainment. They would be given a story about being selected to enter a contest. A lottery in which the winners died. The death would be quick, and not painful. The one who lived would be rich enough to retire, buy the house, the car, the good life. It was full throttle on the risk pedal.

The contest would either take them out of hell or send them directly to hell. Each of the men agreed to throw ten grand into the common pot. One fifty-grand winner took all of the prize money. The police classified the death as a suicide. In Bangkok, suicide among the working *ying*s was not an infrequent event. Police paid little attention to the occasional prostitute who turned up with a bullet in the head. Self-inflicted wounds in working *ying*s happened often enough to be categorized as death by natural causes. All the forensic tests in the world would come back with the same result: the woman shot herself. No foul play.

The women chosen as participants, in the homemade movie of life and death, were not just Thai, but Russians, Poles, Chinese, Burmese, Khmer, a wide open number of nationalities who appeared on the list of eligible candidates; women from totally fucked up beyond recognition countries who had little to lose and much to gain in playing Russian roulette. For the first time in months and months, this small circle of expat men believed that they had found the excitement, which had gone missing in their lives. They placed side bets with each other on the outcome of the evening. They drew straws to see which member won the right to sleep with the winner.

Quentin Stuart's original idea for the script had been inspired from a newspaper story about a Russian prostitute who had been found dead in a short-time room. The police said that she had shot herself to death. She was just another violent expat death. In Reed's mind, however, he had copyrighted the idea, the concept was his and he intended to play for keeps. His plan was to set up one of the scenes that he had written for the screenplay, and one that Quentin had discarded. In this scene, the Russian hooker is seated across the table from a *farang* who has a scarf tied around his forehead just like Christopher Walken in *The Deer Hunter*. The two of them have decided to play. Members of the club had become bored just watching the hookers blowing out their brains, one member had decided to up the stakes and play the game himself.

FORTY-ONE

IT HAPPENED AND it was fated to happen exactly the way that it did. This was Quentin Stuart's firm belief Sam, Reed, and Pauline carefully planned the evening. The handpicked group of guests had assembled in the living room of Ben Nakamura's traditional teak house. Reed, who had known Ben for several years, had convinced him that the party would be a healing experience; and the opportunity would arise for him to break with Sam. They could put an end to the bitterness and disappointment.

The lure for Ben was that he would be accepted back into the right social group; he would be wanted, loved, and respected. Mitchell hit every right chord with Nakamura. The party was planned; the evening was locked in. This was to be the Hollywood party to end all Bangkok parties that pretended to be Hollywood parties. Reed wrapped his arms around Ben's neck, hugged him and confessed that he would get the credit for launching Hollywood into the Asia party circuit, and that certain scenes from the screenplay that Reed and Sam were doing with Quentin would be reenacted in his sitting room.

"I am talking about a first. Something that no one will forget. This party is going to make you famous, Ben," said Reed.

"But famous for what?"

Famous last words in question form.

"As the man who made it all happen. Created the scene. People will talk about you. They will hold you in awe. What do you say?"

Reed and Sam were the first to arrive at Ben's house. Reed had a bottle of champagne. Sam carried red roses. "Doesn't she look great? The girl. The flowers. The film."

A smile flickered across Ben's face, and died like one of those barbecue fires that won't start. "Sam, what can I get you to drink?"

"Gin and tonic," she said, looking him straight in the eye. "It's what I always drink. Have you forgotten?"

"Come on," said Reed, setting down his champagne bottle.

"This man forgets nothing. He has a memory like an elephant."

Quentin arrived a few minutes later with Luk Pla, Ice, and Slugo. Ben Nakamura came out of the kitchen with Reed's bottle of champagne and a bucket of ice. Pauline Cheng came into the room shortly after Sam and Reed; she had been downstairs drinking at the bar. The only stranger in the group was a Russian woman whose street name was Spike. No one knew her real name. Spike was about twenty-five, a tall blonde, slightly overweight as her flesh pushed the seams of her red sequined dress with a slit which revealed enough thigh to make it clear she was a working *ying*. She had large hips, big hands and feet, and a rubbery smile. A brown beauty mark was on her right cheek, and no one was sure whether it was painted on, tattooed on, or was the result of her mother being frightened by a spider while she was still in the womb. None of those details mattered, because Spike had skin so pale that it appeared translucent. The Chinese in the playground had a fetish about pure white-skinned women. That Ivory soap 99.4% pure skin that took you as close to perfection as it was possible to achieve. Spike could have had her nose hair curling over a mustache and it would not have mattered to the Chinese who would have seen nothing but miles of all that white skin.

Reed had brought along a video of The Deer Hunter and arranged with Ben to have the movie playing on his television, one of those modern jobs with a huge flat screen. Reed, who had dressed in a safari jacket, and jeans, with a red scarf tied around his forehead, pressed the VCR remote control and played the Russian roulette scene over and over, three, four times. There was food and drink. And after the first run through of the Russian roulette scene, some of the audience started to talk among themselves. Members of the crowd drifted in and out of the room. Some disappeared into the upstairs washrooms to do drugs. Ice had brought a couple of grams of cocaine after Luk Pla predicted that it could be a heavy, boring night.

"In cyberspace, everyone is a virtual expat," said Slugo, as he put an arm around Ice.

"You give me a thousand baht. I need money," said Ice, with a trace of cocaine on her nostrils.

"Give her money," said Luk Pla.

"You know what I saw in cyberspace the other day?" Slugo had asked Reed, ignoring the plea for money.

"A married woman in Chicago posted a message, *If I sleep with six men in one week, will I still have my integrity?* And I thought that if Ice slept with only six men in one week her integrity would be seriously damaged."

Ben walked among his guests, holding up a bottle of champagne and a bottle of red wine. It was, after all, his party.

"What would you like?" he asked Luk Pla

She pointed at the red bottle. Ben filled her a glass.

"Baby Fish like red wine because you look at glass and see it's wine. You have a glass of champagne, and people, think, what is that girl drinking? She's a stupid girl, don't know that she can drink wine. White wine and champagne don't look like wine."

Ben then turned to Ice.

"You want red, too?" he asked.

"I want the fucking champagne in the ice bucket," she said, grinning.

"Ice continues to develop," said Slugo.

Near the television set was a wooden table and two chairs. Someone had taken the time and devoted the attention to get all the details right. They looked like props out of *The Deer Hunter*. At one point, Quentin stared at his watch, a bored expression crossed his face. Ice and Luk Pla were eating sticky rice and fish paste with their fingers, giggling and whispering about Spike's ugly red dress.

"Let's get started," said Quentin, clapping his hands together.

"Start what?" called Ben from the back.

"Jesus, Ben, it is your party. Aren't you in control?" asked Slugo.

"Art imitates life, and life imitates art," Reed said, pulling back the chair and sitting down. He reached under the table where he found Sam's handbag. Not a conventional handbag, but one of those all-purpose bags that would hold a change of clothes, a couple of books and scripts and still not be filled. He pulled out Quentin's nickel-plated gun.

"Hey, what do we have here?" Reed asked. "Someone has nickel plated an antique gun. An antique purist would weep. Still, it is a lovely weapon."

Quentin no longer looked bored. After the shock wore off, he looked angry and saw Sam a few feet away making a conscious effort to avoid meeting his stare. She stood close to Pauline Cheng, one arm looped around Pauline's waist; both had dipped into Ice's stash of cocaine. The way they stood together, they could have been in another dimension; they might have been surfing cyberspace in a double-seated van.

"Sam, could I have a word with you?" asked Quentin.

Her head jerked around. "You let me borrow it, Quentin. Remember? Please, don't get mad."

"Spike, sit down," Reed said to the Russian.

She had not smiled once since she walked into the room. Turning her head, she coughed into a cupped hand, then obeyed Reed's instructions, sliding into the chair. Reed handed her a silk scarf.

"Tie it around your head just like mine." Reed touched the barrel of the gun to his temple.

Spike blinked, looked down at the scarf. The living room had gone silent and even Ben had moved from the back of the room and joined the others. Beads of sweat, trapped in the ridges of her heavily made-up face, made her forehead glisten in the light. More sweat gathered on Spike's upper lip. She sat in the chair, immobilized, looking at the scarf.

"You do understand English?" asked Reed.

She looked up at *The Deer Hunter* on the television screen just in time to watch a Thai playing a Vietnamese blow his brains out. "Hey, put on the fucking headgear, Spike."

"Stop pushing her," said Sam, coming up behind Reed's chair. "You are being an asshole."

"Of course he's an asshole," said Pauline.

Spike's hands were trembling, she tried to steady her hands by holding onto the edge of the table, but that didn't work; it was like she had grabbed a downed power line and electricity surged through her body. Pure fear froze the Russian woman's face into a mask of horror. She was thinking that no matter how much she struggled to get out of the grim dead-end life in Russia, it didn't matter. The unimaginable stared right into her eyes with a single message: her own death. She did not want to die. She did not want to pretend about dying. No one had any trouble reading her desperation; she had made a bargain with Reed in the cold light of day, in the abstract, it had been just words, just theory—or so it seemed—and when the time arrived, she couldn't go through with it.

"Who's pushing her? She hasn't been forced into servitude. The fact she isn't in Mother Russia shows that she's free. Besides, I bought three hours of her time. Cash up front."

"It's just a game," said Ice, sipping her champagne. "I know, but I can't," said Spike. She pushed the scarf back across the table.

"Why? Because it doesn't match that wonderful dress from Kiev?" Reed reached over and plucked one of the red roses he brought, leaned over, and put it in her hair. He smiled. "Don't you look lovely."

"I am afraid of guns," she said. "The Mafia kill my uncle with a gun. Kill my brother. Kill many people. You don't know Russia. Killing all the time. Guns everywhere. Cheap guns. Cheap lives. No good."

"Okay, go, go. Get out," Reed shouted at her across the table.

As soon as Spike was on her feet and away from the center of action, Sam had whipped around the table and sat down in the chair facing Reed. Spike's rose had fallen from her hair and lay on the table. Sam picked it up and carefully put it in her hair.

"This is what you wanted, isn't it, Reed?"

He watched as Spike, clutching her bag, ran to the end of the sitting room and out the door. No one ever saw her again.

Quentin pressed his fingers on the edge of the table. "Sam, let's go. Take my hand and we will walk out of here together. I am your friend. You don't want to do this. Just take my hand."

She stared at Quentin's outstretched hand, then looked at Reed again.

"Sam has a free will, doesn't she?"

"It's okay, Quentin. Like Ice said, it's just a game." She tied the scarf around her temple. "Winner takes all, right Sam?"

"Meaning the script, dummy."

Luk Pla's eyes were like two black holes. She could not say anything, clutching Quentin's hand and watching what she took to be two very crazy *farang* people playing with a gun.

"Is it loaded?" asked Ben Nakamura. "One blank."

"Reed, I actually hate the idea of guns and violence," said Slugo. "Why do you think I live in Bangkok? I am rich. I could live anywhere. America is full of guns. Can't we drink more champagne and put the gun away?"

"Go online and find an avatar to masturbate with, Slugo," said Reed.

"Reed, put the gun away," said Quentin. "There have been cases where actors have been killed by a blank."

"Hey, you think I am stupid? There's only a quarter load of powder. No one is going to get hurt. Don't forget, we are doing this one for you. Just relax. It's a scene out of a movie. You've been around movie sets all your life. You just have to get into it. Think of Ben's place as a place where we are making a film."

Reed then swung halfway around in his chair, pointed the remote control at the VCR and pressed the button and the characters in *The Deer Hunter* ran backwards until they reached the Russian roulette scene. Then Reed started the scene and turned back to the table. The gun was in the center of the table. For a couple of minutes, Reed and Sam locked eyes, their breathing synchronized; Quentin knew that she was using her ballet training to keep her focus, her balance, and her sense of purpose. Her ribcage moved in and out. Reed took the old Smith & Wesson . 8 first, pressed the barrel against his temple, pulled the trigger. A dull click filled the room, and he handed the gun to Sam. She spun the cylinder and pointed the gun to her head. Her finger hovered near the trigger, she squinted her eyes, never once taking them off Reed. She slowly pulled the trigger. Another dull click. She opened her eyes, and handed the gun back to Reed.

"You are doing well, babe," said Reed. "I like your style."

"Yours stinks," she said.

He gave the cylinder a spin, then another spin for good luck. Putting the barrel to his right temple, he pulled the trigger. On the TV screen, a gunshot rang out loud and sharp, and one of the Asian actors fell dead onto the floor. In the room all that registered was the click of firing a gun with no bullet in the chamber. Once again he passed Quentin's prized handgun to Sam.

She sighed, looked over, a crooked smile on her face, and gave Quentin a wink. A moment later, her finger pressed the trigger and the shot echoed around the room. The pungent smell of cordite spread outward from the table. The sound had nearly ruptured their eardrums. Some were yawning to get their hearing back. Others fell back In shock at the scene. And there was a great deal of blood and brains, as half of Sam's head had been blown off.

A blue haze of smoke stung everyone's eyes. Reed started to say something, then stopped. Ice screamed, her knees crumpled and she passed out on the floor as if someone had shot an arrow into her back. Pauline Cheng wept uncontrollably, running forward to hug Sam's body. Quentin knelt down beside Pauline and put his arm around Sam's lifeless body. The warm blood flowed onto his arm.

"Reed, you sonofabitch. You said that you had put in a blank." Quentin voice dropped to a whisper.

"Of course, I did. Do you think that I would be crazy enough to put a loaded gun to my own head? Fuck, that could have been me."

Reed had turned white, his hands shaking like Spike's hands had been shaking not more than ten minutes earlier. His voice broke as he spoke and his legs were rubbery as he tried to stand up before falling back in his chair. It had happened so fast that it was taking some time for the reality to sink in. Sam McNeal was dead. Not play dead. She was real life dead, out of his world, really gone. Not another word, not another kiss, and not another laugh. The red rose lay on the floor beside her body.

"Someone in this room put a bullet in the gun," said Quentin.

"Maybe it was you, Quentin," said Reed.

The old man hit him across the face with an open hand.

"Shut the fuck up, Reed."

Quentin looked at the faces around the room. He knew everyone: Ice, Luk Pla, Ben, Reed, Slugo, and Pauline. And there was the Russian woman who had fled the scene. Who would have done this? Could someone not in the room have made the change, removing Reed's blank—assuming he used a blank in the first place—and substituted a real bullet? Perhaps someone who wanted the Russian woman dead? But there was no assurance that the Russian would have ended up dead, and there would have been far easier ways to dispatch her. The intellect revolted against the trail of evidence leading to a professional hit ordered by the Russian Mafia; they were not that creative. Before the evening was out, everyone in the room agreed that Quentin would be allowed to take charge of the investigation.

A pact was made by everyone who had been at Ben's house, which no one would speak to the police or another living soul about what happened the night that Sam died. As far as the outside world was to know, the house was empty. Sam had arrived alone, waited for Ben in the living room, become despondent over the end of their love affair, and killed herself. The most important element of the deception was that Sam McNeal had died alone. Had died watching *The Deer Hunter* in the house of her ex-lover. She had intended to send a message. It was not a message of hope; it had been a message of despair and hate. The problem was that anyone close to Sam would have trouble believing that message.

FORTY-TWO

ALAN OSBORN SLUMPED to one side, his nose nearly touching the glass front of the Mermaidium, his breath had fogged a circle about half the size of his head onto the exterior pane. As if he were in deep contemplation, he sat with one arm folded around his mid-section. He was not wearing his glasses. Pulling his head back slightly, he took a long drag from his cigarette, which he held cupped inside the palm of his hand. He had the distinct look of someone with a grievance or someone on the edge of madness as he rocked back on his heels, knocking a long gray cigarette ash onto the floor. As Calvino moved alongside, he discovered the source of Osborn's devout attention was a piece of graffiti. In New York City no one would have looked twice at it. But this graffiti was not scrawled in the subway or on the side of a building. This graffiti had been etched into Osborn's work of art. Someone had used a glass cutter to carve the words "Fuck You" in large letters on the front of the tank. Osborn ran his finger down the back of the letter "F" and sighed.

"Obviously a Cambridge man," he said. "Or an existentialist killer," said Calvino.

Osborn dropped his cigarette on the floor and crushed it with his foot. "You know what the owner said when I showed him?" Calvino shook his head.

"He said, it could have been worse. The killer might have written 'Free Willy.' Have you noticed how every second-rate mind now thinks about the world in terms of movie titles? I actually prefer 'fuck you.' "

"I need to ask you a favor," said Calvino.

Osborn reached into his shirt pocket and took out another cigarette.

"I am flattered, Mr. Calvino."

"I want you to break into a safe."

Osborn sighed, slowly shaking his head, as the smoke rolled out of his nostrils.

"I am in the aquarium and show business fields. Safe-cracking I leave to other artists."

"I saw the way you opened that lock last night. You knew exactly what to do. Who but a pro opens a lock with a couple pieces of wire? I had this insight last night. Maybe you changed careers, you did a little time for opening locks in strangers' houses in England."

"How did you find that out?"

"You just told me. Besides, I had a hunch *The Visitations* was written by someone on the inside and not a visitor. The main clue was the story about the thief who threw the brick through a window to steal a TV. I liked the part about the brick crashing through the screen of a 25" Sony TV."

Osborn nodded. "Leonard had intended to steal the TV, the stupid bugger."

"After throwing the brick, he ran down the street, stole a car that turned out to be a police car. In the narrative, this man had the visitors rolling on the floor with laughter. He told one joke after another after another. But he wasn't any good as a thief. His cellmate taught him the trade, and after a few months, the bad thief turned into a well-trained thief. When that happened he lost his sense of humor. He could no longer make anyone laugh. It was a sad story.

"It was a true story. But somehow I had a feeling that I should leave it out of the collection. Only I couldn't bring myself to pull it. I was weak. Poor Leonard was such a superb comic. His story made the book. Without it *The Visitations* would have been second-rate. The pity is that Leonard would never amount to more than an ordinary thief. Unfortunately for people who lived on King's Road in London, Leonard found that stealing was a more secure way to make money than making people laugh. In a perfect world, people like Leonard ought to be rich. Comedians should run governments, churches, and police forces."

"Some would say that they do," said Calvino.

The Mermaidium had been drained. The empty interior bore no marks of Slugo having been inside. Earl Luce was at the Police Hospital morgue taking photographs of Slugo, thought Calvino.

"Last night was terrible. I can't stop thinking about poor Slugo," said Osborn.

"Will you help me?"

"Let me ask you, are you intending to break into someone's private house?"

Calvino nodded.

"Can you help me?"

"I guess there isn't much more money in being a private eye than being a comic."

"I am not looking for money," said Calvino.

Osborn shook his head and coughed as he pulled the cigarette from his lips.

"Non-monetary break-ins are always the most problematic. Money I can understand. That's a valid reason to commit a crime. Crimes of conviction, crimes of principle are in the realm of politics. In which case you should hire the services of a politician. They have the expertise in such matters."

"You won't help me."

"Don't rush me, Mr. Calvino. I am thinking about how best to remove 'Fuck You' from a work of art and you wish to involve me in crime without monetary reward. I need a moment to reflect."

"I am asking you as an artist," said Calvino. "As a friend of Slugo's."

"You are asking me to break the law. And, besides, what does this have to do with Slugo?"

"I have a plan to catch his killer."

"And what do I get out of it?" asked Osborn. "Except, possibly, being shot at by the killer or arrested by the police?"

"I know someone who can remove that graffiti so you will never know that it was there."

"In that case, of course I will do it," said Osborn.

Calvino crawled over the concrete wall first, then waited until Osborn climbed over and lowered himself down into a small garden. His lungs wheezed from having inhaled too many cigarettes. Calvino watched as Osborn caught his breath.

"Are you all right?" asked Calvino in a whisper.

"I used to be quite fit. But fitness doesn't go with the image of an artist, does it?"

"Let's go," said Calvino, moving across the garden. It was after two in the morning and the neighborhood had a flat Kafkaesque silence. They were deep into a dead-end sub-soi off Soi Chang. Fortunately, the house wasn't inside the usual family compound and, another stroke of good luck, there were no dogs. And the servants' quarters were off in the far corner and away from the main house. Structure was a better description; it was not so much a house as a kind of makeshift bunker—a flat concrete box, a tiled roof with a gentle slope, and in the back, facing the garden, a large sliding door that opened onto a large wooden verandah. Calvino climbed the three steps up to the wooden verandah and knelt down beside a table and a couple of deck chairs. Osborn moved up to the verandah, checking the windows, looking back at the perimeter wall. Dressed in black, Osborn's face was painted black and he wore black gloves so all that was visible were the whites of his eyes and teeth. Along the edge of the verandah were potted flowering plants and large ceramic bowls with small fish inside.

"Who does this house belong to?" asked Osborn. "A client who has failed to pay your fees?"

"Does it matter?" replied Calvino, who had reached into a small tool bag, removed a ring with half a dozen metal augurs attached and resting on one knee, began to pick the lock on the sliding glass door.

Osborn watched for a moment before he removed two thin wires from his trouser pocket.

"Let me do that or we will be here all night. I had no idea that you were such a novice," said Osborn, moving in front of the door and inserting the wires.

"Watch how an expert does it. And you might just learn something about the art of breaking and entering."

In under two minutes, Osborn had them inside an empty room, which was dark except for the ambient dots of red and green lights flashing off and on from a dozen modems stacked in rows, one on top of the other. A penumbra of light from all the computer equipment cast just enough light to illuminate the surface objects: papers, diskettes, coffee mugs, plates, newspapers; this light came from four or five computer screens on two long, intersecting tables.

"Where is the safe?" asked Osborn.

Calvino squatted down beside one end of the tables and pointed a small flashlight at the safe. "That's it."

"You call that a safe?"

"What would you call it?"

"A successful marketing campaign."

"Can you open it?"

"Calvino, don't insult me. Of course I can open it." Osborn rolled himself out flat on the floor, removed more thin wires from his pocket, and had the safe door open in under ten minutes. As he moved back from the opened door, Calvino's flashlight revealed a large Cheshire smile of satisfaction on Osborn's blackened face. He appeared as a small boy who had won his first chess game, only the patchwork of lines around the eyes, deeply shadowed like trenches, distracted from the illusion. He was all eyes and teeth. But his sense of accomplishment managed to shine through his shoe- polish blackened face. Pride sledding down the steep slope to the place where adult approval was waiting to applaud and pat him on the back.

"You did that with wires?" asked Calvino. "You can lever the world with a wire."

Both of them looked inside as Calvino shined the flashlight inside.

"Alas, as you predicted, no money," said Osborn, pulling out a single twenty-baht note, examining it and then putting it back inside. "Nothing but computer diskettes. You haven't taken to software piracy as your game?"

"Shut up, Alan." Calvino removed several rows of magnetic computer diskettes, the kind that were used in optical readers and stored mega amounts of data. The diskettes were in plastic cases. He stacked them on the floor. He shined the flashlight on the labels. He found one marked "Vanuatu Back-up" and another marked "TelecommunicationsProtocol—T-486." He slipped both into his jacket pocket. Finally, as he reached the back of the safe, he found what he was looking for.

It was a box of .8 cartridges. He lifted the lid. Holding the flashlight between his teeth, he counted the rounds. One round had gone missing. As he counted the rounds one more time, the overhead lights came on, filling the room with bright lights. Calvino and Osborn ducked down lower underneath the table. Pauline Cheng entered the room wearing her trademark pair of shorts and a mock Microsoft T-shirt. Calvino leaned forward as he hunched beneath the table, tracking her movement across the room. Pauline, stopped, walked back, and finally sat down in a chair on the opposite side. She turned on a compact disk player and the sound of k.d. lang's "Even Cowgirls Get the Blues" blared out. Osborn put his hands over his ears, sitting with his chin on his knees and his eyes closed.

"Don't tell me, it's the police," whispered Osborn.

"No," Calvino whispered back. "Relax. We'll be out of here soon."

Calvino crawled out from underneath the table, clutching the box of cartridges. He stood up and cleared his throat. At first, he received no reaction; Pauline was deeply absorbed as her fingers raced over the keyboard, her eyes on the screen. He suspected that she might be replying to an e-mail.

"Pauline, it is time for a D&M," Calvino said.

She turned around, one hand touching her throat, and for the first time, he thought that just maybe he had caught her with her guard down. Her hand came down and she knocked a coffee mug onto the floor and the shards flew across the room. She was shaking, wrapping her arms around herself in a childlike embrace.

"A what?"

"A deep and meaningful conversation," Calvino said. "I am going to phone the police," she said. There was little conviction in this threat.

"Not a bad idea. Phone them. Ask for a Colonel Pratt. You know the colonel, he's been in this room before. Looking at Shakespeare websites. And all of the time these were only a couple of feet away."

He held up the box of .8 shells and rattled it. As stand-offs went, this was a relatively short, easy one. Pauline's eyes were glued to the box as Calvino opened it and removed one of the bullets. He had called her bluff and she stood, shaking, staring at the phone. She held the receiver not like someone intending to make a phone call but as a possible weapon to hurl. Finally, as they locked eyes, she put the receiver down. Osborn crawled out on all fours from under the table and stood up, rubbing his knee and grimacing.

"I have cut my knee," Osborn said, as he took away his hand and a trickle of blood appeared on his fingers. He lowered himself to the floor, tore up his pant leg and took out a piece of broken coffee mug.

"It was an accident," said Pauline, looking at the box of . 8s.

"We surprised you," said Osborn, looking at the piece of ceramic shrapnel.

"She means Sam's death," said Calvino.

"An accident? I thought she killed herself," said Osborn.

"She had no intention of killing herself, did she, Pauline?" Calvino had moved to within a couple of feet of Pauline Cheng, who had slumped down into a chair.

Osborn limped off to the bathroom, leaking droplets of blood from his cut.

"Wounded in the line of duty. I'll be back," he said. But neither Calvino nor Pauline were listening.

She had gone from fear to a raging anger in a matter of seconds. Whatever lapse of confidence Pauline had suffered in discovering the intruders was restored. She was ready for action.

"Don't pretend you really care anything about Sam McNeal," she said to Calvino. "Men in this city see women, all women, as entertainment. They are objects rotated according to your crude instincts. Men like you and your friend put young women into aquariums for the amusement of men."

"You didn't happen to write 'Fuck You' on my Mermaidium?" asked Osborn as he opened the bathroom door.

Pauline shouted at him, "You're a disgusting pig."

"Why did I think you would adopt that point of view?" asked Osborn as he slammed the door behind him, leaving Pauline to square off alone with Calvino.

She was not even close to being finished.

"*Farang* men in Bangkok are a parody of what men should be for women. I am not just talking about promiscuity. You are selfish, careless, unfeeling. It's about your attitude about sleeping with as many women as possible and taking no responsibility for your actions."

"Are you saying that you're different? You are going to take responsibility for your action in putting a live round in the gun before Sam and Reed played Russian roulette?"

"The men in Bangkok are psychopaths. They live pornographic lives."

"Killing a Slugo rids the world of another psychopath?"

"Of moral pollution, yes."

"Let's take the murders one at a time. It wasn't a man who was responsible for Sam's death," said Calvino.

That did nothing to silence her rage.

"What do you want? And what right do you have to break into my office?"

Calvino ignored both questions. "Sam confided in you about her relationship with Ben Nakamura, and you used your friendship to try and swing a deal with one of your *guanxi* offshore connections. You pressured Sam until she wrecked her relationship with Ben. Then you brought in WULF to take revenge on him because he wouldn't go along with what you wanted. You set up a team to flame Ben, sending each piece of e-mail to a long list of his friends and colleagues. You tried to destroy him.

"When Sam began seeing Reed Mitchell, she told you every intimate detail of the affair, how he was pressuring her over the script, trying to get a meeting with Quentin Stuart. You told her to dump the guy and get a real life. She wanted to; she even tried to follow your advice, but she wasn't strong enough to do it. You told Sam that her relationship was destructive. How it was destroying her self-esteem and that Reed was only using her to get to Quentin. Once he got direct access to Quentin, the next step would be for him to dump her altogether.

"You pleaded with her; you begged her to break off with him. You wanted her to go back to Ben so you could have a second try. But that relationship was finished. And you didn't get the Japanese company to sign off on the T-486 component. They didn't want to touch it. They knew about the Chinese Long March -B rocket and the sub-contractor on that project was also the T-486 manufacturer. That must have been a loss of face as big as the Great Wall of China.

"While you are trying to build the new China, Sam was doing the best that she could to keep her relationship with Reed going. It wasn't much of a relationship, but it was all that she had. Of course Ben and Reed being in the same business, Ben told him about your pressure to fall in behind the decision to change from the American components to the Chinese T-486 rocket killer. That made Sam's relationship even more dangerous for you. With the help of WULF, you had neutralized Ben. What about Reed? Sam kept going back to him no matter how many times she promised that she had decided never to see him or call him again.

"Sam told you about Reed's idea to arrange a Russian roulette game. He had hired a Russian hooker and Reed planned to sit across the table from the hooker while The Deer Hunter played on a VCR. The inner circle of friends would witness Reed's play-acting. You also knew that Quentin Stuart was going along to watch because Sam told you. You knew that Sam had arranged to borrow Quentin's antique Smith & Wesson, and she told you it was a . 8, and you saw your opportunity. A bullet-proof way to advance the cause of WULF and protect your Chinese friends with their defective components. This was far more effective than knocking out one of Slugo's virtual reality avatars in cyberspace. This was gonna be the real thing. There will be so much publicity that you would become a legend in your own time.

"Isn't it one of the great strategies from *The Art of War* that you find a third hand to destroy your enemy for you? But you thought that you had found a foolproof way: that Reed's plan would allow the enemy to destroy the enemy. It was a fail-proof scheme to advance the cause of women and free your friend Sam from Reed Mitchell. All you had to do was buy a box of bullets, remove the blank that Reed had put in the chamber and replace it with a live round. Then you could stand back with the others and watch as the Russian prostitute and

Reed played what they thought was a pretend game of Russian roulette.

"If the Russian blew out her brains, then you and your friends at WULF would have found your new martyr. Her face would have been on every electronic bulletin board that Chinese money could buy. And if Reed took the hit, then, even better, an abusive man, a packaged *farang* in Bangkok becomes the dead creep who got what he deserved. You have a great message for the media: Reed Mitchell, killed in a sordid attempt to kill prostitutes for pleasure. It's no longer just the lower classes satisfying their animal desires with young Asian women, but *farang*s from the privileged, elite class who were paying women not only for sex but for the opportunity to blow out their brains for money.

"But something went wrong at the party. Everyone watched as the Russian sat across from Reed. There was a hitch. The Russian had some sixth sense about the gun, the set-up, the game, and she backed out. What I don't understand is why you didn't stop the game when Sam sat down? Was it because as you saw her at the table, you saw she made even a better victim than the Russian prostitute? Sam was from the upper class, just like Reed, and that meant that the game was on an equal footing. They each had a fifty-fifty chance of winning. And they had an equal chance of dying. You could have grabbed the gun from Sam and emptied the live round. Why didn't you?"

Pauline hadn't attempted to interrupt once as Calvino had laid out his version of the case. She waited a few seconds after he finished to reply to his questions. The anger had receded and she looked more reflective.

"You don't think that I haven't asked myself that question a hundred times? And each time, I come back with the same answer. She had free will, free choice. She made a decision about life. Who was I to tell her it was wrong? Or can't a woman make a decision about life and death without someone even taking that away from her?"

"Is it possible that Sam was of more value to your cause dead than alive?"

"I don't believe that. Sam wanted to die," said Pauline Cheng.

"And Slugo, he wanted to die, too?" asked Calvino. "Men can be such fools. Look at the last six months of Sam's life. Sooner or later she would have done it. I knew her better than anyone else. Being her friend was like being on a deathwatch. She tried to overdose twice. Each time I took her to the hospital. Each time they pumped out her stomach. That was after Nakamura took away her dignity. She was tired of living, of trying to make men like Ben and Reed happy."

"The law may take a different view," he said.

"The law. You say that word as if it is in all capital letters. Well, it's not. Not for women anyway. And many laws were made by men to oppress women."

"Unlike the laws in China, which force them to have abortions."

"You don't understand."

"Because I'm an Italian-Jew who happened to be born in America, and you do because you happen to be ethnic Chinese and born in America. What I do understand is that China has been building great walls against the outside world for centuries. When the Chinese ventured into the world long before Columbus had even been born, who did they send to discover the world? The emperor sent his chief eunuch, Cheng Ho. He led a flotilla of hundreds of ships and thousands of men, and he made it to India, Indonesia, Africa, Arabia. You know the purpose of his seven voyages, Pauline? They were to show others that the Chinese were superior. They took some feathers and buttons from the local barbarians and in return gave them gold. See, we are better than you. And nearly five hundred years after in the spirit of Cheng Ho, the emperors of China launched another voyage. This time the captain's a woman, an NGO living in Thailand, and this time no one is giving away gold or anything else; the mission is to show China's morality and values are superior to the barbarians of the West."

"Chinese culture finds pornography repulsive. Do you expect me to apologize for that?"

"No, because when you are working for a higher cause, even standing by while a friend kills herself is all right so long as it advances that cause."

"A female Stalin," said Osborn, who had finished cleaning his wound and had returned very quietly so as not to disturb the exchange.

"Stay out of it, Alan."

"Sam put in the bullet in the gun herself."

"She did what?" asked Calvino.

"You heard what I said. Sam loaded Quentin's gun herself. Ask Ice. She was in the bathroom. She saw Sam taking out the blank and pushing in the live round."

"Ice is your witness? The *ying* who you have killed in cyberspace three times."

"Four times. Though with Slugo unfortunately dead, I doubt that Ice will be a problem in the future,"

411

said Pauline. "That night, Ice came into the bathroom wanting to fight me. That is, until she saw the gun. She looked at Sam, the gun, then at me, watched Sam slip in the bullet, and then she flew out of the bathroom. It was one of the rare times that Sam ever showed any true courage."

Calvino was wondering whether Slugo knew about the incident, and was thinking the script idea was a scam to divert attention from Ice, his new Eve, his Alpha Domo project. Pauline sat on the edge of the computer table, arms folded around her waist.

"But you gave Sam the round," said Calvino.

"Who cares whether I gave her the bullet. I am saying when she sat down at that table she knew there was a live round in the gun. It was her fucking choice."

"Fuck," said Osborn in a low voice. "Without the 'you.'"

"Now would both of you get out of my office?"

"Why did you have Slugo murdered?"

She smiled, sat back and shook her head.

"You don't understand anything. Slugo was enemy number one. He was commercializing sex in cyberspace. Nothing would stop him. So he had to be stopped."

"Will you tell Quentin what you've told me tonight?" asked Calvino.

"Why should I tell him anything?" she asked. "He's part of the monster Hollywood exploitation machine. He used Sam. Used Sam's mother and father. He discarded them like they were nothing more than worthless objects. Whatever he did for Sam, he was doing for himself. I don't believe for a moment he cares at all what happened to Sam."

Calvino pulled a tape recorder from his jacket pocket.

"I am sure when Quentin hears your views on Hollywood, he will be crushed."

"And your friend Colonel Pratt will be most pleased," said Osborn.

FORTY-THREE

LUK PLA OPENED the front door only a crack—
she was too short, even on tiptoes to look through the
peephole—and when she saw Calvino standing in the
hallway, she swung the door wide open. She wore a pair
of four-inch, red high heels and a gold mini-dress; her hair
was done up in ringlets which curled over her ears, and
she looked about eighteen. No one would have thought
that Luk Pla was the mother of a two-year-old and a
gunshot victim with an ex-husband in prison. All the
gold given to her by Quentin was carefully displayed on
her neck and arms and she smiled as Calvino came into
the anteroom where there was a table with a large green
vase filled with fresh flowers. The entrance to Quentin's
penthouse was intended to create drama, an unfolding of
expectation as the guests removed their shoes.

"You want to see my scar?" she asked.

Without waiting for a reply, Baby Fish hiked up her
dress, holding it to her chin. Calvino still had on one

shoe and Luk Pla had flashed him. She wasn't going to drop her dress until he took a look. Underneath Luk Pla's mini-dress, she wore a pair of red bikini briefs, and above the briefs, a crooked red line the thickness of a Timberland shoelace, marked one side of her body.

She quickly dropped her skirt. In the Big Weird, anything was possible, and there was a class of *ying*s who had lost their shyness; their body was an object to be displayed and they applied make-up, clothes, jewelry to stress various features. Wishing to share a crooked scar left over from a gunshot wound was in the nature of sharing a biographical moment.

"You think it look very ugly?"

Calvino shook his head.

"Ugly is dead. You're alive."

"Ice say I never work again."

"Ice is wrong. You are working. On the job."

"Hey, you are right. Ice go back to bar. She very jealous of me. More gold, more everything. Come on. Follow me."

Calvino followed her downstairs to Quentin's office. "Darling, you look so beautiful, doesn't she, Vincent?"

Baby Fish ran over and jumped onto his lap, and wrapped her arms around his neck. Reed Mitchell sat in an armchair opposite Quentin's desk, and Quentin turned to him, smiling. "You know, when I lived in LA I had fridge magnets that weighed more than Luk Pla."

"I show Khun Vinny my scar," she said.

Quentin looked up at Calvino. "It's not that bad, is it?"

"With a little make-up, you would think it was a sleep mark from a rumpled sheet," said Calvino. "Something acquired in the line of fire."

"There. You see, Luk Pla. That's what I said. The very same words and Khun Vinny agrees. It's not a problem. So you can stop pulling your dress up in front of strangers and getting another second opinion, okay?"

"Baby Fish, the flasher chick from the Plaza," said Reed Mitchell. "She ought to be in movies."

"I wanted to thank you for the tape. It was a life saver. Of course, Pauline refused to talk to me. She referred me to her lawyers. I gather Colonel Pratt has hit the same brick wall. At least, Rebecca is off my back. She has lost her leverage. I instructed my lawyer that if she were to leak a single word to the press, I would sue her until I had recovered everything she ever ripped off me. Minus, of course, her paintings. And now, thanks to you, Mr. Calvino, I am back at work. Thank God, that awful business is behind us," Quentin said, seeing that Calvino had not taken his eyes off Reed Mitchell.

"Reed is working on a project with me," said Quentin. He avoided looking at Reed.

"We have changed the ending. She knows that a live round has been loaded into the gun. She is on a suicide mission. So it's a plus for her. She's desperate. It's either her or her boyfriend, and she is having the showdown in front of all of their friends," explained Reed.

"Just like in real life," said Quentin.

"You know, she could have killed me. The bitch." Calvino closed his eyes, held his breath for a count of five, before he swung around with a right crossover punch that knocked Reed Mitchell off his chair. He had feared losing control; he had been afraid that somehow Pauline Cheng might have been right. Sam McNeal's death was being wrapped like a gift: she existed in the imagination of screenwriters. Her thoughts and feelings would be on film one day, and the climax of her life, the meaning of her life, the only event which would survive and be remembered, would be the moment that she could have put down the gun, walked out of the room, but instead chose to risk pulling the trigger. What Calvino had recorded from Pauline's explanation was insufficient evidence to charge her with Slugo's death. It was open to argument that she had said nothing more than Slugo had enemies, and sooner or later, in the Big Weird, a *farang* with enemies could end up under water, dead.

Luk Pla hunched over Reed. He lay still, eyes closed. The punch had knocked him out cold. "I guess the bastard deserved it," said Quentin.

"But don't tell me, even though he's a bastard, it's a good story you are working on with him," said Calvino.

Quentin smiled. "When you are at the end of your life and you've lived as long as I have, you realize just how important a good story is. And working with a bastard is the essence of Hollywood. You can't only not avoid bastards; you can't get a film made without them."

"What about all that talk about alienation? Getting away from Hollywood because all the people were sick with greed, power, and games? That their sickness was far more dangerous than The Sickness?"

"I meant that. I stand by it. But do you want to know a secret of the business?"

"I don't want to know it."

"I will tell you anyway. Failure is not being heard. It is not being seen. If you want to create a psychological bulletin board, then you have to post on the system that is out there. The only system is the Hollywood system.

Maybe guys like Slugo are the future; but the future isn't here yet. And neither is Slugo. I don't like Reed any more than you do. He is a motherfucker. But you know what? I have worked with worse assholes. And unless I'm knocked out of action in the next couple of months, then the chances are that I will work with guys that will make him look like the Dalai Lama."

Calvino headed for the door.

"Vincent, why don't we have lunch tomorrow? You can tell me about this film idea you've been dancing around for a week or so. I know you've got something you want to see on the screen. I owe you. Let's see if we can make it happen."

"Make what happen?" asked Calvino.

"Your dream. What else?"

"Mr. Stuart, like Luk Pla, I work for people who live in dreams. Sam had her dreams. So did Slugo. Big dreams. But, at the end of the day, all that is left is a handful of dust shaped like a stickman laid out for a few friends and strangers. Do you know what they are looking for when they view the ashes?"

Quentin looked away as if he didn't want to really hear the answer. "What do they look for?" he whispered.

"If the ashes are white, the cremated person had no sin, she is not reborn. But if they are gray, then some sin is in the bones, and if the ashes are black, then the sin is without doubt, and the dead person comes flying back to this world, the cycle starts over again, and it continues for as long as it takes for the ashes to turn white. Between now and the day when people read the color of my ashes, I prefer living close to the hard reality of life, life as it is, because maybe that's the way we were meant to live and die."

He turned and looked back. The old man had tears in his eyes.

"Sam's ashes were white. You have to believe me. I loved her like a daughter."

"The irony is," Calvino paused, "no man ever sees the color of his ashes. The best he can do is make an educated guess."

In a rational universe love must have meant something, thought Calvino. In the Big Weird it was just another virtual reality device, another avatar that floated on the night, from the Plaza to the other venues, skipping from a spiritual world into a commercial world as if there was no real boundary between the two.

"See you around," said Calvino.

As Calvino walked along the street, passing people who were all eyes, their mouths and noses covered by surgical masks, he saw fatigue and fear in their eyes. He looked up at the sky, wondering about the fungi and bacteria breeding inside airborne colonies, and his thoughts turned to his next visa run: should he renew for another ninety days in this strange and mysterious tribal land?

The truth was, like the temple sparrows released from their cage as a merit-making exercise, he would return, knowing it was weird and that staying in such a fouled enclosure was even weirder. Yet, in some deep part of his soul, he knew that it was the weird that had made him self-sufficient and kept him on the job.

After midnight, Calvino checked in at the Plaza for a nightcap. No sooner had he ordered a drink, than he turned around and looked at the Mermaidium. At first he saw legs, stomach and breasts, then a face. Ice's face. She had shaved her head. In one way she was no longer recognizable. It was as if she had gone into a religious order, one that had separated her from the world, one that promised rebirth and enlightenment. Deep underwater, she sat on the pirate's treasure chest, leaned forward and pressed her lips against the glass in the form of a kiss, her head shaped like a sea creature. Then Ice kicked back, and her underwater face was full of shock, of loss, of grief.

Ice had recreated herself as a new form of being. No longer digital, no longer human. Osborn had once said, when he thought no one was listening, that the nature of water was to exploit the weak point and escape. And no matter how smart a man was he could never predict where the water would make its break to freedom. He had also said that the nature of the *ying*s was like the nature of water.

Water had no will to break, no pain of loss, no heartache to endure. Water was relentless, indifferent, beyond suffering. Looking at Ice, Calvino thought how she exhibited the true nature of water. She was like her name, Ice: frozen, solid, without the means to escape.

As his drink arrived, Calvino was certain he saw the impossible, a woman weeping underwater. He asked himself how it was possible for a woman to cry totally submerged in a tank, then he remembered: this was the same tank that Slugo had been drowned in, the same tank in which Ice had lost her dreams, the same tank to which she had been forced by circumstances to return.

Chances were that whatever dreams she would have would be inside that water kingdom, inside a space from which she once thought she had escaped only to find herself thrown back into the sea. Could she have killed her creator? Not likely, he thought. Calvino raised his drink to her and smiled.

Whoever had killed Slugo, one thing was for certain—the woman at the bottom of the Mermaidium hadn't been his killer. She would be occupying Slugo's space, his dead space, wondering what might have been had he not died, wondering how many lifetimes she would have to occupy his watery tomb before she might be reborn into that place of the D avatars, a cyberspace presence. A digital wonderland where the illusions were more real than life and the money rolled in. A cosmic aquarium where Ice, timeless and ageless, would always be a star.

ABOUT AUTHOR

Christopher G. Moore is a Canadian writer who once taught law at the University of British Columbia. After his first book His Lordship' Arsenal was published in New York to a critical acclaim in 1985, Moore became a full-time writer and has so far written 23 novels and one collection of interlocked short stories.

Moore is best known by his international award-winning Vincent Calvino Private Eye series and his cult classics Land of Smiles Trilogy, a behind-the-smiles study of his adopted country, Thailand. His novels have been translated into eleven languages. His Vincent Calvino novels are published in the United States by Atlantic Monthly Press and in Great Britain and the Commonwealth by Atlantic Books.

He lives with his wife in Bangkok. For more information about the author and his work, visit his official website: www.cgmoore.com. He also blogs regularly with other cirme authors at www.internationalcrimeauthors.com

THE VINCENT CALVINO P.I. SERIES

CHRISTOPHER G. MOORE's Vincent Calvino P.I. series began with *Spirit House* in 1992. The latest, eleventh, in the series is *The Corruptionist* first released in Thailand in 2010

Moore's protagonist, Vincent Calvino is an Italian-Jewish former lawyer from New York who left his practice to turn P.I. in Southeast Asia. Calvino's assignments take him inside the labyrinth of local politics, double-dealing and fleeting relationships. Unlike typical tough-guy sleuths, Calvino admits he would never survive without his guardian angel, his Shakespeare-quoting and saxophone-playing buddy, Colonel Pratt, an honest and well-connected Thai cop who helps him find hidden forces, secret traps and ways to keep him alive in a foreign land.

The twelves novels in the Vincent Calvino P.I. series are: *Spirit House, Asia Hand, Zero Hour in Phnom Penh, Comfort Zone, The Big Weird, Cold Hit, Minor Wife, Pattaya 24/7, The Risk of Infidelity Index, Paying Back Jack, The Corruptionist,* and *9 Gold Bullets.* The novels are published in Thailand by Heaven Lake Press, in the United States by Grove/Atlantic and in Great Britain by Atlantic Books.

The third installment in the series *Zero Hour in Phnom Penh* won the German Critics Award for Crime Fiction (Deutscher Krimi Preis) for best international crime fiction in 2004 and the Premier Special Director's Award Semana Negra (Spain) in 2007 or the author's website: www.cgmoore.com.

SPIRIT HOUSE
First in the series

The Bangkok police already have a confession by a nineteen-year-old drug addict who has admitted to the murder of a British computer wizard, Ben Hoadly. From the bruises on his face shown at the press conference, it is clear that the young suspect had some help from the police in the making of his confession. The case is wrapped up. Only there are some loose ends that the police and just about everyone else are happy to overlook.

The search for the killer of Ben Hoadley plunges Calvino into the dark side of Bangkok, where professional hit men have orders to stop him. From the world of thinner addicts, dope dealers, fortunetellers, and high-class call girls, Calvino peels away the mystery surrounding the death of the English ex-public schoolboy who had a lot of dubious friends.

"Well-written, tough and bloody."
　　—Bernard Knight, *Tangled Web* (UK)

"A worthy example of a serial character, Vincent Calvino is human and convincing. [He] is an incarnate of the composite of the many expatriate characters who have burned the bridge to their pasts."
　　—*Thriller Magazine* (Italy)

"A thinking man's Philip Marlowe, Calvino is a cynic on the surface but a romantic at heart. Calvino ... found himself in Bangkok—the end of the world for a whole host of bizarre foreigners unwilling, unable, or uninterested in going home."
　　—*The Daily Yomiuri*

ASIA HAND
Second in the series

Bangkok—the Year of the Monkey. Calvino's Chinese New Year celebration is interrupted by a call to Lumpini Park Lake, where Thai cops have just fished the body of a *farang* cameraman. CNN is running dramatic footage of several Burmese soldiers on the Thai border executing students.

Calvino follows the trail of the dead man to a feature film crew where he hits the wall of silence. On the other side of that wall, Calvino and Colonel Pratt discover and elite film unit of old Asia hands with connections to influential people in Southeast Asia. They find themselves matched against a set of *farangs* conditioned for urban survival and willing to go for a knock-out punch.

"Moore's Vinny Calvino is a worthy successor to Raymond Chandler's Philip Marlowe and Mickey Spillane's Mike Hammer."
—The Nation

"The top foreign author focusing on the Land of Smiles, Canadian Christopher G. Moore clearly has a first-hand understanding of the expat milieu ... Moore is perspicacious."
—Bangkok Post

ZERO HOUR IN PHNOM PENH
Third in the series

In the early 1990s, at the end of Cambodia's devastating civil war, UN peacekeeping forces try to keep the lid on the violence. Gunfire can still be heard nightly in Phnom Penh, where Vietnamese prostitutes try to hook UN peacekeepers from the balcony of the Lido Bar.

Calvino traces leads on a missing *farang* from Bangkok to war-torn Cambodia, through the Russian market, hospitals, nightclubs, news briefings, and UNTAC headquarters. Calvino's buddy, Colonel Pratt, knows something that Calvino does not: The missing man is connected with the jewels stolen from the Saudi royal family. Calvino quickly finds out that he is not the only one looking for the missing *farang*.

"Political, courageous and perhaps Moore's most important work."
   —*CrimiCouch.de*

"Fast-paced and entertaining. Even outside of his Bangkok comfort zone, Moore shows he is one of the best chroniclers of the expat diaspora."
   —*The Daily Yomiuri*

"A brilliant detective story that portrays—with no illusion—Cambodia's adventurous transition from genocide and civil war to a free-market economy and democratic normality. A rare stroke of luck and a work of art."
   —*Deutsche Well Buchtipp,* Bonn

COMFORT ZONE
Fourth in the series

Twenty years after the end of the Vietnam War, Vietnam is opening to the outside world. There is a smell of fast money in the air and poverty in the streets. Business is booming and in austere Ho Chi Minh City a new generation of foreigners have arrived to make money and not war. Against the backdrop of Vietnam's economic miracle, Comfort Zone reveals a divided people still not reconciled with their past and unsure of their future.

Calvino is hired by an ex-special forces vet, whose younger brother uncovers corruption and fraud in the emerging business world in which his clients are dealing. But before Calvino even leaves Bangkok, there have already been two murders, one in Saigon and one in Bangkok

"Moore hits home with more of everything in Comfort Zone. There is a balanced mix of story-line, narrative, wisdom, knowledge as well as love, sex, and murder."

—*Thailand Times*

"Like a Japanese gardener who captures the land and the sky and recreates it in the backyard, Moore's genius is in portraying the Southeast Asian heartscape behind the tourist industry hotel gloss.

—*The Daily Yomiuri*

"In Comfort Zone, our Bangkok-based P.I. digs, discovering layers of intrigue. He's stalked by hired killers and falls in love with a Hanoi girl. Can he trust her? The reader is hooked."

—*NTUC Lifestyle* (Singapore)

THE BIG WEIRD
Fifth in the series

A beautiful American blond is found dead with a large bullet hole in her head in the house of her ex-boyfriend. A famous Hollywood screenwriter hires Calvino to investigate her death. Everyone except Calvino's client believes Samantha McNeal has committed suicide.

In the early days of the Internet, Sam ran with a young and wild expat crowd in Bangkok. As Calvino slides into a world where people are dead serious about sex, money and fame, he unearths a hedonistic community where the ritual of death is the ultimate high.

"An excellent read, charming, amusing, insightful, complex, localised yet startlingly universal in its themes."
—*Guide of Bangkok*

"Highly entertaining."
—*Bangkok Post*

"Like a noisy, late-night Thai restaurant, Moore serves up tongue-burning spices that swallow up the literature of Generation X and Cyberspace as if they were merely sticky rice."
—*The Daily Yomiuri*

"A good read, fast-paced and laced with so many of the locales so familiar to the expat denizens of Bangkok."
—*Art of Living* (Thailand)

COLD HIT
Sixth in the series

Five foreigners have died in Bangkok. Were they drug overdose victims or victims of a serial killer? Calvino believes the evidence points to a serial killer who stalks tourists in Bangkok. The Thai police, including Colonel Pratt, don't buy his theory.

Calvino teams up with an LAPD officer on a bodyguard assignment. Hidden forces pull them through swank shopping malls, run-down hotels, the Klong Toey slum, and bars in the red light district as they try to keep their man and themselves alive. As Calvino learns more about the bodies being shipped back to America, the secret of the serial killer is revealed.

"The story is plausible and riveting to the end."
    —*The Japan Times*

"Tight, intricate plotting, wickedly astute ... Cold Hit will have you variously gasping, chuckling, nodding, tut-tutting, oh-yesing, and grinding your teeth throughout its 330 pages."
    —*Guide of Bangkok*

"City jungle, sex, drugs, power, but also good-hearted people: a complete crime."
    —*Zwanzig Minuten Zürich*

"Calvino is a wonderful private detective figure! Consistent action, masterful language ... and Anglo-Saxon humour at its best."
    —Lutz Bunk, *DeutschlandRadio,* Berlin

MINOR WIFE
Seventh in the series

A contemporary murder set in Bangkok—a neighbor and friend, a young ex-hooker turned artist, is found dead by an American millionaire's minor wife. Her rich expat husband hires Calvino to investigate.

While searching for the killer in exclusive clubs and not-so-exclusive bars of Bangkok, Calvino discovers that a minor wife—mia noi—has everything to do with a woman's status. From illegal cock fighting matches to elite Bangkok golf clubs, Calvino finds himself caught in the crossfire as he closes in on the murderer.

"What distinguishes Christopher G. Moore from other foreign authors setting their stories in the Land of Smiles is how much more he understands its mystique, the psyche of its populace and the futility of its round residents trying to fit into its square holes."
—*Bangkok Post*

"Moore pursues in even greater detail in Minor Wife the changing social roles of Thai women (changing, but not always quickly or for the better) and their relations among themselves and across class lines and other barriers."
—*Vancouver Sun*

"The thriller moves in those convoluted circles within which Thai life and society takes place. Moore's knowledge of these gives insights into many aspects of the cultural mores. Many of these are unknown to the expat population. ... Great writing, great story and a great read."
—*Pattaya Mail*

PATTAYA 24/7
Eighth in the series

Inside a secluded, lush estate located on the edge of Pattaya, an eccentric Englishman's gardener is found hanged. Calvino has been hired to investigate. He finds himself pulled deep into the shadows of the war against drugs, into the empire of a local warlord with the trail leading to a terrorist who has caused Code Orange alerts to flash across the screen of American intelligence.

In a story packed with twists and turns, Calvino traces the links from the gardener's past to the doors of men with power and influence who have everything to lose if the mystery of the gardener's death is solved.

"Calvino does it again ... well-developed characters, and the pace keeps you reading well after you should have turned out the light."
—*Farang Magazine* (Thailand)

"A compelling, atmospheric and multi-layered murder investigation set in modern-day Thailand. The detective, Calvino, is a complex and engaging hero."
—Garry Disher, award-winning author of *The Wyatt Novels*

"We enjoy the spicy taste of hard-boiled fiction reinvented in an exotic but realistic place—in fact, not realistic, but real!"
—*Thriller Magazine* (Italy)

"A cast of memorably eccentric figures in an exotic Southeast Asian backdrop"
—*The Japan Times*

THE RISK OF INFIDELITY INDEX
Ninth in the series

Major political demonstrations are rocking Bangkok. Chaos and fear sweep through the Thai and expatriate communities. Calvino steps into the political firestorm as he investigates a drug piracy operation. The piracy is traced to a powerful business interest protected by important political connections. A nineteen-year-old Thai woman and a middle-aged lawyer end up dead on the same evening. Both are connected to Calvino's investigation.

The dead lawyer's law firm denies any knowledge of the case. Calvino is left in the cold. Approached by a group of expat housewives—rattled by the "Risk of Infidelity Index" that ranks Bangkok number one for available sexual temptations—to investigate their husbands, Calvino discovers the alliance of forces blocking his effort to disclose the secret pirate drug investigation.

"Moore's flashy style successfully captures the dizzying contradictions in [Bangkok's] vertiginous landscape."
    —Marilyn Stasio, *The New York Times Book Review*

"A hard-boiled, street-smart, often hilarious pursuit of a double murderer."
    —*San Francisco Chronicle*

"Humorous and intelligent ... a great introduction to the seamy side of Bangkok."
    —Carla Mckay, *The Daily Mail*

"Taut, spooky, intelligent, and beautifully written."
    —T. Jefferson Parker, author of *L.A. Outlaws*

PAYING BACK JACK
Tenth in the series

In *Paying Back Jack*, Calvino agrees to follow the 'minor wife' of a Thai politician and report on her movements. His client is Rick Casey, a shady American whose life has been darkened by the unsolved murder of his idealistic son. It seems to be a simple surveillance job, but soon Calvino is entangled in a dangerous web of political allegiance and a reckless quest for revenge.

And, unknown to our man in Bangkok, in an anonymous tower in the center of the city, a two-man sniper team awaits its shot, a shot that will change everything. Paying Back Jack is classic Christopher G. Moore: densely-woven, eye-opening, and riveting.

"[*Paying Back Jack*] might be Moore's finest novel yet."
    —Barry Eisler, author of *Fault Line*

"*Paying Back Jack* is so tightly woven and entertaining it is hopeless to try to put it down. Not only was it new and fresh, but I feel like I have taken a trip to the underbelly of Thailand. It is impossible not to love this book."
    —Carolyn Lanier, *I Love a Mystery*

"A vivid sense of place ... the city of Bangkok, with its chaos and mystery, is almost another character. Recommended."
    —*Library Journal*

"Moore clearly has no fear that his gloriously corrupt Bangkok will ever run dry."
    —*Kirkus Review*

THE CORRUTIONIST
Eleventh in the series

Set during the recent turbulent times in Thailand, the 11th novel in the Calvino series centers around the street demonstrations and occupation of Government House in Bangkok.

Hired by an American businessman, Calvino finds himself caught in the middle of a family conflict over a Chinese corporate takeover. This is no ordinary deal. Calvino and his client are up against powerful forces set to seize much more than a family business. As the bodies accumulate while he navigates Thailand's business-political landmines, Calvino becomes increasingly entangled in a secret deal made by men who will stop at nothing—and no one—standing in their way. But Calvino refuses to step aside.

The Corruptionist captures with precision the undercurrents enveloping Bangkok, revealing multiple layers of betrayal and deception.

"Moore's understanding of the dynamics of Thai society has always impressed, but considering current events, the timing of his latest [The Corruptionist] is absolutely amazing."
—Mark Schreiber, *The Japan Times*

"Politics . . . has a role in the series, more so now than earlier. What with corruption during elections and coups afterwards, the denizens watch with bemusement the unlikelihood of those in office serving their terms. Moore captures this in his books. Thought-provoking columnists don't do it better. . . . Moore is putting Thailand on the map."
—Bernard Trink, *Bangkok Post*

"An achievement . . . interpreting modern, fast changing Thailand with its violent political power struggles. . . . [T]he levels and depths of observation and insight reach an epic nature in [The Corruptionist]. . . . The new characters are stunning. . . . The ending is superb."

—Richard Ravensdale, *Pattaya Trader*

"Very believable . . . A 'brave' book . . . Another riveting read from Christopher G. Moore and one you should not miss."

—Lang Reid, *Pattaya Mail*

9 GOLD BULLETS
Twelfth in the series

A priceless collection of 9 gold bullet coins issued during the Reign of Rama V has gone missing along with a Thai coin collector. Local police find a link between the missing Thai coins and Calvino's childhood friend, Josh Stein, who happens to be in Bangkok on an errand for his new Russian client. This old friend and his personal and business entanglements with the Russian underworld take Calvino back to New York, along with Pratt.

The gritty, dark vision of 9 Gold Bullets is tracked through the eyes of a Thai cop operating on a foreign turf, and a private eye expatriated long enough to find himself a stranger in his hometown. As the intrigue behind the missing coins moves between New York andBangkok, and the levels of deception increase, Calvino discovers the true nature of friendship and where he belongs.

CPSIA information can be obtained
at www.ICGtesting.com
Printed in the USA
LVHW021738180219
607895LV00046B/1835/P